# WHY IT'S STILL KICKING OFF EVERYWHERE

## The New Global Revolutions

### Revised and Updated Second Edition

## PAUL MASON

**VERSO**

London • New York

This revised and updated second edition first published by Verso 2013
First published by Verso 2012
© Paul Mason 2012, 2013

1 3 5 7 9 10 8 6 4 2

**Verso**
UK: 6 Meard Street, London W1F 0EG
US: 20 Jay Street, Suite 1010, Brooklyn, NY 11201
www.versobooks.com

Verso is the imprint of New Left Books

ISBN-13: 978-1-84467-028-4

**British Library Cataloguing in Publication Data**
A catalogue record for this book is available from the British Library

**Library of Congress Cataloging-in-Publication Data**
A catalog record for this book is available from the Library of Congress

Typeset in Fournier by MJ Gavan, Truro, Cornwall
Printed by CPI Group (UK) Ltd, Croydon, CR0 4YY

To my mother

# Contents

CONTENTS

# Introduction

It was a cold Friday night in early 2011, sometime between the fall of Ben Ali in Tunisia and the fall of the Egyptian president Hosni Mubarak. I got a call: would I do a lecture on the history of the Paris Commune for something called 'The Really Free School' in Bloomsbury? I turned up to the venue to find it was a squat. They'd formed an ad hoc university, occupied an eighteenth-century townhouse in the heart of London and stuck a sign on the door saying 'Journalists Fuck Off'.

Here was the hard core of the student protest movement: dedicated eco-warriors, veterans of suicidal sit-downs in front of tanks in Gaza, the demobbed Clown Army and, as my host put it, 'the Situationist Taliban'.

Did they know this had all been done before? They had a vague idea. I watched their eyes widen—sixty of them, cross-legged on the Jane Austen–era floorboards—as I explained the debates between Proudhon, Blanqui, Marx and Garibaldi in the years before 1871, scarcely needing to draw out the parallels with Climate Camp, the Black Bloc, Naomi Klein and the Zapatistas.

Afterwards, a few of us wedged ourselves into the nearby Museum Tavern, where Marx had been a regular. There was @spitzenprodukte and @benvickers_, both art activists; @dougald—the inventor of the term 'collapsonomics'; @digitalmaverick, a schoolteacher and 'moodle

1

evangelist'; and Tim, who'd dedicated his life to fighting for human rights in the Niger Delta.

The discussion buzzed: is it the technology, the economics, the mass psychology or just the zeitgeist that's caused this global explosion of revolt? I inclined to a technological-determinist explanation: 'Look how your eyes shine when we talk about the network. It's the network!' Glancing at my iPhone, I realized why they seemed occasionally distracted: they were tweeting the entire conversation, live, to their friends.

The next morning I wrote a blog post based on the conversation: 'Twenty Reasons Why It's Kicking Off Everywhere' (see page 63). It went viral.

Within a month I met a hacker from Boston, Massachusetts, who told me that 'there are discussion groups in the USA studying your blog'. Later, I found out that a global collective of protesters were working on a book critiquing the blog[1]; later still I met some of them, as they tried to avoid having their heads bashed in by Greek riot police. This has created a degree of circularity between the reporter, the reported-on and the events which I am still struggling to get my own head around.

In this book I explore the reasons why numerous protest movements, revolutions, civil wars and internet-based revolts 'kicked off' in 2009–11. I've travelled from Cairo to Manila to Athens and beyond to write it. It's not a comprehensive history, and of course the events are not over.

The book makes no claim to be a 'theory of everything', linking LulzSec to global warming and key dates in the Mayan calendar. And don't file it under 'social science': it's journalism.

Some ideas in the original blog have been expanded, others ditched. Some theatres of the conflict have been ignored, simply because I couldn't get there. The original post—written on 5 February 2011 when Mubarak was still in power and Greece was still scheduled to pay its debts (and with my head throbbing thanks to the Museum

2

Tavern)—was just a snapshot and so is this, albeit with more pixels and depth of field. Though events have moved on fast, the essence of my argument remains unchanged. We're in the middle of a revolution caused by the near collapse of free-market capitalism combined with an upswing in technical innovation, a surge in desire for individual freedom and a change in human consciousness about what freedom means. An economic crisis is making the powerful look powerless, while the powerless are forced to adopt tactics that were once the preserve of niche protest groups.

If you're skilled at chaining yourself to fighter planes, or know how to launch a 'denial of service attack', there will be parts of this book that make you think, 'Yeah, right, of course, I knew all that.' The aim, as with the original blog, is to capture the moments of crisis and revolution, to give them context and to explain what links these apparently disparate, worldwide upheavals.

Many of the activists I've interviewed are hostile to the very idea of a unifying theory, a set of bullet-point demands, a guru or a teleology. I'm not trying to provide any of these. For the youth, increasingly, knowledge is drawn, on demand and free, from online articles and commentaries and—often breathless—tweets. And for many, politics has become gestural: it is about refusing to engage with power on power's own terms; about action, not ideas; about the symbolic control of territory to create islands of utopia.

The format of the book reflects the zeitgeist: it brings together reportage, essay, tweet, anecdote and cyber-psychology; plus some economic insights gathered amid clouds of tear gas.

And the role of 'the book' itself is changing. Writers of my generation stood in awe of the New Journalism of the 1960s, when the sudden swing to truthful reportage could end presidencies and terminate wars. But the equivalent in this era will not be like the grand reportage of the Sixties at all. Rather, it is the combined input of thousands of people into the freely accessible public record of social media: the thoughts they tweeted, the jokes they cracked as their friends panicked in the crush of crowds, the football shirts they wore as they toted Kalashnikovs through liberated Tripoli. There is a great river of human hope flowing, and all I am trying to do is dip my fingers in it.

The essence of why it's kicking off was put into words by a student protester in the USA. Federal police had tried to arrest somebody on a university campus, so a group of students sat down around the police car. A twenty-one-year-old with curly blond hair took off his shoes and stood on the car's roof, to begin a mass meeting that would last several days. Later, he said:

> The act of sitting around the police car, of getting up on the car and starting to speak, of physically structuring the possibility of a community ... all of a sudden there is a self-justifying factor to it. In a way, once it's been established, there might be other reasons for sitting around the car than keeping it from moving—namely participating in the community. I have never experienced that anywhere nearly so strongly as around the police car.[2]

But that was not in 2011. Those words were spoken in 1964 by Mario Savio, a student leader in Berkeley, California, in a protest that kicked off a decade of campus revolts throughout the USA.

You may have thought such days were gone—such idealism, such eloquence, such creativity and hope. Well, they're back.

London, 26 October 2011

# 1

## 'Now There Is Freedom':
## Why Egypt's Revolution Is Not Over

*Cairo, May 2011*

The ground floor of Musa Zekry's house is head-high with garbage and thick with flies. The floor above is home to the widow of his brother, shot dead during the revolution. Musa will live in the top floor, above her, when it is finished—but for now it's a shell, choked with rubble, dust, more garbage and more flies.

A dead brother, several fear-filled days in Tahrir Square, weeks of danger and distrust: that's the balance sheet of Musa Zekry's revolution. All he's got to show for it is a banner slung across the street outside, hailing his brother as a martyr, alongside a portrait of Jesus Christ. Plus freedom.

And it is this freedom, so unexpected and so viscerally felt, that lights his face and energizes his five-foot frame as he steers me through streets filled with *shisha* smoke, donkey crap and a blizzard of flies:

> The Central Security forces now are non-existent—because we have freedom! Now everybody has a voice and wants to speak. Before, under Mubarak, if you raised your voice they would kill you in the street. Now there is freedom.

5

Cairo's Moqattam slum, in the south-east of this vast metropolis, is home to 65,000 *zabbaleen* or 'garbage people'. The young men and children collect the garbage in the twilit streets of downtown Cairo. The women sort it into separate sacks: bone, metal, cloth and plastic in all their subsets: water bottles, oil containers. A whole family just down the street from Musa specializes in smashing plastic knives and forks into a crisp white rubble. The *zabbaleen*'s world is one of rank alleyways, face-stinging heat, cheap bread eaten fresh out of grubby fingers.

The *zabbaleen* are mainly Coptic Christians: the face of Jesus gazes down on every workshop and rubbish pile. But in the street, as Musa leads me to a makeshift factory where they are using vats and blowers to turn plastic bottle shreds into translucent snow, two men embrace each other, gesturing at the religious symbols tattooed on their wrists: 'I Christian, I Muslim,' they chime. 'We together.'

The Egyptian revolution may have begun on Facebook, but when it reached these alleyways, mobilizing men whose whole lives are stratified by religion, family and caste—well, that was the point that things got serious for Hosni Mubarak.

'Two men came to us and said, let's go down to Tahrir, to ask for change,' says Musa. He's reluctant to name them even now, but he clasps his palms together above his head to demonstrate what they did. 'They told us: let's make a demonstration with the people in Tahrir Square. One was Muslim, one Christian. One hand! We went by car: ten or twenty cars. When we got there I realized that our goal was right: to make a revolution and get freedom.'

Some of the bottle shredders did not go: 'We have our own square here,' laughs one, pointing to a patch of dust and dog-dirt. 'We waited for Tahrir to come to the *zabbaleen*!'

It did, but not in the way they had expected. On 7 March 2011, less than a month after Mubarak had fallen, and the garbage people had symbolically cleansed Tahrir, thugs from the old regime organized a Muslim mob to attack the slum. These hired gangs are known as the *baltagiya*:

My brother ran to tell my Dad—he works in a garage in the place the *baltagiya* were marching to. But my Dad had already run away. Then we got a phone call: your brother is in the hospital, he is dead. He was shot but nobody knows who did it.

Relations between the Copts and the Muslim slums nearby were always fraught, but, despite his brother's death, Musa is not scared to go there. It's the city centre, where law and order has been minimal since the revolution, that frightens him: 'I can walk through the Muslim slum, no problem. The problem is, now, if I go downtown I am worried somebody's gonna shoot me; somebody is gonna wave a pass—I don't know whether it's fake or real—and tell me to give money, or kill me.'

For Musa, as for millions of others from the slums and tenements of Cairo, this has been no 'social media revolution'. It's been a chaotic, frightening implosion of order. Policing, he says, is lax; security is 'just decorative':

Economically nothing has changed. We went to Tahrir to make a change, but so far, nothing's improved. What we need is for Egypt to be like America—so that if you have an idea, if you want to start a business, you can do it freely. We need social justice. That was what we chanted for.

To see how far from social justice Mubarak's Egypt was before 25 January 2011, the Moqattam slum is a good place to start. It's crammed into a sloping gully beneath a sandstone cliff. If you stand at the top, near one of the caves they use for churches, you're confronted by a landscape of wooden shacks, twisted metal rods, crumbling concrete and hundreds of rusted satellite dishes. But this is just the unfinished roofscape, the top layer of misery. Plunge down into the alleyways and it becomes dark. The *zabbaleen* build their shanty-dwellings five or six floors high; each new son or marriage adds another layer of brick and concrete to create a warren of urban canyons—like a miniature New York, with donkeys for traffic.

And there is intense noise: machines shredding and crushing plastic; blacksmiths hammering old metal into something new. Coptic ballads of death and resurrection wailing out of tinny radios mingle with the braying of donkeys and goats. When the garbage arrives—in 1970s-model Datsun trucks whose windshields and brakes are long gone—they tip it into the alleyways, right next to where people live. The women come out, accompanied by any children old enough to walk, squat down in the middle of the garbage and start picking through it. They rummage deftly, looking for valuable stuff amid the refuse. The women's hands and faces are grey with grime, but they're swathed in acid-coloured scarves and headbands, while their ears are weighed down with yellow gold.

And then there are the flies. If you painted the Moqattam slum you would have to fill the canvas with small dots of brown light, like *pointillisme* done with flying dirt. But no picture, not even a video, could capture the intensity of the insect life which swarms across your gaze, inhibiting your inward breath.

Like all modern slums, Moqattam is really a giant informal factory: its micro-economy is both essential to global capitalism and in the process of being destroyed by it.

For sixty years, the *zabbaleen* had run Cairo's trash collection system. They picked up the waste door to door, fed their pigs with the rotting organic matter and recycled the rest for cash, trading with a traditional caste of middlemen. But in 2003, as part of a privatization programme overseen by Mubarak's son Gamal, three sanitation companies—two Spanish and one Italian—were brought in to 'modernize' the city's waste collection.

These outside firms were given cleaning contracts valued at US$50 million a year. Instead of door-to-door collection, they placed big plastic bins on street corners. Instead of recycling 80 per cent of solid waste—as the *zabbaleen* had managed to do—their contracts required that only 20 per cent be recycled, with the rest tipped into landfill. The transformation of Cairo's refuse system was to be crowned by the eviction of the *zabbaleen*, whose slum was adjacent to a new residential property development planned by friends of Gamal Mubarak.

'The old system worked. The recycling process was one of the most efficient in the world,' says Ezzat Guindi, born and raised in the slum, where he now runs an NGO. 'And', he goes on, 'people could live. There was no sub-dollar-a-day poverty among the *zabbaleen* until the multinationals came. Now, about 30 per cent are destitute; and it's those who've been displaced and made redundant by the sanitation companies who are the poorest.'

But the new system wasn't working. Cairo's residents refused to use the bins; in fact, many of the high-grade plastic containers were stolen and, with poetic justice, ended up being shredded and recycled by the *zabbaleen*. People began to dump their rubbish onto the streets or into the disused and abandoned buildings that scar Cairo's streetscape.

So, the new system needed an extra push. When the global swine flu epidemic broke, in 2009, the Mubaraks spotted an opportunity. The Egyptian parliament, circumventing its own health ministry and in defiance of UN advice, ordered all the *zabbaleen*'s pigs to be slaughtered. There had been no recorded transmission of swine flu from pigs to humans. No other country in the world had ordered the mass eradication of domestic pigs. But that did not deter Hosni Mubarak.

Across Egypt, an estimated 300,000 swine belonging to *zabbaleen* households were slaughtered; the government paid between $15 and $50 per pig in compensation, compared to the $80 to $300 they'd been selling for on the market. Soon, two things happened. With no pigs to eat the rotting food, the *zabbaleen* stopped collecting it, leaving it to pile up on the streets. Then malnutrition appeared among their children. For, says Guindi, though the multinational companies were getting $10 a tonne for waste, and the middlemen $2 out of that, the *zabbaleen* received nothing from the contract—only what they could make from the sale of recycled waste, and their pigs.

Now something else happened, equally novel: the *zabbaleen* rioted. They hurled rocks, bottles and manure (there was plenty of that to

9

hand) at the pig-slaughtering teams. In response, Mubarak deployed riot squads into the slums—followed, as always, by Central Security and its torturers.

That is how a mixture of repression, greed, corruption and neo-liberal economic doctrine managed to turn the *zabbaleen* into latent revolutionaries. All it needed was a spark, and that came on 25 January 2011.

## *Cairo, 25 January 2011*

'Something's going to happen in Egypt,' Hossam el-Hamalawy had told me when we talked in a Bloomsbury café two years before. 'Mubarak will try to hand over to his son, Gamal, but Gamal might lose the next election.'

Hamalawy spoke softly. He'd been detained and tortured by Mubarak's secret police for selling socialist literature and was active around the uprising on 6 April 2008 in the Delta city of Mahalla. Then, like a tremor that should have warned of the earthquake to come, a city of 400,000 people rioted for three days in response to the suppression of a textile strike and the rocketing price of food.

It was around the Mahalla strike, too, that the April 6th Youth Movement was formed, by mostly young activists, liaising by Facebook, email and Flickr. They were drawn from Egypt's fragmented opposition: secularist youth from the left, the liberal opposition parties, the human rights community.

When I met Hamalawy in 2009, screwing up Gamal's election campaign was the limit of his ambition. But in January 2011, once the revolution in Tunisia was under way, the horizon for Egypt's opposition groups broadened rapidly. Hamalawy (who tweets as @3arabawy) was among those that initiated the call for a demonstration in Cairo's Tahrir Square on 25 January, again made through a Facebook page.

Meanwhile, the downtrodden and the desperate had begun to react to

Ben Ali's overthrow in more direct ways. On 17 January, three days after the Tunisian president's fall, a fifty-two-year-old lawyer in central Cairo shouted slogans about food price rises, then set himself on fire. A man in Alexandria did the same. A third man—a restaurant owner—immolated himself outside the Egyptian parliament after quarrelling with officials about the cost of bread. The next day, a twenty-five-year-old business graduate named Asmaa Mahfouz (@AsmaaMahfouz) posted a video blog on YouTube. 'Four Egyptians have set themselves on fire', she announced,

> to protest humiliation and hunger and poverty and the degradation they've had to live with for thirty years, thinking that we could have a revolution like in Tunisia. Today one of them has died … People, have some shame! I, a girl, posted that I will go down to Tahrir Square, to stand alone, and I'll hold a banner. All that came were three guys. Three guys, three armoured cars of riot police and tens of *baltagiya* … I'm making this video to give you a simple message: we're going to Tahrir on 25 January.[1]

During the following days, activists frantically refreshed the Facebook page advertising the 25 January demo, as news spread it was gaining thousands of followers per second. Many had also joined the 'We are all Khaled Said' page, dedicated to a youth beaten to death by police in Alexandria for posting evidence of police corruption on YouTube.

The veteran activists knew the stakes. They knew the Central Security would crack down hard on any attempts at demonstration. They had no idea whether the tens of thousands of names on Facebook would translate into anything more than the usual forlorn and harassed protests. That they did was thanks, in the first place, to a new generation of young people—many of whom had previously been active only in student politics, and who simply decided they'd had enough.

Sarah Abdelrahman (@sarrahsworld), a twenty-two-year-old drama student at the American University of Cairo, had never been on a demonstration and had never been politically active beyond the student union. On the 25th itself, knowing that the advertised start-points on Facebook would be mere 'camouflage' to fool the police, she hooked up with a friend more experienced in political organization and headed for the slum settlement of Naheya, just outside downtown Cairo.

> We had to walk in twos at first—this was my first protest and I didn't know why, but they said it's because of the Emergency Law: more than two is illegal. Then someone gave me a paper with lawyers' numbers 'in case you get detained'—and I am going: 'Whoa, whoa, whoa!'

Her eyes whiten as she relives it. She speaks perfect American English, dresses like any student in London or New York, and has that confident tone of voice you hear in the Starbucks of the world:

> We were roaming around; people started hiding in alleys, walking in twos and you could look at another two people, the other side of the street and know they don't belong here. And I'm thinking, 'I know why you are here'—there's a moment of eye contact. Someone started chanting and then all of a sudden people came from the alleys and we were about 200 people, in this tiny street. And people came onto the balconies to see what was happening.

Among the crowd she spotted Abd El Rahman Hennawy (@Hennawy89). The twenty-five-year-old is hard to miss: he sports a large beard, a red Bedouin scarf and a t-shirt bearing the word 'social-ism'. He seemed surprised to see her: 'Before then, whenever Hennawy called us out to protest, in the university, I'd be like, sorry, man, I can't. He saw me and said, what are you doing here? This is *my* stuff, it's what I do!' Hennawy was part of the core of protesters who knew what was going to happen. On the night before, 24 January, he had attended a packed meeting in a private flat. Then, like all the activists there, he'd organized a cell of six people to sleep on the floor of his own apartment and to wait there for information.

They'd been working like this since Mahalla in 2008: misdirecting the police by planning spoof marches openly on their cellphones and then failing to turn up, or launching flash demos out of the radical coffee shops in the alleyways around Tahrir. Recently they'd switched from demonstrating in the centre to demonstrating in the slums and suburbs. 'On 25 January,' Hennawy recalls,

> we put three things together for the first time: the surprise demonstration, plus going to the slums instead of downtown, plus the chants. We chanted about economics, not politics. If you are shouting 'Down with Mubarak!' in the slums, nobody cares. They care about food and shelter. So we chanted: 'How expensive is bread; how expensive is sugar; why do we have to sell our furniture?' And people joined in. We had no idea it was going to be a revolution, though. I thought it would be just a demonstration.

Hennawy estimates that the 200 activists who went to Naheya were able to mobilize up to 20,000 people on the day. The urban poor responded to two issues in particular: police brutality and the price of bread.

As this crowd, and others, marched to Tahrir Square, a pattern developed: they would hit a wall of riot police, and the wall would break. The scenes would be posted on YouTube later, but if you track back through the Twitter feeds of the leading activists (in English, because the world was watching), you can see it happen:

> 13:21:56: @Sandmonkey: Huge demo going to Tahrir #jan25 shit just got real
> 13:42:45: @norashalaby: Fuck got kettled almost suffocated till they broke cordon
> 14:08:55: @Ghonim: Everyone come to Dar El Hekma security police allow people to join us and we are few hundreds[2]

When they got to Tahrir, the fighting started. Sarah says: 'I was getting hit with water cannons, tear gas and bricks, and getting very close to being detained, and that's the moment'—she snaps her fingers—'when it hit me.'

> Someone who knows nothing about history, the opposition, nothing about freedom in Egypt and how it's been suppressed—because I've been so disconnected—you see all these people around you chanting the same thing and it triggers something in your mind ... You see people running towards the police, hurling bricks at them—and wow: the normal scenario would be to run away. I went home and I told my mother—I am not myself. I am somebody new that was born today.

The demonstrators took Tahrir Square. They fought the police, held impromptu meetings, gave sound bites to the world's media and, by nightfall, the Egyptian Revolution had begun. Twitter was blocked by the Egyptian government around 5 p.m., but the main activists were back on via a proxy (hidemyass.com) around 9 p.m. It was—as some of the activists proclaimed—a revolution planned on Facebook, organized on Twitter and broadcast to the world via YouTube. The global news channels, above all Al Jazeera, became a massive amplifier for the amateur reports and videos, spreading the revolution's impact across the world.

The farther away you stood, the more it looked like this was an uprising of secular youth with perfect teeth, speaking the kind of English you hear at Princeton or Berkeley. Even the Mubarak regime convinced itself that the revolt was something imposed from outside: tales of 'foreign agents with an agenda' were spread via the state-run rumour networks. On the night of 27 January, the government switched off the Internet. It was then that the world found out the revolution was neither digital nor alien.

## Day of Rage, 28 May 2011

Next day, Friday the 28th, the Muslim day of prayer, tens of thousands streamed out of the mosques and headed for Tahrir Square. This was the 'Day of Rage': the day the Mubarak clique effectively lost control, though it would take two more weeks to oust the man from power. The moment was captured on mobile phones and posted on YouTube.

In one video, a crowd of around three thousand pushes the riot police back over the Qasr al-Nil bridge—the main route from Zamalek Island, in western Cairo, into Tahrir Square.[3] Arcing over their heads are white plumes of tear-gas canisters. Two water-cannon trucks speed forward and swerve into the crowd, doing U-turns and jerks to flatten as many demonstrators as possible, but the security forces are unable to stop the crowd, now so big it fills the bridge.

The water cannons fire. The crowd halts. An imam appears, clad in white. The men at the front form a row and now, soaked through and shielding their eyes, just yards from the police, they kneel and pray. Those behind them do the same. Everybody is clawing at their faces as the water concentrates the tear gas, spraying a burning cocktail onto their skin.

Now, police trucks drive directly into the crowd; the praying ends, the crowds scatter. Police shoot a man in the face with a tear-gas grenade, point-blank (later, video footage of him on the operating table shows up on YouTube, smashed teeth protruding from a hole where his mouth had been). The crowd panics, pursued by four trucks and the far end of the bridge is engulfed in smoke, and now flames, as somebody has torched a car.

It seems like game over, but it's not. Soon the police are in full retreat, back across the bridge: the crowd has armed itself with traffic barriers and a tube-shaped metal kiosk, which they roll before them on its side like a tank. A water-cannon truck has been captured and the rioters turn this, too, into a moving barricade. The police beat a headlong, terrified retreat. If the crowd pursuing them look like football fans, that's because many of them are: the 'ultras' of Zamalek Sporting Club.

Mahmoud, who I met in Tahrir Square a few weeks later, draped in the flag of Zamalek SC, was among them. 'There was me and about four thousand others at Qasr al-Nil bridge,' he recalled. 'It was a beautiful feeling: to know that Egypt is finally free of all the corruption, the rule of the iron fist.'

The 'ultras'—named after the notorious Italian football hooligan gangs—had organized for years in the face of police repression, at all big soccer clubs. The police accused the ultras of fostering terrorism and organized crime, and they, in turn, found ways of getting their banners, flares and weapons into the stadiums. They would meet up at pre-arranged venues, ready to fight each other and the cops. On 28 January they were initially summoned to go and smash the demonstration, says Mahmoud, in response to rumours that it was organized by foreign agents:

> We came down to see what was the truth behind what the media had been telling us, and found it was all wrong. The club HQ kept telling us the protesters were traitors, foreigners, and urging the ultras to go down there and do something about it. But when we got there, to Tahrir, we formed our own opinion: we bonded with the protesters and became part of them.

Ultras from rival club al-Ahly also joined in the fighting. By the end of the day numerous police cars had been torched, the headquarters of Mubarak's National Democratic Party was on fire, and protesters controlled Tahrir Square.

He's thin, Mahmoud, with a cheeky smile poking out from beneath his red-and-white Zamalek scarf. He says: 'Why don't you ask me about football?' So I throw him some inane question about Zamalek's position in the league. He chuckles: 'Since the revolution I've been neglecting football hooliganism for a bigger cause: the revolution. I can speak for both myself and every ultra. We all have.'

## A soft coup

On 29 January, with several hundred protesters killed across Egypt, the demonstrators forced the riot cops of the Central Security to vacate the streets; the ordinary police force withdrew too, in a calculated tactic to promote lawlessness. Army units were positioned at strategic points, but having refused an order from the interior ministry to use live ammo on the demonstrators, they took no part in the maintenance of law and order. All across Cairo, neighbourhoods responded by creating vigilante squads armed with clubs and small firearms. The main aim of these groups was to fend off the *baltagiya*—essentially a network of civilian thugs paid and organized by the police to carry out such beatings, rapes and tortures as are necessary to pacify a city of 22 million people without rights or decent livelihoods.

The moment was essentially a soft coup by the army against the parts of the regime loyal to Mubarak, but at the same time it created 'fragmented power' on the streets: not so much the 'dual power' of Marxist theory, but the kind of deconstructed power we saw taking shape in the vacuum left by Hurricane Katrina and would see, at isolated moments, in Greece and London later in 2011.

Though the precise details of how the military then seized power remain shrouded, there can be few clearer examples of an economics-driven split within a ruling class. Gamal Mubarak's neoliberal programme of privatizations and corporate land grabs had been actively championed by the IMF and by leading European politicians: from Tony Blair and Peter Mandelson to French industry minister Eric Besson and, of course, Silvio Berlusconi, as well as many of the business leaders who gather annually at Davos.

Gamal and his brother Alaa had built a personal fortune for the family, estimated at around $70 billion, by extracting stakes in the newly privatized enterprises. Like many of the morally dubious enterprises that have collapsed in chaos since 2008, it was run from a business address in London.

But decades before the Mubaraks created their neoliberal fiefdom, the army had created its own economic empire: factories, tourist resorts and service businesses, replete with a supply chain of privately held companies dependent on army patronage. The politicians and media types aligned with this section of Egyptian capital saw the state, not global capitalism, as their meal ticket. The generals, together with this 'national' faction of Egyptian capital, had material reasons to resent the Mubarak clique—above all the impending stitch-up of the presidential succession—and they saw their moment.

While the masses were on the streets, these two factions fought a Shakespearean death-tragedy behind closed doors, and the army won. First, they forced Mubarak to concede the appointment of a vice president; next, the sacking of his cabinet and its replacement with army-aligned politicians. On 1 February, with a million people in Tahrir, they forced Mubarak to announce he would no longer seek re-election. The next day, Mubarak-loyal politicians paid camel drivers to gallop into Tahrir Square to attack protesters: the aim was to present to the world the illusion of a mass backlash, an 'enough reform and lawlessness' movement.

When, after two days and nights of hand-to-hand fighting, the camel-backed counter-revolution failed, Tahrir began to fill with a much wider demographic of protesters who, day by day, rejected the various compromises and reshuffles offered by Mubarak. Who can forget the old man holding up a placard that read: 'Mubarak: Go! My arms are tired'?

Finally, on 10 February, at the demand of the first meeting in decades of the Supreme Council of the Armed Forces (SCAF), Mubarak recorded a speech announcing he would step down. But Gamal stormed into the presidential palace and forced his father to scrap the recording and make a new one. This promised only elections by September.

It was to be the final straw for the masses, who were flooding into Tahrir in their hundreds of thousands, and for the army, which was now beginning to split openly under pressure of demands from Tahrir and because of its fraternization with the protesters. The generals forced Mubarak's departure—without further ado or speeches—on 11 February, to be replaced in power by General Tantawi and the SCAF itself.

But by now a new force was making itself heard: the working class.

## *The collapse of invisible walls*

The Egyptian working class bears the birthmarks of its creation, first under British rule and then during the state capitalist regime of Gamal Abdel Nasser: it is concentrated in the public sector, in army-owned factories and in recently privatized enterprises. On the eve of the revolution, 28 per cent of the workforce was employed by the state and just 10 per cent in the 'modern' sector—that is, in textiles, construction, energy, transport and services. More than a third of workers were 'informal', and the rest worked on the land.[4]

Though shrunk by twenty years of privatization, and further diminished by job losses after 2008, the Egyptian working class had a clear demographic identity under Mubarak. You could see it on the picket lines that formed in early February.

At the gates of the Suez Canal Port Authority, it was middle-aged men and their sons in orange overalls. Big-chested guys who'd had to fight for these jobs—and defy the state-run union to go on strike and occupy the port. Among the Real Estate Tax Authority Workers in their blue baseball caps, who marched into Tahrir calling for Mubarak to go, there were more women: but that same confident, educated culture was evident. They'd been the first to break from Mubarak's state-run union federation in 2008.

This is a class with status: the men seem physically larger than the urban poor, and the demographic is discernibly centred on the age group 35–55. And they have a culture of solidarity. For Mubarak, the price of maintaining the state-run union as an organ of control within the workplace had been to hold congresses, maintain the NDP's membership of the Socialist International, to keep the ILO onside, and to deliver material concessions. In 2008, 5.9 million government workers won a 30 per cent pay rise in 2008, while Mubarak was forced to double food, health and education subsidies, from LE64 billion to LE128 billion (\$22 billion).[5]

By 9 February the pattern of action was clear: workers were beginning to form unions separate from the state-run union, often seizing the workplace and kicking out the boss. At a textile factory in Daqahliya they sacked the CEO and began self-management. At a printing house in Cairo, they did the same. In Suez, where there had been heavy repression, the steel mill and the fertilizer factory had declared all-out strikes until the fall of the regime.[6]

Egyptian activists are split over the significance of this late-stage strike wave: some think it was a second-order effect of the mass unrest, others believe it was decisive in beginning to split the army—and thus forcing the SCAF to depose Mubarak. What is not in doubt is that, after 11 February, worker unrest took off.

Mohammed Shafiq, a psychiatrist at the Manshiyet el Bakri hospital in Cairo, had been in Tahrir Square as a volunteer medic from day one, treating the injured in one of the makeshift clinics:

I had been in Tahrir for about ten days. I'm tired, I'm hungry, so I decided to go to my own hospital as there was a standstill between the regime and the protesters. In the hospital there was a revolutionary mood. Even those who supported Mubarak knew the situation could not go on. I started a petition, with some of the demands I'd been hearing in Tahrir Square: all the doctors signed and then, amazingly, nurses started coming to me, saying: 'You are demanding a cut in hours and an increase in wages—what about us?'

Shafiq describes what happened next as 'the collapse of invisible walls': the nurses, the technicians, the porters added their demands.

Then he returned to Tahrir: the last days of Mubarak, followed by days of chaos and celebration, were frantic for the medics. But when he went back to the hospital in mid-February, the workers asked: 'What happened to our petition?' By now the entire workforce of 750 people, including managers, had signed it. They formed a cross-professional trade union. The nurses staged a sit-in over unpaid wages. The doctors also joined: junior doctors in a public hospital earned just LE300 a month basic, while hospital administrators could earn LE2,000. Shafiq says:

> The manager in every hospital is like a small dictator, they are a 'Mubarak in the workplace'. But we'd just decapitated Mubarak! After four weeks we decided to sack the manager. We told him not to come to work, and told the security guards to lock him out. He went to the ministry and complained—but the union ran the hospital for two weeks until we elected a new manager. It was the height of dual power except it was not dual power, it was only one power, and it was us.

When I meet Shafiq in April, he's hosting a delegation of British trade unionists, sweating into their souvenir Tahrir t-shirts in the garden of the Doctors' Union. The doctors are about to launch a national strike call, but the union is controlled by the Muslim Brotherhood, which doesn't want to strike. Another young doctor comes over.

'My colleague favours an immediate all-out strike,' Shafiq informs the British postmen and train drivers huddled under the palm trees. 'But I favour a warning strike to start with. What would you do?' A bloke from London Underground asks: 'What are your plans for picketing?' Both men look blank. There is further puzzlement among the hijab-clad young female medics who have joined us. After a few minutes back and forth in Arabic and cockney, the Brits explain the idea of blocking access to the workplace to prevent strike-breakers. 'This had not occurred to us,' say the Egyptians.

On May Day 2011, as Shafiq and the secular medics jostle with the Brotherhood for control of the stage at the Doctors' Union, workers begin filling Tahrir Square. It is, says Hossam el-Hamalawy, the first real May Day since 1951. The red flag does not predominate: instead people arrive with homemade banners, always with middle-aged men in the lead, chanting and singing. One banner says: 'Fight for social justice, not your own demands'. At the edge of the square, the top-selling items on the souvenir stands are A4 posters showing Mubarak and all his ministers in orange jumpsuits, with nooses around their necks.

A loud delegation from the Masry Shebin El-Kom textile factory surrounds me. Mahmoud el-Shaar, who's led a thirty-five-day occupation at the plant, says:

> We're striking to remove the imperialist presence of foreign elements. Mubarak privatized the company to Indonesian owners and they've shut four out of seven units. We want the prosecution of the corrupt officials who ran the cotton industry, and we want to terminate the contract with the Indonesians because it's destroying our lives. Our average wage is between LE360 and LE700 a month.

The company was the target of a classic Mubarak-era deal: the Indorama group paid LE174 million for 70 per cent of the assets, the state kept 18 per cent and the NDP-run trade union would own 12 per cent. 'The old, Mubarak union did nothing but corrupt the situation: we're finished with them,' el-Shaar says.[7] Rifat Abdul, in the t-shirt of the public transport union, grabs my arm. His banner demands a minimum wage of LE1200. What's changed?

> I feel free. We all feel we can say what we think without getting detained for it. At work, though, nothing has changed: wages, conditions, work hours, nothing. But there is a spirit of optimism between all workers, in every sector. During the revolution, we were here from

22

day one. But now it's reached the point where we look around and we recognize these other delegations from the days in Tahrir Square, people from totally different sectors: we know each other's faces, we shake each other's hands, we slap each other on the back.

His mate, Wasim, rips the baseball cap off his bald head. 'Look,' he says. 'We're not going anywhere. I'm 100 per cent sure the whole world is behind us. We'll stay here in the sun and heat until it's done.' But it's not done yet.

### The question for Musa Zekry

Back in the Moqattam slum, Musa Zekry's future revolves around a single type of shampoo, brand name Pert. To prevent counterfeits, Procter & Gamble pay the *zabbaleen* to shred every Pert bottle they collect, in return for cash. With the cash—supplemented by money from Bill Gates—they run a school. At the school the kids learn Arabic, English, computing and how to shred the Pert bottles. Zekry learned English at this school and now mentors the kids.

They are bright-eyed and cheerful, but decide to sing me a doleful Coptic song whose refrain asserts the inevitability of being poor and the certainty of salvation. One kid, aged thirteen, explains his daily routine: 'I go rubbish collecting from 2 a.m. to 8 a.m., and at 8 a.m. I go to school.' With free English lessons he's one of the lucky few, so what are his ambitions? 'To collect so much rubbish we can pay for another school.'

Will he leave the slum? He shakes his head. The combined efforts of Bill Gates, Procter & Gamble and thirty years of Mubarak's rule never managed to raise the aspirations of the Cairo poor beyond a better kind of poverty. By contrast, twenty-one days of revolution have brought freedom.

And freedom poses questions philanthropy does not bother with. Will Musa Zekry get healthcare, a living wage, free education for his kids *as of right*, instead of through charity? Will the 'Mubaraks-in-every-enterprise' be toppled? Will Egyptian society be scarred by rampant corruption and inequality forever? Or will they get something better?

These are questions which, for twenty years, the policy elite believed were closed. The great surge of freedom that carried Musa Zekry into Tahrir Square has reopened them.

But I'm rushing ahead. We need to backtrack, to the old world, where everything was stable and imagination was dead ...

# 2

# Nobody Saw It Coming: How the World's Collective Imagination Failed

President Zine El Abidine Ben Ali fled Tunisia on 14 January 2011. By 11 February, Hosni Mubarak was gone, and protests were spreading across the region: to Yemen, where the first 'day of rage' took place on 27 January; to Bahrain, where protesters occupied the Pearl Roundabout on 14 February. Then, on 17 February, security forces started shooting marchers in Bahrain and the Libyan people rose up against Gaddafi. On 25 March the long, tortured battle for freedom in Syria began.

Nobody had seen this coming. Nobody with any influence, anyway. The stock image of Arabs in the Western media was of a passive but violent race, often filed under the categories of 'terrorism' and 'insoluble problems'. The Middle East specialists in the diplomatic and intelligence communities worked with a scarcely more sophisticated version of the same view. The *Economist* magazine's celebrated yearbook, published in December 2010, contained just four predictions for North Africa and the Middle East: Sudan would split; Iran's economy would suffer; Iraq would continue to be a headache; and there would be new peace talks over Palestine.[1] Mubarak, Ben Ali, Gaddafi, Saleh and Assad were deemed to be of no interest.

Even after the fall of Ben Ali, they failed to see it coming. In an article titled 'Why the Tunisian revolution won't spread', Stephen M. Walt,

Harvard professor of international relations, opined that: 'The history of world revolution suggests that this sort of revolutionary cascade is quite rare, and even when some sort of revolutionary contagion does take place, it happens pretty slowly and is often accompanied by overt foreign invasion.'[2]

Even when Tahrir Square was occupied, they could not see it coming. On the night of 25 January, Hillary Clinton told reporters: 'Our assessment is that the Egyptian government is stable.'[3] On the same day, Israel's military intelligence chief told the Knesset much the same thing. He predicted that Mubarak would 'be able to keep the demonstrations in check', and echoed Clinton's words: the regime was 'stable'.[4]

And even when the revolution was all but over, some could still not see it. Peter Mandelson, the former Labour minister, made an extraordinary plea to the global elite to save the Egyptian dauphin, Gamal Mubarak:

> Gamal Mubarak … has been the leading voice in favour of change within the government and the ruling party. Of course, it is easy to cast him as the putative beneficiary of a nepotistic transfer of family power, the continuation of 'tyranny' with a change of face at the top. This analysis, in my view, is too simplistic.

For a good six months, then, the Western political elite, media, academia and intelligence services were effectively driving with a shattered windscreen. But why?

The specific myopia over the Arab states is not hard to explain. Decades ago, Edward Said tried to warn the West about the self-deluding nature of its narrative on the Middle East:

> Very little of the detail, the human density, the passion of Arab-Moslem life has entered the awareness of even those people whose profession it is to report the Arab world. What we have instead is a

series of crude, essentialized caricatures of the Islamic world presented in such a way as to make that world vulnerable to military aggression.[5]

Said's words were written in 1980: long before 9/11, before two invasions of Iraq had laid the basis for sectarian civil war there, and before the West began to conflate the narrative of Islam with al-Qaeda's narrative of ruthless, nihilistic terror. For Carnegie scholar Tarek Masoud, the misapprehension goes deeper than the problem of cultural stereotypes:

> Those of us who study the region not only failed to predict the [Mubarak] regime's collapse, we actually saw it as an exemplar of something we called 'durable authoritarianism'—a new breed of modern dictatorship that had figured out how to tame the political, economic, and social forces that routinely did in autocracy's lesser variants.[6]

This gets closer to the root cause of disorientation, and holds lessons valid beyond the Middle East. A flaw in the West's political psyche had convinced people that dictatorships could be stable and sustainable, flying in the face of a 200-year-old doctrine equating capitalism and freedom. But none of this explains the depth of the disorientation: something in the intellectual Kool-Aid had atrophied our ability to think beyond the present.

Indifference to class, the one-dimensional mindset of the professional 'Arabists' and outright self-interest all played a part in misleading the political right. But the left, too, was disoriented. The key problem was spelled out by the theorist Fredric Jameson in 2003: 'It is easier to imagine the end of the world than it is to imagine the end of capitalism.'[7]

*Twenty years of capitalist realism*

When a cheetah catches a gazelle there is always a moment where the prey gives up: it goes floppy, bares its neck, becomes resigned to its fate. You have got me, it seems to say, but now you have to kill me; in the meantime I will try to think about something else.

This has been the relationship between the right and the left since the early 1990s. The organized working class of the Fordist era was smashed, the Soviet Union—if no longer a role model, then at least a pole of opposition to US dominance—was gone. State capitalism and Keynesian economics had been supplanted. Modernism, the beloved republic that had begun with Picasso and Kandinsky, had been overthrown by such geniuses as Tracey Emin and Damien Hirst. Rock and roll was dead several times over; the airwaves now sizzled with litanies to rape and murder by black dudes with diamond earrings. What to do?

If we look at the main intellectual contributions from the left in this period, they are effectively rationalizations of defeat. Jameson's seminal 1991 account of postmodernism defines it as a 'condition', reliant on new technology, a new mass psychology of passivity and the fragmentation of meaning within culture. In this condition, he writes, there is

> an unparalleled rate of change on all the levels of social life and an unparalleled standardization of everything … What we now begin to feel … is henceforth, where everything now submits to the perpetual change of fashion and media image, that nothing can change any longer.[8]

On top of this there was the media: vast, powerful, impervious to criticism, corporate, and monopolized by the rich. Chomsky and Herman's celebrated book on the media, *Manufacturing Consent*, outlined the ways in which control over the media allowed capitalism to assert a new cultural dominance:

The beauty of the system, however, is that such dissent and inconvenient information are kept within bounds and at the margins, so that while their presence shows the system is not monolithic, they are not large enough to interfere unduly with the domination of the official agenda.[9]

While that may have been correct when the book was first published, it is striking that the emergence of the Internet did not fundamentally change its authors' analysis. In their 2002 introduction to a revised edition of *Manufacturing Consent*, Chomsky and Herman concluded that the Internet, while a powerful tool for activists, would make no difference to the ability of corporate interests to control the media, or to its essential role as propagandist for big corporations. They judged that the rapid commercialization and concentration of the Internet 'threatens to limit any future prospects of the Internet as a democratic media vehicle'.

When it came to philosophy, leftists who had railed against 'bourgeois ideology' now abandoned the very concept. Slavoj Žižek rejected the idea that ideology was 'false consciousness', arguing, effectively, that ideology *is* consciousness: it is impossible to escape the mental trap created by capitalism, because one's life inside the system constantly recreates it. Instead of rebellion we are reduced to perpetual cynicism: we are trapped, like Neo in *The Matrix*, in a world we know to be half true. But we can't escape: 'Even if we do not take things seriously, even if we keep an ironical distance, we are still doing them.'[10]

Add it all up and you get the mindset of the left in an era of defeat. Nothing can change. Dissent is not strong enough to break the media's stranglehold; only irony or flight are possible.

By the late 1990s, Western mass culture was dominated by this zeitgeist of impotence. Future movie historians will look at the Hollywood catalogue and see this as the dominant theme of the 2000s: from *The Matrix* and *The Truman Show* to the Bourne movies, from *The Eternal Sunshine of the Spotless Mind* to films as various as *Avatar* and *Inception*, through all of them there flows the notion of 'manipulated consciousness': the suspicion that the hero is trapped within a malevolent system that controls his mind, but which he cannot defeat. This is no longer the external control of Orwell's *1984*, but a pre-programmed alternative reality against which the hero cannot deploy core human values like love and decency.

In an influential essay, cultural commentator Mark Fisher describes the impact of all this on a generation that has known nothing else. He calls the resulting phenomenon 'capitalist realism', defined as

> the widespread sense that not only is capitalism the only viable political and economic system, but also that it is now impossible even to *imagine* a coherent alternative to it ... a pervasive atmosphere conditioning not only the production of culture but also the regulation of work and education, and acting as a kind of invisible barrier constraining action.[11]

Up to 2008, the left's inability to imagine any alternative to capitalism was like a mirror image of the right's triumphalism. The establishment's tramline thinking on Islam and its theories of 'durable authoritarianism' conformed, like the rest of its ideology, to Francis Fukuyama's 'end of history' thesis and the paeans of various commentators—Thomas Friedman foremost among them—to the triumph of globalization. Together, left and right created a shared fatalism about the future.

The right believed that with indomitable power it could create whatever truth it wanted to. In a famous phrase, Karl Rove, senior advisor to then US President George W. Bush, scorned those without power as the 'reality-based community'. Study reality, if you will, in search of solutions, Rove is said to have told a journalist, but

> That's not the way the world really works anymore. We're an empire now, and when we act, we create our own reality. And while you're studying that reality—judiciously, as you will—we'll act again,

creating other new realities, which you can study too, and that's how things will sort out. We're history's actors … and you, all of you, will be left to just study what we do.[12]

But then Lehman Brothers went bust. Here was a reality the neocons had not created, and against which they were powerless. The date was 15 September 2008. Suddenly, it became possible to imagine the end of capitalism. Indeed, faced with a 50 per cent loss of global stock market value in six months, the scale of the disaster forced even some investors to contemplate it. But few, even now, were prepared to imagine an alternative.

If the rule of men like Mubarak, Gaddafi and Assad had been seen as somehow separate from the rule of free-market capitalism, maybe political science would not have become trapped in the same fatalism as economics. But support for these pro-Western dictators—or more especially for their sons—had always been sold on the basis that they were 'liberalizers': freeing up their home market for corporate penetration and, one day soon, reforming their constitutions. This was the theme of the famous essay by Anthony Giddens, which declared Gaddafi to be a follower of the Third Way and Libya on the road to becoming 'the Norway of North Africa'.[13]

Consequently, the failure of imagination leaked easily from economics into politics, diplomacy and social affairs. Few could conceive the fall of Mubarak or Gaddafi; the collapse of Rupert Murdoch's political leverage; the appearance of half a million young demonstrators on the streets of Tel Aviv, or Arab teenagers shouting 'Fuck Hamas' in the streets of Gaza City.

In my book *Meltdown*, in June 2010, I grappled with the reasons for this deep psychological complacency:

It appears—because it has been the case for twenty years—that every problem is solvable … that no matter how badly the world economy slumps there is a pain-free way out of it. Once the realization dawns

31

that there is not, and that the pain will be severe, the question is posed that has not really been posed for twenty years: who should feel it?[14]

Now, that question had become concrete. On 17 December 2010, a street vendor called Mohamed Bouazizi walked into the traffic in the Tunisian backwater of Sidi Bouzid, carrying a can of gasoline, and set himself on fire: he had, he claimed, been slapped by a corrupt local official, and his street goods had been confiscated. Within eight months, what began with Bouazizi had ripped away the fabric of autocratic rule across the Middle East.

And with hindsight we can now see that the fabric had already begun to fray elsewhere.

## Athens and Gaza

From late 2008, events began to happen in which the new predominated over the old; in which the forces that would defy fatalism began to flex their limbs. Almost simultaneously the neocon faction of the US political elite lost the ability to 'create reality' as described by Karl Rove— starting with the loss of the White House.

The clearest precursor event for the new unrest was the December 2008 uprising in Athens. For three weeks after the police shooting of fifteen-year-old Alexandros Grigoropoulos in the student district of Exarcheia, students rioted, struck and occupied their universities, their actions eventually drawing in parts of the Greek labour movement.

The disturbances in Athens created a template of 'social explosion': an uncontrolled and randomly provoked reaction to economic crisis, in which students and uneducated urban youth come together to make mayhem. One second-generation Greek immigrant remembered:

This was my first time ever to cast a stone, first time I covered my face … I had been before in demonstrations and protests but never before I had participated in riots. It was something like an initiation for me and

I have to admit I felt liberated, you know. It made me feel like I regained control over myself.[15]

The next precursor moment is the Israeli invasion of Gaza, which began two days after the Greek riots ended, on 27 December 2009. Operation Cast Lead would radicalize many Egyptian youths and discredit sections of the mainstream media in the eyes of young people both in the West and in North Africa. Though in fact a military victory for Israel, it appeared as a moral defeat to the Arab youth, and to Muslim youth in Europe. In the West it would bring onto the streets the same core alliance of anti-capitalists, inner-city youth and the labour-orientated left as had staged mass protests over Iraq earlier in the decade. On 9 January 2009 a quarter of a million people took to the streets of Madrid; big demos occurred in every European capital, plus huge protests in Jakarta and Manila. The London demonstrations ended with violence and large-scale arrests: more than sixty Muslim men aged between seventeen and twenty were jailed.

One of the few commentators to predict the Arab Spring was the sometime adviser to Venezuelan President Hugo Chávez, Alan Woods. As demonstrations flared across the Middle East during the Gaza war, Woods observed that 'all the pro-Western regimes there are hanging by a thread ... Saudi Arabia ... Egypt ... Lebanon ... So is Jordan, so is Morocco. These ruling elites were terrified by the demonstrations that took place during the Gaza war.'[16]

The invasion of Gaza even struck home among some sections of the Western political elites. 'Our policy is disgusting,' one Labour ministerial aide told me in January 2009. 'If I were not a government adviser I would be on the anti-war demonstrations myself.'

### Iran: The 'Twitter Revolution'

Then came Iran. On 13 June 2009 the incumbent president, Mahmoud Ahmadinejad, was re-elected with 62 per cent of the vote. Turnouts above 100 per cent in two provinces, massive discrepancies between pre-election polls and the results, plus widespread ballot-rigging, sent supporters of the reformist candidate Mir-Hossein Mousavi onto the streets within hours. 'If Iran sleeps tonight,' tweeted @mehri912, 'it will sleep forever.' It did not sleep.

The first of the iconic cellphone videos shows a crowd of protesters moving swiftly down Tehran's Valiasr Street, chanting: 'Mousavi, take back my vote!' These are office workers: men with briefcases, women wearing the minimum headgear required to avoid harassment from the religious authorities. Another YouTube video, fifty-eight seconds long and shot on a cellphone, shows what happened next.[17]

It starts with a crush of people against a shop façade, women screaming as they fight for space. Now the camera-holder, like the men in front of him, elbows his way forward as uniformed cops start batoning protesters, none of whom show any sign of belligerence. This is pure dictatorship: the collective punishment of a crowd for the act of being there. Riot police with shields run after them as they flee, beating their legs and backs, and on the soundtrack, again, we hear women screaming.

Next the cameraman spins round; the visored face of a policeman looms into shot as he hits the cameraman on the leg and tells him to get lost. Off-camera you hear the repeated thud of truncheons on flesh and more screaming. Then the shot becomes of running feet.

By nightfall, that video was zipping around the global Farsi networks via blogs, YouTube, Twitter and Facebook. If it had been taken by a TV cameraman, that fifty-eight-second single shot would have won awards. It captures reality in a way you rarely see on TV news: terror, chaos, innocence, the sudden tremor in the policeman's face as he bottles out of hitting the cameraman again. But the point about the video is that it was not shot by a news crew, nor was it shown in full on any TV network.

Social media's power to present unmediated reality has never been better demonstrated. And the Iranian demonstrations produced hundreds of similar videos, both of the protests and the crackdown that confronted them. Thanks to Twitter, these images exploded like a virus onto the screens of young people all over the world. The *Washington Times* called it 'Iran's Twitter Revolution':

> Hackers in particular were active in helping keep channels open as the regime blocked them, and they spread the word about functioning proxy portals. Eventually the regime started taking down these sources, and the e-dissidents shifted to e-mail. The only way to completely block the flow of Internet information would have been to take the entire country offline, a move the regime apparently has resisted thus far.[18]

Though the Ahmadinejad regime now took down Twitter, Facebook and SMS, it could not prevent the imagery circulating. No revolution in history had been recorded so comprehensively, and in such minute detail. In one video, police pick on a bystander at a bus stop; as they baton him a woman in a headscarf, about five feet tall, karate-kicks the police, two of whom then turn on her. One batons a car bonnet, randomly, in frustration. Then they stop and the woman merges again into the queue at the bus stop.[19]

Future social historians will gorge themselves on evidence like this, the micro-detail of social responses to unrest: but for now, its importance lies in the way it enables participants to judge what kind of history is being made in real time. Banned from reporting in Iran, the mainstream media quickly began to realize the value of this user-generated content, and to run it. The momentum of the protests fed off this cycle of guerrilla newsgathering, media amplification, censorship and renewed protest.

By the time the death of protester Neda Agha-Soltan was shown on YouTube, on 20 June 2009, the once-forlorn slogan of the anti-globalization movement had become a reality: the whole world actually *was* watching.

Bystanders posted three separate videos of Neda's shooting by a member of the regime's Basij militia: *Time* magazine called it 'probably the most widely witnessed death in human history'.[20] Blood trickles over her face. Her eyes roll sideways. She says, 'I'm burning.' Her grey-haired singing teacher vainly tries to staunch the flow of blood. Later, the crowd detains the alleged perpetrator and his security pass is photographed: this too gets uploaded to YouTube.

Another image resonated across the world that summer from Tehran: the so-called 'rooftop poems'. As demonstrations were repressed, student dorms invaded and young men handed over to the Basij rape-gangs and torture squads, protesters retreated to the roof-tops by night to call out *Allah-o-Akbar*. On 16 June an anonymous young woman, whose YouTube username is Oldouz84, began impro-vising poems as she filmed the rooftop cries. In the last clip, taken the day after Neda's death, she whispers:

> *Allah-o-Akbar* is no longer about being a Muslim. It's become a call for unity, whether Muslim, Jew, Zoroastrian, faithless or faithful. The voices are coming from far away: they leave you shaken ... Too many children will not hold their parents tonight. It could have been you or me.[21]

It's delivered in the style of an art-house movie narration: Wim Wenders in Farsi, with Tehran instead of West Berlin. But it is real—just as Neda's death, the karate-kicking woman, the surging crowds and baton charges are all real. The reality of protest, self-sacrifice and solidarity surged through the songlines of the Internet. Not everybody saw them: only the netizens sitting up late at night in Santa Cruz, in Marrakech, in Beijing, in Cairo, dipping beneath the barriers of Internet censorship in search of a better world. And it turned out there were more of these netizens than anybody thought.

The Iranian uprising was defeated: in part because the youth and the professional classes overestimated the break the poor were prepared to make with the hardliners; in part because the workers—having created strong, semi-legal organizations in defiance of repression, and having staged a wave of strikes which would continue into 2011—were not prepared to stake everything on an alliance with Mousavi.

But all the ingredients were present of the uprisings that would, eighteen months later, galvanize the Middle East and beyond: radicalized, secular-leaning youth; a repressed workers' movement with considerable social power; uncontrollable social media; the restive urban poor. And there was an élan, a poetry about it, an absence of postmodern cynicism. If you had met Neda Soltan or Oldouz84 in a Starbucks in New York, they would be just like you.

But still the media and the politicians failed to see it coming. Most reports placed Gaza and Iran in the category 'Islam versus the rest of the world', and heard Greece as merely sound and fury, signifying nothing.

### Communiqué from an absent future

last night around midnight, there was an out of control electrocommunist dance party with maybe 300 people dancing to justice in quarry plaza with glow sticks chanting STRIKE! STRIKE! STRIKE! i'm not kidding. i don't drink but i think it's pretty awesome that we violated every single party regulation the university has for 4 or 5 hours and there was no police action.[22]

On 24 September 2009, students at University of California Santa Cruz occupied their own common rooms and held a dance party. By November, student occupations had spread to Los Angeles, California, Fresno, Davis, Irvine and Berkeley. While students have always sporadically protested over politics, this was an economic movement, and its targets were spelled out on the banners they had hung at the rave in Santa Cruz: 'Take over the city, Take over campus, End capital'. The occupation movement continued to gather momentum throughout the winter of

2009, culminating in a coordinated walk-out on campuses across America on 4 March 2010.

Something new was happening. Throughout the first decade of the twenty-first century, students had been told they were society's new archetype. Their knowledge work would ensure a prosperous future; their passion for personal electronics would keep China's factories in business; and their debt repayments would fuel Wall Street for half a century.

But by 2010, students all over the developed world were coming under economic attack, through a combination of fee increases, hikes in the cost of student credit and a jobs downturn that had seen casual work dry up. If the students who led the struggles at Berkeley in the 1960s had been a prosperous, nerdy elite fighting for the rights of African Americans, their successors were now themselves victims, on an economic front line. 'The arriving freshman', they complained, 'is treated as a mortgage, and the fees are climbing. She is a future revenue stream, and the bills are growing. She is security for a debt she never chose, and the cost is staggering.'[23]

Among students and graduates, this sudden loss of confidence in the future was tangible. One of its most eloquent expressions was penned by the Research and Destroy group of activists at UC Santa Cruz. Entitled *Communiqué from an Absent Future*, it became required reading among student radicals everywhere. It perfectly captures the impact of 'capitalist realism' on the youth of the 2000s: 'Safety ... and comfort have been our watchwords. We slide through the flesh world without being touched or moved. We shepherd our emptiness from place to place.' But now the postmodernist dreamtime was at an end:

'Work hard, play hard' has been the over-eager motto of a generation in training for ... what?—drawing hearts in cappuccino foam, or plugging names and numbers into databases. The gleaming techno-future of American capitalism was long ago packed up and sold to China for a few more years of borrowed junk. A university diploma is now worth no more than a share in General Motors.[24]

And General Motors, by this point, had gone bust. As the stimulus packages ran out, and the first waves of post-Lehman austerity began to hit public-sector pay and pension rights in 2010, those in power comforted themselves with one thought: that postmodern society had eradicated solidarity. The young would never go out onto the streets to fight for the rights of the old, established workforce; the feral youth of the inner cities would never combine with the educated elite. There might even be an 'age war' between the baby boomers and the iPod generation. There would be strife, but it would never be coherent.

On 19 October 2010, the Paris bureau of Associated Press issued the following newswire: 'Masked youths clad in black torched cars, smashed storefronts and threw up roadblocks Tuesday, clashing with riot police across France as protests over raising the retirement age to 62 took a radical turn.'

The age of capitalist realism was over. Things would now kick off in the most unlikely places, and involve people nobody ever expected to resist.

# 3

## 'Trust Is Explosive':
## Britain's Youth Rebel Against Austerity


*London*. She walks into Soho's Bar Italia looking like a postmodern Sally Bowles: black top, black skirt, black tights; bobbed black hair. Black cowl modelled on an outfit worn by Lady Gaga. Outsize black sunglasses. Blue glitter beneath the eyes. She says,

> I was at a dinner party the night before the occupation and they said to me if you don't come with us you will have to stay in the flat on your own and you won't like it. You can tweet as much as you want. They kind of tricked me because we were on this march, and I was tweeting, and then suddenly we were in a room and that was the occupation.

This was on 'Day X', 24 November 2010, and the venue was University College London: just the kind of place a privately educated, Lib-Dem-voting twenty-one-year-old might go to get an English degree, in between drinking large amounts of gin and attending Paris Fashion Week:

> The people who sat down at the media table turned out to be a working group: I knew most of them on Twitter but had never met them in person before. I think they recognized me from my Twitter picture because it's, er, quite distinctive. Then, once we started tweeting, we

41

got loads of messages of support and I started replying with this hashtag: #solidarity. I had no idea of, like, its historical meaning. I just thought: that's a great word.

Had she heard of the Polish trade union Solidarity? Shakes her head. Nothing at all: only three weeks later somebody told her. Had she heard of the song 'Solidarity Forever'? Ditto, but she can sing it now.

I had no politics. I still don't subscribe to any. I'd probably say I was quite far left now—although I am not radical. I don't read newspapers. I bought the *Guardian* once because there was a picture of me. I read blog posts. The books I read, apart from coursework, are mainly chick-lit.

Guy Debord? Toni Negri? Any of the books traditionally found strewn on the floors of student occupations? 'I haven't and I wouldn't,' says @littlemisswilde, whose real-life name is Jessica Riches.

I would rather read new stuff: the old ideas are nice to know; they're context. But I would rather know what's happening now. I can't believe there are still people who read articles. If everybody had a Twitter feed you could just see the news as it happens. You don't need 100 words of background.

If the political elite had understood the power of the militantly unread socialite with a Twitter feed, they might have salvaged something out of the clash they provoked with Britain's youth. But they had no idea.

### Millbank gets deconstructed

'Millbank' is journalistic shorthand for the unofficial nexus of power in British politics. The street, right by the River Thames, houses the political studios of the main TV networks, the party HQs, the offices of lobby firms and think tanks and, at the end of it, parliament.

But on the cold, clear afternoon of 10 November 2010, as around 200 students broke away from a student march to gather outside Conservative Party HQ at Millbank Tower, the word 'Millbank' was about to acquire another meaning. Because Millbank was where they lost control. The Coalition lost control of the political agenda; the NUS leadership lost control of the student movement; the police lost control of the streets.

Millbank was staffed by that narrow group of graduates who'd bought into the whole story of mainstream politics: the bad suit, the neat hair, the drug-free lifestyle led in hopes of one day becoming an MP. Now they found themselves besieged by their alter egos: girls dressed like Lady Gaga, boys wearing pixie boots and ironic medallions.

By 2 p.m. the cackle of circling media helicopters alerted the whole of central London that something was going on. Students had pushed their way into the forecourt of Millbank Tower. Police, in pitifully small numbers, found themselves squashed against its plate-glass windows. Now the protesters surged into the building using side entrances, fire-doors and eventually—after smashing the glass—the actual windows. Soon, a crowd of students were milling about on the roof. Others had already made it to the floor where the Conservative apparatchiks, locked inside, were watching it all on television.

Edward Woollard, an eighteen-year-old further education student, recklessly threw a fire extinguisher off the roof towards the police lines.[1] In the forecourt the chant went up: 'Stop throwing shit.' The police, outnumbered, looked helpless.

Then things petered out. The students hung around a bit, lit fires with placards, painted some graffiti and then went home. But on their flame-lit faces you saw the look of people who had discovered the power of mayhem.

Millbank was one of those unforeseeable events that catalyze everything. The Liberal Democrats under Nick Clegg had ridden a wave of centre-left support in the May 2010 general election. The party's MPs had signed a pre-election pledge not to raise university tuition fees; after gaining power as part of the Conservative-led coalition, they promptly signed up to support the tripling of fees, to £9,000 a year, and to abolish a small weekly grant for low-income school students.

The reaction among working-class school students went beyond outrage: they panicked. It was an impossible sum to comprehend. One told me: 'My mum only earns £9,000 a year.'

Both the political and media classes anticipated that opposition to the fee increase would be led by the usual 'student leader' types, eager to join the Millbank set themselves. They thought Nick Clegg's residual popularity with students—who, like @littlemisswilde, had voted massively for the Lib Dems in May 2010—would hold things together. They assumed, above all, that the youth were too engrossed in their iPhones and their Twitter feeds, too in thrall to postmodernist insouciance, to notice the freight train of economic doom coming at them.

Millbank shattered all these certainties. The mainstream media decided that, even if this student movement came to nothing, they had better start covering it as if it were part of something bigger—though they did not yet know what that something would be.

### Spontaneous horizontalists

*29 November 2011*. At the London School of Oriental and African Studies, they had occupied a room in the library, which they'd plastered in hand-crayoned manifestos. Their demands were modest, focused on the running of the school, the non-victimization of the protesters and, finally, a request for the college management to state its public opposition to the fee increase.

In the corner was a prayer area for Muslim students. On the floor lay those iconic books: Hardt and Negri's *Multitude*; a Foucault primer; Debord's *Society of the Spectacle*, Fanon's collected works.

They'd called a mass meeting about 300 strong, a young guy with a beard officiating. To his right huddled a small group of hard leftists; at the back were some of the college staff, including a few veterans of 1968 with long grey hair and beards. The question was whether to continue the occupation—they had been going for a week—but very few people spoke to the issue. One man, a young Syrian, stood up to say: 'What we're doing is having a global impact. This French journalist came up to me and said, this is amazing, this never happened before. What are the Brits doing? I said—what, you think the French are the only ones who can riot?'

The method, as people speak, is to waggle your hands: upwards if you agree, downwards if not, more vigorously if you agree more, etc. I first saw it used in the late 1990s by the anti-globalization movement. But in the space of ten years the whole menu of 'horizontalist' practice —forms of protest, decision-making, world view—has become the norm for a generation.

And the meeting we are attending is not the only meeting: there is another one going on, in the form of tweets and texts that people are sending to their friends in other colleges. This is normal in the student movement: 'virtual' meetings that will never be minuted or recorded. As @littlemisswilde describes it: 'We use Twitter to expand the room.'

It comes to the final vote. Shall they stay in occupation? One of the Sixty-Eighters pipes up with a last-minute call for a strike and occupation of the main admin block. He is applauded—almost as if it is okay to applaud somebody whose politics and hairstyle date from the epoch of applause instead of hand-waggling.

But this is a blip. Most of the meeting is conducted in an atmosphere of flat-faced calm. This is an obvious but unspoken cultural difference between modern youth protest movements and those of the past: anybody who sounds like a career politician, anybody who attempts rhetoric, espouses an ideology, or lets their emotions overtake them is greeted with a visceral distaste. The reasons are hard to fathom.

First, probably, it's because there is no ideology driving this movement and no coherent vision of an alternative society. Second, the potential for damage arising from violence is larger than before: the demos, when they get violent, immediately expose the participants to getting jailed for serious offences, so they will go a long way to avoid getting angry. Third, and most important, it seems to me that this generation knows more than their predecessors about power. They have read (or read a Wikipedia summary of) political thinkers like Foucault, Deleuze, Dworkin. They realize, in a way previous generations of radicals did not, that emotion-fuelled action, loyalty, mesmeric oratory and hierarchy all come at an overhead cost.

At the end of the meeting, the consensus is to stay in occupation for another night. 'That's good,' smiles the bearded guy announcing the result, 'because my house is shit anyway.'

## Day X: Kettled youth

After Millbank, in the occupations, squats and shared houses, the makeshift ideology of the students had veered rapidly towards a kind of makeshift anarchism. 'Don't underestimate this generation, Paul,' one chided me. 'Unlike you, they've had to do tests every month of their lives; some of them were working for the Lib Dems and Labour six months ago, but they are so angry now, some of them are heading in the direction of insurrectionary violence.' As the mood changed, students started to talk about a 'Day X'. The posters proclaiming this new demonstration, slated for 24 November, had begun to borrow the imagery of Paris 1968.

But since Marx is out of fashion, and Lenin and Mao have been branded left fascists, who else is there to study but the Frenchman whose musings have become required reading in the era of Lady Gaga: Guy Debord?

Many students were familiar with Debord and his Situationist movement, for the simple reason that he is taught on every art course, and the big London art schools—Slade and Goldsmiths—were centres of militancy. But also because, as we will see, some of the Situationist tactics that failed in May 1968—basically, spreading out to create chaos—do not look so ludicrous if you own a Blackberry.

While the undergraduate occupation movement grew, the sixteen-to eighteen-year-olds at further education colleges (the British equivalent to high school) were facing a double hit. If they got to university, they would be the first to pay the fee increases. But in the interim the government had decided to cut the Education Maintenance Allowance, a payment of up to £30 a week Labour had introduced in 2004 to combat —or conceal, depending on your viewpoint—structural youth unemployment. At the time of its abolition, 647,000 under-eighteens were receiving EMA. Though conceived as a kind of paternalistic 'pocket money', most of those I talked to were so poor that they were spending the money on essential groceries for their family.

On 24 November at 11 a.m., school walkouts began in towns and cities all across the UK. 'They're taking away our future. They're rich, they don't care about us' was the theme of the vox pops as the twenty-four-hour news channels televised it all. Rough kids from Newham in London; polite kids from Dundee; Asian kids from Birmingham; white kids from Truro, Cornwall. In Morecambe, Lancashire, 200 students blocked the traffic and beat drums. In Liverpool they blockaded Lime Street station. 'The police are outnumbered, they don't know what to do,' one participant texted.

Instead of Guy Debord, the under-eighteens opted for Anglo-Saxon literalism. They swarmed into Trafalgar Square, off buses from London's poorest neighbourhoods, clambered over the lion statues and chanted: 'David Cameron, fuck off back to Eton!'

Then they surged down Whitehall, trashed an abandoned police van, covered it in graffiti, smoke-bombed it, attacked the police and danced. The iconic image of the day is the police van being protected by a cordon of schoolgirls who thought the violence had gone too far.

The police, in response, repeatedly 'kettled' the protesters, and at one point charged at them on horseback. The experience of getting kettled would be central to the process of radicalization. It was not a new tactic: it had been deployed against protesters on various anti-globalization demos, and at the G20 Summit in April 2009. But for most of the students it was new and shocking: you can tell this from the vividness of the language, the way first-person accounts spark into life when they describe it. Taught throughout their lives that their rights were primarily individual, not collective, but at the same time inalienable, kettling seemed to many like an offence against the person. Sophie Burge, aged seventeen:

> We waited and waited. Kettling does work when you have no choice about where you move; you start to feel very desolate and very depressed. People were crying. It was horrible; it was freezing and there were no toilets … we all just had to wee in a specific corner.[2]

Activist Jonathan Moses spelled out the political conclusion many of them drew: 'that property comes before people; the rights of the former supersede those of the latter'.[3]

With the momentum and the radicalism increasing, the school students staged a Day X-2 on 30 November, again clashing with police and attacking property in central London. Now the stage was set for Day X-3: the demo to coincide with the final parliamentary vote on the fee increase.

### The Dubstep Rebellion

*9 December 2010.* I start 'Day X-3' in the occupation at UCL, where young men are fashioning makeshift armour for their arms and shins out of cardboard. Sleeping on the floor I find Chris, a school student from Norwich who has 'just turned up' for the demonstration. He doesn't know anybody at UCL, but they have let him stay the night. 'I'm from the lower middle class, you could say. Not poor enough to get a grant under the new system so, though I was hoping to go to university, I really might not go.'

Lingering at the entrance to the occupation are four young boys from a nearby Camden estate: three black, one white. They are still wearing school uniform trousers, though they have swapped blazers for hoodies and face masks. They avoid my gaze. They smoke. When I catch the eye of one, he snickers wildly, staring into the distance. Though there are hours to go, they're twitching in anticipation of the violence to come.

At 2 p.m. about 40,000 people set out peacefully in the biting cold, marching from the University of London's Senate House to Parliament Square. At the Square they deviate from the agreed route, break through a line of cops who try half-heartedly to baton them, and tear down the six-foot metal fences protecting the grassy centre.

Then they dance. The hippy in charge of the sound system is from an eco-farm and has, he tells me, been trying to play 'politically right-on reggae'. However, a new crowd—in which the oldest person is maybe seventeen—takes over the crucial jack plug. A young black girl inserts this plug into her Blackberry (iPhones are out for this demographic) and pumps out the dubstep. Or what sounds to me like dubstep.

Young men, mainly black, grab each other around the head and form a circular dance to the digital beat—lit, as dusk gathers, by the distinctly analog glow of a bench they have set on fire.

While a good half of the marchers are undergraduates from the most militant college occupations—UCL, SOAS, Leeds, Sussex—the key phenomenon, politically, is the presence of youth: *banlieue*-style youth from places like Croydon and Peckham, or the council estates of Camden, Islington and Hackney.

Meanwhile, the pushing and shoving at the police line has turned into fighting. There are of course the anarchist, Black Bloc types, there are the socialist left groups—but the main offensive actions taken to break through police lines are by small groups of young men dressed in the hip-hop fashions of working-class estates.

Some of them will appear a few days later in the *News of the World*, their mugshots released by the Met: a black kid in a Russian fur hat; other young black boys in hoodies. Exhilarated eyes, very few bothering to mask up.

As it gets dark, there are just two lines of riot police and about thirty yards between the students and the parliament building. The Met has adopted a first-ditch-equals-last-ditch defence: Britain's only full-time riot squad, the Territorial Support Group, is all that's preventing the youth from clambering over the medieval walls of Westminster.

Inside parliament, MPs are debating the fee increase. Outside, getting nowhere with the TSG, the students change direction. They swarm up Victoria Street, which leads away from parliament, pushing back a line of mounted police and breaking through police attempts to form a cordon. But then, in successive charges, both the mounted police and the riot squads fight back. There is now toe-to-toe confrontation.

Heavy objects land among the police, amid a much larger volume of paint, fireworks and flash-bangs. At one point the horses are unable to cope, and a policeman falls off his mount, getting dragged away on a stretcher by colleagues.

A girl steps through a break in the police line and gets batoned. She crumples to the ground, where the police continue beating her. Afterwards she stays there, inert for a long, long time, so that the press photographers in their crash helmets stop shooting and cluster around her. She doesn't speak. Her face is screwed up, disbelief mingled with terror.

At the point of the wedge, alongside the estate youth, are the self-styled 'Book Bloc'. They've gone into battle in green helmets with mattress-sized mockups of book covers: *Endgame*, by Samuel Beckett; *Negative Dialectics* by Theodore Adorno; Debord, of course; and—for levity—the tales of an unruly school-kid, *Just William* by Richmal Crompton. They've copied this tactic from a group of Italian students, who are at the same moment lobbing firebombs into the side-streets of Rome.

Soon the books-cum-shields are torn out of their hands, and it is metal and bone and Kevlar that is making that clunk-clunk sound.

Together with the constant strobe of camera flashes and the throb of the dubstep —or what sounds like dubstep—it's become like a macabre outdoor nightclub.

For the police this is an 'only just' moment: a couple of officers get knocked to the ground and the students break through. Reinforcements arrive: dismounted motorcycle cops, many without helmets but wielding long batons. One runs straight at me, face snarling. But he's aiming for someone else. Clunk.

I decide to get out. There's one of the Fleet Street photographers covered in green paint; his Nikon's covered in paint too: irreparable. He shows it off to the others. It's like shift work, because as we're pulling out others are going in. The journos are clad in black, like many of the protesters, and we smile at each other as if this is somehow funny.

On the east corner of Parliament Square, people climb up to smash the windows of the HM Revenue and Customs building. On the west side they scale the façade of the Supreme Court, smash the leaded windows and push lighted materials inside. On the wall, someone sprays Debord's aphorism: 'Be Realistic—Demand the Impossible'.

Outside a pub there is a line of injured protesters being triaged by ambulance crews. Everybody has a head wound and a white bandage. And now the kettling's started. Some will end up trapped for hours in the freezing cold. Those who can escape go back to the student occupations to discuss where the campaign goes next.

By nightfall a student called Alfie Meadows is undergoing brain surgery after allegedly being batoned by police. Television footage shows another student—Jody McIntyre, who has cerebral palsy— being dragged from his wheelchair by an irate policeman, who's being restrained by his own colleagues. Elsewhere, in the West End, a breakaway group has surrounded a vintage Rolls Royce carrying Prince Charles and Camilla, Duchess of Cornwall to a function at the Palladium Theatre. As the protesters rock the car to and fro and throw paint bombs at it, somebody leans through the open window and prods

Camilla with a stick. The royal protection squad, it emerges later, were on the point of drawing their guns.

A few hours later, after I've blogged all this under the headline 'The Dubstep Rebellion', some protesters make vigorous representations to me via Twitter: they present a detailed playlist of the tracks blasted out in Parliament Square, which proves the music was not dubstep but grime.[4] It was the Grime Rebellion, doh.

Grime is music seen as so dangerous that it's effectively banned in the clubs teenagers frequent, and its performers shunned by all but pirate radio stations. Grime is hip-hop with a Cockney accent and a dirty bass-line; its most important instrument is the cracked-vowel voice of the London street kid. The same kind of voice that is now heard gabbling with rage on the evening news: 'We're from the slums of London, yeah, and how do they expect us to pay uni fees—of nine thousand pounds? And the maintenance allowance: that's what's keeping us in college. What's stopping us from doing drug deals on the streets anymore? Nothing.'[5]

This, it turns out, is the most prescient statement made that day.

At six o'clock the next evening, with the Met police chief, Paul Stephenson, facing calls for his resignation over the breakdown of law and order, I return to the scene of the battle. Whitehall and Parliament Square are still strewn with rubble and missiles; boarded-up windows line the route and the atmosphere is tense, the police on edge.

Suddenly, out of the dark comes the sound of drumming and wailing. Seven or eight figures emerge, dressed in black and wearing elaborate crows'-head masks. They do a dance across three lanes of stalled traffic into the middle of Parliament Square and approach the statue of Liberal Prime Minister David Lloyd George. And they lay a black wreath.

'We're here to mourn the death of the Liberal Party,' croaks the guy holding the drum, as he beats out a tocsin surrounded by the masked, mainly female, wailers. This goes on for about five minutes. At no point do they attempt to photograph, film or otherwise record the performance. It is purely gestural, vanishing into obscurity the moment it's over. Though the area is swarming with police, none interferes.

'We're art students from Slade and Goldsmiths,' explains the drummer. Why are they doing this? 'We felt we had to.' Did they, I ask, know about the teach-in at the National Gallery, at the height of last night's riot?

'Yes, that was us: the *Hive Manifesto*.'

## *The* Hive Manifesto

A spectre is haunting Europe—the spectre of debt slaves refusing to pay. All the powers within Europe have entered into a holy alliance to regenerate a failing economy, to realise a lethal dream of returning to business as usual, and to level the education and culture, to transform the educational and cultural sectors into a consumer society success story.[6]

At 4:45 p.m. on Day X-3, while clashes raged around parliament, art students and their professors had invaded the National Gallery and staged a sit-in beneath Manet's *Execution of Maximilian*. Earlier they had held an impromptu rave on Ai Weiwei's pebble sculpture at the Tate Modern. After a couple of lecturers gave speeches about the meaning of modern art, the students began scribbling. They produced *The Nomadic Hive Manifesto*, a parody of Marx and Engels which quickly becomes a bullet-point list of exhortations for protesters to remain non-hierarchical and fluid, to communicate 'using dancing and pheromones'.

The point about the *Hive Manifesto* is not that it is in any way a special literary document but that it sums up the change that people were feeling globally by late 2010, especially youth:

If you listen carefully, all that moaning, the sound that can be heard just behind the drone of everyday life, cars and the slurping of lattes, has become a little more urgent: a humming of dissatisfaction becomes dissent. The Holy Alliance fears that this noise has become a song on the lips of all?[7]

The art students had grasped that the fees protest would catalyze a far wider dissatisfaction with the effects of the economic crisis. The experience would show that refusal to cooperate with a system could be a more effective method of fighting it than an ordinary political campaign.

On the website Critical Legal Thinking, which published the Hive text, PhD student Rory Rowan surveyed the experience of kettling. Bearing in mind the tendency of kettling to provoke people into anger, and to provide a negative spectacle for the heliborne TV cameras, he suggested:

> A form of protest is needed that places dispersal over concentration, mobility over stasis and perhaps even disruption over symbolism. If multiple smaller mobile groups were to simultaneously occupy key strategic sites and disrupt vital processes, the momentum of symbolical opposition could be maintained without the police being able to herd opposition toward spectacle.[8]

Now, once the vote in parliament was over and the student movement had demobilized, sections of the discontented public seemed to sense that the moment for such protests had arrived.

### Tactics of the powerless

The first UK Uncut action took place on Wednesday, 27 October 2010, when about forty protesters occupied and closed down a Vodafone store in London's Oxford Street. A mixture of old and young, they crime-taped the entrance, holding up banners claiming that Vodafone's unpaid tax bill—reported to be £6 billion—was just short of the £7 billion of public spending cuts now being made. Three days later, on Saturday, 30 October, there were similar actions in fifteen UK cities. By 18 December the movement reached a peak, with actions in over seventy UK towns and cities.

The core activists were committed horizontalists who had learned their methods in the Climate Camp movement. They would occupy a store, create a narrative there (for example, declaring it to be a 'library' and handing out books), and then get thrown out—displaying enough resistance to sabotage the business operation, but not usually enough to get arrested.

Though it coincided with the student unrest, the most remarkable thing about Uncut was its spontaneous replication by groups with no connection to the students nor to the anarchist protesters. The spectacle of grandmothers sitting down in the Boots pharmacy of quiet provincial towns, arm-in-arm with their teenage granddaughters, alarmed public-order specialists because there was little or no sanction they could bring against it.

The think tank Policy Exchange convened a panel of law-and-order specialists to ask: 'Do these actions portend a dangerous new trend towards the use of physical force? If so, what can and should be done to prevent this phenomenon becoming a regular feature of the national landscape?'[9]

Actually, the answer is: very little. Ewa Jasiewicz, a thirty-something veteran of the anti-globalization movement, has been involved with UK Uncut from the start. An organizer for the Unite Union, she's been jailed and deported twice from Israel, most recently during the Gaza Flotilla of May 2010, and helped to set up an oil workers' union in Iraq after 2003. She is therefore used to being part of an activist minority, and interprets the recent adoption of radical tactics by large numbers of people as the result of a new feeling of powerlessness:

I feel like there is a lot of reaction to 'the future': there is a sense that the present is so bad, and conditions of austerity being imposed, pensions undermined, services undermined—that we can't have any more of this. And if this is what the present is, what's the future?

Social media, she believes, have been the key to turning what was once a niche, lifestyle form of protest into an accessible method for everybody else:

> The anti-road movement of the late 1990s didn't ask you to sign up to an ideology, just to put your body in the way of a JCB. The difference is that then, we didn't have a media strategy. UK Uncut is the best example of social media carrying ideas into maximum participation on a localized, decentralized scale.

Horizontalism, she argues, provides the most useful methods for people with no power. If trade-union activists and grandmothers alike were drawn to dressing up and committing civil disobedience in the high streets of small towns, it was because they saw the old ways of trying to influence politics as closed off. Jasiewicz describes succinctly what this kind of protest is designed to achieve: 'A lot of our resistance as unarmed and powerless people is based on creating moments where the state is forced to respond to a scenario we are putting forward that is problematic for them; that creates a crisis of legitimacy.'

UK Uncut actions were 'fun, good-natured', easy to join in with—but they also allowed people to 'see the repression in their lives', says Jasiewicz.

> Once you can take the struggle out of the corridors of power and distil it—so that you can see capitalism, personified, in your high street—it becomes more tangible. It becomes easier to respond to an oppression you could not name. Now you can. And social media says to people who are alienated and disparate: you are like me; these things are everywhere.

I ask Jasiewicz the same questions I asked Riches: what she reads, and what has influenced the way she thinks and acts. It turns out that, like many fellow activists, she has a deep hostility to theory. 'I don't like talking about what I think; it's bullshit. It's this action, this protest, Iraq, Palestine, Deptford'—where she organized a post-riot cleanup and solidarity demo in August 2011. 'And even social media is not the central thing. The things that are central are off the radar: social interaction, relationship building, trust. Talk to people. Trust is explosive.'

In the space of six months, the impact of austerity in Britain had created a mass constituency for these ideas, above all among school students and undergraduates. But the old, hierarchical forms of protest had not gone away. Slowly, the trade unions moved from lobbying to action. On 26 March 2011 they called what would become the biggest trade-union demo in post-war history.

However, just as the events in Tahrir Square had demonstrated the potential for synthesis between students, workers and urban poor, 26 March would be a case study in the lack of synthesis. It would throw the horizontalist movement in Britain into a crisis of direction that it is still struggling to recover from.

### Three tribes go to war

*London, 26 March 2011.* It's clear early on it's going to be massive. The leaders of Unison—which represents local government and health workers—have massively mobilized their people, bringing in whole trains and hundreds of coachloads of workers, printing t-shirts and professional-looking banners. On the south bank of the Thames, a group called 'Croydon Filipino Nurses' is lining up for a photo call. Further on, under a banner saying 'Nurses Uncut', a group of women—long-time workmates from various hospitals—meet up, ready to march. They've organized it on Facebook: 450 have signed up, some not even in a union. They've spent the past few days reassuring each other because of the lurid tabloid headlines about anarchists and violence. 'There won't be any trouble,' they tell each other.

Getting across the river is hard: some bridges are closed, others crammed with people. Shoulder to shoulder are teachers from Devon, firefighters in red t-shirts, balloon-holding binmen from Glasgow, Norwich, Gloucester; home helps from Renfrewshire. They shuffle their way across Waterloo Bridge. The demonstration is already massing along the Thames and you can hear whistles, drums and vuvuzelas.

By the time the march sets off, with a clear half million on the streets, it has turned into the biggest trade-union demo for more than thirty years.

Among the marchers, you can see what the new mood created by the student movement and UK Uncut has achieved. 'Where's Ed Miliband?' representatives from a special needs school—students and teachers linked arm-in-arm—ask me. 'We don't trust him! He needs to get his act together. It's the bankers, the profit system. The big companies should stop evading tax!' There's a festive atmosphere. The schoolkids are singing a re-scripted version of 'I Will Survive'.

But at Piccadilly Circus, the edges of the demo are swarming with youths dressed like members of the anarchist Black Bloc. Really young kids: buzzing with the newness of it all, some change from their normal clothes into black hoodies and scarves right there in front of the police. The police begin to talk urgently into their walkie-talkies.

A veteran riot photographer texts me with the time and place where it will kick off: Regent Street, a vast curve of nineteenth-century architecture and luxury retail. When I get there, it's deserted. In the distance I can make out a tight phalanx of black-clad protesters, about 400 strong, filling the width of the street. They tramp forward, masked, some carrying the red-and-black flags of anarcho-syndicalism. This, one of them tells me later, is the biggest Black Bloc ever assembled in the UK. And though there are certainly numerous anarchists from Europe here, it is the students and school students from December who have really swelled the numbers.

They veer off into a side-street and start lobbing paint, billiard balls and smoke flares at various boutique shops: Victorinox gets it, so does an art gallery. There are only about twenty police around, none in riot gear. In a futile gesture, they try to protect the Victorinox shop, receiving the full barrage of paint, bottles and—according to the Met's later report—an acid-filled light bulb.

It's mayhem. And it is clear the police tactic is not to deploy fully and fight the protesters. For the next few hours the Black Bloc will roam around the West End, attacking shops, breaking into groups, running away, re-forming—with a Genoa-style, 'fluffy' contingent of non-violent direct action people trailing along behind.

I stop some of the latter: the women are dressed in multicoloured wigs, faces painted, tinsel in their hair, bare midriffs; the men are long-haired, thin, and non-aggressive. Why are they doing this?

Boy: 'Because Top Shop's owner hasn't paid billions of pounds of tax.'
   Girl (off her head): 'We're just dancing with flowers. We're protesting in favour of beauty, against all this fucking shit in the window. We don't want to spend all our money on clothes.'
   Boy: '... and because capitalism is a damn lie. That's why we're throwing stuff at these fucking shop fronts.'

I buttonhole a second group, students; two young men and a woman. One of the guys, wearing a hipster low-neck t-shirt and a plaid duffle coat:

We're sick with the government in general. For decades nobody legitimately can tell the truth; the nature of the hierarchy means only the imbeciles, the suck-ups, only the scumbags ever get to the top. So to truly be free is for everyone to take our part and decide for our freedom.

This is weird English but that's exactly how he says it, and he is not drunk or foreign, just furious. 'We need to all get together and create a community. All government is just an infrastructure, when we get government out of our vision we can start from the ground up, without corruption.'

At Oxford Circus a thirty-foot Trojan Horse made of wicker is wheeled in by protesters and goes up in flames. The police do nothing, because at this point there are none in attendance.

Along Oxford Street, all the stores targeted by UK Uncut in previous weeks—Topshop, Nike, HSBC—are closed in anticipation of the protests. In front of a branch of Boots, a peaceful picket of Uncutters (everybody dressed as doctors or patients) is busy sealing off the store with tape. Their symbolic message—the death of healthcare and Boots' non-payment of tax. Nearby, police video them and take notes.

A few hundred yards away is Hyde Park, where hundreds of thousands who have stayed to listen to the speeches hear civil service union leader Mark Serwotka call for a general strike. Ed Miliband makes a speech. He is not so well received, and by now the networks are split-screening him with something more televisual.

Anarchists have gathered outside the Ritz Hotel on Piccadilly, pelting and daubing the famous landmark. A few doors down, hundreds of UK Uncut activists invade the upmarket grocer's Fortnum & Mason. This moment—which unfolds across my Twitter feed, with people messaging from inside Fortnum's and from within Ed Miliband's press team—turns out to be the crest of the wave of protest that began at Millbank in November. After this climax comes the crisis.

The police kettled the Fortnum's protesters and, as night fell, 145 of them were arrested one by one. Many were held for the full twenty-four hours allowed by law and then released, in paper jumpsuits like terror suspects, their clothes impounded.

No serious act of violence had been committed at Fortnum's, though some protesters had chalked messages on the shop front. But there had been a mass outbreak of Black Bloc violence and destruction elsewhere. Virtually none of the Bloc had been arrested—but almost all of Fortnum's invaders had.

This posed, point-blank, two problems for the core of activists who had launched UK Uncut. Did they condone or condemn the actions of the Black Bloc, and how would they now function, since most of them were on bail? Of the total of 201 protesters arrested over the entire day, 145 were at Fortnum & Mason. At time of writing, all but thirty have seen all charges dropped.

Meanwhile, in Hyde Park, half a million trade unionists began drifting away to their coaches, oblivious to—but later horrified to learn—what the Black Bloc had done. Half a million low-paid public servants had been eclipsed by the actions of four hundred people: the news bulletins were dominated by images of masked kids, broken windows and a smouldering wicker horse in Oxford Circus.

## Towards the English Summer

In the period between Millbank and the trade-union demonstration of 26 March 2011, three social forces had been on the streets that we will meet time and again in the new global unrest: enraged students, youth from the urban underclass, and the big battalions of organized labour. In each phase, social media had helped the movement grow with dizzying rapidity.

The police, still smarting from the condemnation of their tactics at the G20 Summit in 2009, were in crisis. First, they had failed to anticipate Millbank, and their repeated use of kettling had radicalized large numbers of young people. Soon, the *News of the World* phone-hacking scandal would end the careers of London's two top policemen, and the Met would stumble into the 2011 summer of riots seemingly directionless.

But the protest movement was also in crisis. Students got wrapped up in their exams; the trade unions began negotiations over pensions; the small group of activists behind UK Uncut went into a defensive huddle; and the anarchists engaged in mutual recrimination, the Black Bloc openly declaring their 'right' to be violent. The momentum had gone.

Meanwhile, a third demographic group had gone missing. The urban youth crept back to their estates where, as spring turned into summer, they cranked up the Grime. They pondered the meaning of all the Situationist slogans they had heard, and watched as the Met Police leadership self-destructed during the Murdoch scandal. Then, in August, as a shaken political class retreated to the Tuscan hills, the urban poor staged an insurrection of their own.

After police shot alleged gang member Mark Duggan, on 6 August 2011, riots erupted in thirty English towns and cities. Despite the relatively small-scale participation in the uprisings, they were concentrated and devastating, leading to widespread looting and arson. In the first two days, in most places, police lost control of the streets. In some areas, where the rioting overlapped with ethnic tension between black youths and Asian or Turkish small businessmen, the latter formed protection squads, which found themselves also in tension with law enforcement.

It became clear the rioters across Britain had organized through social media; above all the Blackberry instant messaging service.

Though occasionally led by organized crime, and often by the disorganized petty criminals who form the youth gang fraternity, the overwhelming social characteristic of those arrested was poverty. The events, whose precise significance is still being disputed by criminologists and social theorists, formed a coda to the British winter of discontent.

Because—from Millbank to the summer riots—the scale of British discontent looks small beside the Arab Spring, it's been possible to ignore its significance. But it was significant, both sociologically and politically. Not only did it demonstrate the almost total disconnect between official politics and large sections of young people; it was also the moment that protest methods once known to a committed few were adopted by the uncommitted mass. But it also showed how, in developed societies, organized labour is still capable of channelling and overwhelming the more chaotic, spontaneous protests.

And it was an advance preview of the problem which youthful, socially networked, horizontalist movements would have everywhere once things got serious: the absence of strategy, the absence of a line of communication through which to speak to the union-organized workers. The limits, in short, of 'propaganda of the deed'.

Despite all this, what was obvious by late 2010 is that we were dealing with something new: something produced by bigger changes in society. But what?

# 4

## So, Why Did It Kick Off?
## The Social Roots of the New Unrest

If the Arab Spring had happened in isolation, it might have been categorized as a belated aftershock of 1989; if the student unrest had been part of the normal cycle of youth revolt, it could have been quickly forgotten. But as the momentum gathered, from Iran to Santa Cruz, to London, Athens and Cairo, the events carried too much that was new in them to ignore.

The media began a frantic search for parallels. Nigel Inkster, former director of operations for Britain's Secret Intelligence Service, told me: 'It's a revolutionary wave, like 1848.' Others found analogies with 1968 or the fall of the Berlin Wall in 1989. In late January 2011 I sat with veteran reporters in the newsroom of a major TV network and discussed whether this was Egypt's 1905 or its 1917.

As I will argue, there are strong parallels—above all with 1848, and with the wave of discontent that preceded 1914. But there is something in the air that defies historical parallels: something new to do with technology, behaviour and popular culture. As well as a flowering of collective action in defence of democracy, and a resurgence of the struggles of the poor and oppressed, what's going on is also about the expanded power of the individual.

For the first time in decades, people are using methods of protest that do not seem archaic or at odds with the modern contemporary world;

the protesters seem more in tune with modernity than the methods of their rulers. Sociologist Keith Kahn-Harris calls what we're seeing the 'movement without a name':

> A trend, a direction, an idea-virus, a meme, a source of energy that can be traced through a large number of spaces and projects. It is also a way of thinking and acting: an agility, an adaptability, a refusal to accept the world as it is, a refusal to get stuck into fixed patterns of thought.[1]

Why is it happening now? Ultimately, the explanation lies in three big social changes: in the demographics of revolt, in technology and in human behaviour itself. And without ignoring the specifics of Europe, North Africa or the global south, I will attempt here to summarize (as in the original 'Twenty Reasons' blog) what is common to these situations.

## The graduate with no future

At the centre of all the protest movements is a new sociological type: the graduate with no future.

In North Africa there is a demographic bulge of young people, including graduates and students, who are unable to get a decent job—or indeed any job. By 2011 there was 20 per cent youth unemployment across the region, where two-thirds of the population is under the age of thirty. In Libya, despite high GDP growth, youth unemployment stood at 30 per cent.

But youth unemployment is not a factor confined to North Africa. In Spain, in 2011 youth unemployment was running at 46 per cent, a figure partially ameliorated by the tendency for young Spaniards to live off their extended families. In Britain, on the eve of the student riots of 2010, youth unemployment stood at 20 per cent.

The financial crisis of 2008—which would bankrupt states as well as banks—created a generation of twenty-somethings whose projected life-arc had switched, quite suddenly, from an upward curve to a downward one. The promise was: 'Get a degree, get a job in the corporate system and eventually you'll achieve a better living standard than your parents.' This abruptly turned into: 'Tough, you'll be poorer than your parents.'

All across the developed world, the generation that leaves university in the 2010s will have to work longer because the guarantee of a comfortable income in retirement can no longer be met, either by private investment or the welfare state. Their disposable income will fall, because the financialization of public services demands a clutch of new debt repayments that eat into salaries: student loan repayments will be higher, private health insurance costs will rise, pension top-up payments will be demanded. They will face higher interest rates on home loans for decades, due to the financial crash. They will be burdened with the social costs of looking after the ageing baby boomers, plus the economic costs of energy depletion and climate change.

For the older generation it's easy to misunderstand the word 'student' or 'graduate': to my contemporaries, at college in the 1980s, it meant somebody engaged in a liberal, academic education, often with hours of free time to dream, protest, play in a rock band or do research. Today's undergraduates have been tested every month of their lives, from kindergarten to high school. They are the measured inputs and outputs of a commercialized global higher education market worth $1.2 trillion a year—excluding the USA. Their free time is minimal: precarious part-time jobs are essential to their existence, so that they are a key part of the modern workforce. Plus they have become a vital asset for the financial system. In 2006, Citigroup alone made $220 million clear profit from its student loan book.[2]

When in 2010 I attended Warwick University's prestigious Economics Conference, it was populated by young men and women dressed in box-fresh versions of 'business attire'—hypersexual retakes on the cocktail dress, Mormon-sharp suits, neutral ties—worn amid the routine squalor of a university campus. They were trying to live the dream—but a glance at their Facebook pages told you it was just for show. This was the lifestyle they'd been sold.

These students were aspiring to be the 'ideal workers' of the global age. The sociologist Richard Sennett describes how, starting in high-tech industries, a particular type of employee has become valued by corporations: 'Only a certain kind of human being can prosper in unstable, fragmentary social conditions ... a self oriented to the short term, focused on potential ability [rather than actual skill], willing to abandon past experience.'[3]

For employers, Sennett writes, the ideal product of school and university is a person with weak institutional loyalty, low levels of informal trust and high levels of anxiety about their own competence, leading to a constant willingness to reinvent themselves in a changing labour market. To survive in this world of zero loyalty, people need high self-reliance, which comes with a considerable sense of individual entitlement and little aptitude for permanent bonding. Flexibility being more important than knowledge, they are valued for the ability to discard acquired skills and learn new ones.

However, Sennett observes, such workers also need 'a thick network of social contacts': their ideal habitat is the global city, at whose bars, coffee shops, Apple stores, dance clubs and speed-dating events they can meet lots of equally rootless people.

The revolts of 2010–11 have shown, quite simply, what this workforce looks like when it becomes collectively disillusioned, when it realizes that the whole offer of self-betterment has been withdrawn. In revolts sparked or led by educated youth—whether in Cairo or Madrid —a number of common traits can be observed.

First, that the quintessential venue for unrest is the global city, a megatropolis in which reside the three tribes of discontent—the youth, the slum-dwellers and the working class. The estates, the gated communities, the informal meeting spaces, the dead spaces between tower blocks just big enough to be blocked by a burning car, the pheromone-laden nightclubs—all combine to form a theatrical backdrop for the kind of revolts we've seen.

Second, members of this generation of 'graduates with no future' recognize one another as part of an international sub-class, with behaviours and aspirations that easily cross borders.

I saw the Egyptian revolutionary socialist Gigi Ibrahim (@GSquare86), an iconic figure in the 25 January revolution, speak to London students a few weeks after Mubarak fell. There was no noticeable difference between her clothes, language and culture and theirs. She didn't mind that the meeting was small, that people came and went at random, depending on their other social commitments; she was not put off by their texting and tweeting during her speech.

The boom years of globalization created a mass, transnational culture of being young and educated; now there is a mass transnational culture of disillusionment. And it transmits easily. When activists like Ibrahim began to appear on TV in vox pops from Tahrir Square, youth all over the world—above all in America, where the 'image' of the Arab world has been about Islam, terrorism and the veil—simply said to themselves: 'Heck, that kid is just like me.'

Soon the activists were making physical links across borders. I had interviewed British student protester Simon Hardy during the wave of college occupations in London and had seen him carrying a red flag emblazoned with the word 'Revolution' on the 9 December demo; I was astonished to find him tweeting from Tahrir Square on 2 February. He reported:

We're quite near the front line where the pro-Mubarak forces are throwing sticks and stones at us. Around us people are breaking up paving stones with metal sticks to get ammunition. This is wrapped in carpet and taken to the front line to defend the square against the pro-Mubarak militias. Everyone here comes up to us as we walk past. They say how much they love freedom and hate Mubarak.[4]

In the twentieth century, revolutionaries would ride hanging from the undersides of railway carriages to make cross-border links like this. Today, information technology and cheap air travel makes them routine; shared global culture makes the message easy to convey.

But there is a third social impact of the 'graduate with no future': the sheer size of the student population means that it is a transmitter of unrest to a much wider section of the population than before. This applies both in the developed world and in the global south. Since 2000, the global participation rate in higher education has grown from 19 per cent to 26 per cent; in Europe and North America, a staggering 70 per cent now complete post-secondary education.[5]

In Britain, the Blair government's policy of getting half of all school-leavers into higher education meant that, when it broke out, student discontent would penetrate into hundreds of thousands of family homes. While the middle-class student activists of 1968 thought of themselves as external 'detonators' of the working class, the students of 2010 were thoroughly embedded both in the workforce and in low-income communities.

At the same time, in the developed world at least, the 'graduates with no future' often live in close proximity to the urban poor. Many dwell in the hidden modern slum—a.k.a. the 'student house'—where every room contains a bed, or in flats rented in the terraced streets and inner-city neighbourhoods where the unemployed and the ethnic minorities live. Once the housing and jobs markets collapsed, the student house became the young accountant house, the young lawyer, teacher and other struggling professional's house.

At the dance clubs students frequent there's always some urban poor youth: this is true even in smart American college towns. But in the mega-cities of youth culture—London, Paris, Los Angeles, New York—the cultural proximity is more organic. And in no-hope towns where the college is the only modern thing in the landscape, everyone rubs shoulders in the laundromat, the fast-food joint, the cramped carriages of late-night trains.

70

In North Africa, though many of the college students who led the revolutions were drawn from the elite, you find this same blurring of the edges between the educated youth and the poor.

The story of Mohamed Bouazizi, the street trader whose self-immolation on the morning of 17 January 2011 sparked the revolution in Tunisia, illustrates this well. He can't get a job because, in a corrupt dictatorship, he lacks the right connections. He's a street vendor earning $140 a month, but he's using the money to put his sister through college.[6]

The 2008 uprising in Mahalla, Egypt, saw this same overlap of worker, student and urban poor. Although a strike initially caused the rising, when the strike was banned the revolt was led by the urban poor: jobless youths, street traders and women. As the blogger and activist Hossam el-Hamalawy told me:

> In the poor neighbourhoods of Egypt you will usually find one son unemployed, another working in a factory, another at university. The issues of poverty and repression overlap; in each poor neighbourhood the police station is basically a torture centre.

The organized labour movement itself is wedged between the discontented middle class and the urban poor. In the developed world, organized labour has been weakened by anti-union legislation and is in numerical decline; in the developing world, labour organization is increasing, but the size of the formal workforce can be, as in Egypt, small compared to the other plebeian classes. For all these reasons, we've seen, in a variety of locations, a growing tendency for workers to take action outside the workplace and against targets that are not their direct employers.

Indeed, in the developed world the whole concept of 'working class' has come to describe two distinct sets of people. There is the skilled workforce, which is no longer dominated by blue-collar male workers with manufacturing skills, but by a different demographic: more ethnically diverse, more clerical and admin, sometimes predominantly female. And then there are those that in British popular culture have come to be labelled 'chavs' (much like those President Obama inadvisedly called 'rednecks'): the lowest-skilled, poorest-educated white workers, whose lifestyle has been dissolved by globalization and inward migration. This second group is often prey to right-wing ideologies dressed up with 'class' rhetoric, which repulse the more educated salariat. Among such workers, levels of resentment were already high, even during the boom of the mid-2000s.

Though it differs from country to country, this division within the developed-world workforce—which is largely a function of someone's exposure or otherwise to modern, globalized work—poses a strategic problem for the left. It makes it hard for social-democratic and left-liberal parties to create a unified narrative or programme around 'class' or 'class interest'. And it poses an acute challenge for any resistance movement trying to base itself on a common 'working-class' culture.

In Egypt and Tunisia—where the organized workforce still maintained elements of a 'pre-globalized' lifestyle such as state-owned factories, or communist traditions in the case of Tunisia—the problems were posed differently. Here the organized workforce is small in relation to other classes: socially powerful, but culturally distinct both from the urban poor and from the frappé-sipping graduates in the city-centre cafés.

Both the urban poor and the organized working class have—as we will see—crucial parts to play in shaping the course of the global unrest. But it was to the 'graduates without a future' that it fell to kick things off. From the rich world to the poor world, it is educated young people whose life chances and illusions are now being shattered. Though their general conditions are still better than those of slum-dwellers and some workers, they have experienced far greater disappointment.

This new sociology of revolt calls to mind conditions prior to the Paris Commune of 1871: a large and radicalized intelligentsia, a slum-dwelling class finding its voice through popular culture, and a weakened proletariat, still wedded to the organizations and traditions of twenty years before. This has major implications for the kind of revolution people make, once they take to the streets. And it makes the social order of the modern city highly fragile under economic stress.

The Athens uprising of December 2008 was a case study in how the three parts of the plebeian mass interact. A group of participants wrote that the rioters

> ranged from high school students and university students to young, mostly precarious, workers from sectors like education, construction, tourism and entertainment, transport and even media. [Older workers] were a minority … very sympathetic towards the burning down of banks and state buildings, but were mostly passive.[7]

The French historian Hippolyte Taine understood the essential danger of this social mix. When it comes to revolution, he warned, forget the poor and worry about poor lawyers:

> Now, as formerly, students live in garrets, bohemians in lodgings, physicians without patients and lawyers without clients in lonely offices … so many Brissots, Marats, Dantons, Robespierres, and St Justs in embryo. Only for lack of air and sunshine they never come to maturity.[8]

Taine put his finger on what, in 1789, had turned the normal rebelliousness of impoverished graduates into a force that would reshape the world. He saw that the 'worm-eaten barriers [had] cracked all at once'. Technology, social change, institutional decay had unleashed something bigger than teenage angst.

If this sounds like an eighteenth-century version of the 'death of deference' complaint, well, it was. A deep social crisis was under way, then as now. But with one big difference: today, in every garret there is a laptop.

## The Jacobin with a laptop

There has been high prominence given to technology and social media in explanations of the global unrest—and for good reason. Social media and new technology were crucial in shaping the revolutions of 2011, just as they shaped industry, finance and mass culture in the preceding decade. What's important is not that the Egyptian youth used Facebook, or that the British students used Twitter and the Greek rioters organized via Indymedia, but what they used these media for— and what such technology does to hierarchies, ideas and actions.

Here, the crucial concept is the network—whose impact on politics has been a long time coming. The network's basic law was explained by Bell Telephone boss Theodore Vail as early as 1908: the more people who use the network, the more useful it becomes to each user. This is known as the 'network effect': what it describes is the creation, out of two people's interaction, of a 'third thing' which comes for free. Because network theory originated in the boardroom, this 'third thing' has tended to be identified in terms of economic value. But, in recent years, it has become clear it can provide much more than that.

There's another difference: when it was first theorized by Vail's technologists, the 'network effect' seemed like a by-product, a happy accident. Today we are conscious users and promoters of the network effect. Everyone who uses information technology understands that they are—whether at work, on Facebook, on eBay or in a multiplayer game—a 'node' on a network: not a foot-soldier, not a bystander, not a leader, but a multitasking version of all three.

Vail's customers probably had no idea that, by buying and using telephones, they were enhancing the technology's value for others and creating spin-off effects for Bell's other businesses (what are now termed 'network externalities'). Nowadays, many of us have a very clear understanding of all this. The result is that, in the past ten years, the 'network effect' has blasted its way out of corporate economics and into sociology.

The most obvious impact has been on the media and ideology. Long before people started using Twitter to foment social unrest, mainstream journalists noticed—to their dismay—that the size of one's public persona or pay cheque carried no guarantee of popularity online. People's status rises and falls with the reliability and truthfulness of what they contribute. This is a classic network effect—but it is not measurable as profit and loss.

If you look at the full suite of information tools that were employed to spread the revolutions of 2009–11, it goes like this: Facebook is used to form groups, covert and overt—in order to establish those strong but flexible connections. Twitter is used for real-time organization and news dissemination, bypassing the cumbersome 'newsgathering' operations of the mainstream media. YouTube and the Twitter-linked photographic sites—Yfrog, Flickr and Twitpic—are used to provide instant evidence of the claims being made. Link-shorteners like bit.ly are used to disseminate key articles via Twitter.

And the democracy of retweeting (or sharing on Facebook) filters out the trash. In this way, key contributions to the dialogue that's going on around the action get promoted as if by acclaim, as happened to the original 'Twenty Reasons' blog post. Activists describe this process as 'memetic', drawing on Richard Dawkins' proposal of information 'memes': ideas that behave like genes, fighting for survival and mutating in the process.

Underpinning the social media is mobile telephony: in the crush of every crowd we see arms holding cellphones in the air, like small flocks of ostriches, snapping scenes of repression or revolt, offering instant and indelible image-capture to a global audience. Cellphones provide the basic white sliced bread of insurrectionary communications: SMS. SMS allows you to post to Twitter, or to microblogs, even if you don't have Internet access and can't read the results. Texting is traceable, of course. But as all fans of *The Wire* understand, you can thwart surveillance if you use a cheap, pay-as-you-go handset, which you can throw away if you're in a tight corner. What's more, for many of the impoverished youth and slum dwellers, pay-as-you-go is all they can afford.

Finally, there is blogging. Though blogging was an early form of social media and has been heavily colonized by the mainstream press, 2011 saw a revival of what was essential about the format: the ability to express your own agenda through montaging stills, movies, words and links to create indelible statements of attitude and contempt. In some countries, residually, bulletin boards have played a role: the Athenian revolt of December 2008 was initially organized through newsflashes on the Indymedia bulletin board.

Blogs have been most influential in the Arab world, where the mainstream press has been subject to various degrees of censorship and self-censorship. But in all the theatres of revolution, blogs have offered that vital resource: somewhere to link to. They have become, like the newspapers of the nineteenth century, journals of record. Their impact can be measured by the fact that, in 2011, 7 per cent of Middle Eastern bloggers surveyed reported they'd been arrested by their respective security forces.[9]

The ability to deploy, without expert knowledge, a whole suite of information tools has allowed protesters across the world to outwit the police, to beam their message into the newsrooms of global media, and above all to assert a cool, cutting-edge identity in the face of what Auden once called 'the elderly rubbish dictators talk'. It has given today's protest movements a massive psychological advantage, one that no revolt has enjoyed since 1968.

Suddenly, the form of today's protests seems entirely congruent with the way people live their lives. It is modern; it is immune to charges of 'resisting progress'. Indeed, it utilizes technology that is so essential to modern work and leisure, governments cannot turn it off without harming their national economies. And, as Mubarak, Gaddafi and the Bahraini royals discovered, even turning it off does not work.

Because—and here is the technological fact that underpins the social and political aspects of what's happened—a network can usually defeat a hierarchy.

The pioneer of network theory, Walter Powell, summed up the reasons for this as follows: the network is better at adapting to a situation where the quality of information is crucial to success, but where information itself is fluid; a hierarchy is best if you are only transmitting orders and responses, and the surrounding situation is predictable. Above all, 'as information passes through a network, it is both freer and richer [than in a hierarchy]; new connections, new meanings are generated, debated and evaluated.'[10]

However, the early network theorists were only studying the advantages of, say, collaborative workshops in the textile industry versus big factories. Now we are studying networks with many millions of individual nodes, and they are in conflict with states. Once information networks become 'social', the implications are massive: truth can now travel faster than lies, and all propaganda becomes instantly flammable.

Sure, you can try and insert spin or propaganda, but the instantly networked consciousness of millions of people will set it right: they act like white blood cells against infection so that ultimately the truth, or something close to it, persists much longer than disinformation.

In fact, this quality of Twitter means, according to the South Korean authors of the first data-based study of it, that it is not really a 'social network' but more like a news service. Services like Flickr, MSN and Yahoo involve a high level of 'reciprocity', since about 70 per cent of relationships are two-way. Facebook is constructed in such a way that this reciprocity is 100 per cent: I 'friend' you, you 'friend' me. On Twitter, by contrast, only about 22 per cent of relationships are two-way—there is a much higher ratio of 'followers' to those being followed.[11]

A second implication is that forms of protest can change rapidly. Whereas the basic form of, say, a Leninist party, a guerrilla army or even a ghetto riot has not changed in a century, once you use social networks the organizational format of revolt goes into constant flux. Even in the period between the Iranian uprisings of July 2009 and the time of writing (autumn 2011), changes have taken place in the way protesters use social media, in the way rioting is directed (as with the 'Blackberry riots' in England in 2011), in the way people evade Internet shutdowns and in the tools used for 'denial of service' attacks by hackers.

Indeed, during the actual course of the Iranian uprising of 2009, the ways of using social media visibly evolved. Protesters called the process 'wave creation', using email, blogs and SMS to evolve the protests in real time. Looking at this phenomenon, Stanford scholar Saeid Golkar concludes:

> The Internet enables users to suggest new mechanisms to expand protests and gather feedback on these suggestions. On one hand, this makes the movement more flat and democratic, and on the other hand, it makes its activities more rational, with lower costs of action.[12]

As the real-world revolt was suppressed, activists took to the digital rooftops: launching 'Googlebombs' against Ahmadinejad and cyberattacks on government websites, while putting psychological pressure on members of the repressive forces by naming them and disseminating their details. In response—in what remains the best-documented example outside China of cyber-repression—the regime trawled Facebook for the identities of activists, unleashed cyber-attacks against their networks and instructed 10,000 members of the Basij militia to set up their own, rival, blogosphere.[13]

The new technology, then, makes possible a new relationship among protesters themselves and between protesters and the mainstream media, and gives protest movements increased leverage over NGOs, multilateral bodies and guarantors of international law. It provides instant evidence of truth and can facilitate swift neutralization of lies, including those of state propaganda. All this, however, is only a side-effect of the much bigger change this technology has brought about: the change in human behaviour.

The iconic image of this decade is a young person sitting in Starbucks, her face blue from the screenlight of a MacBook. She could be hanging out, composing chart-busting electro-pop, creating more value than the whole Starbucks branch with some high-tech research project; or planning a revolution.

To an older generation, steeped in the culture of collectivism, these Starbucks Kids were the epitome of egotistic isolation. But it turns out these young people were not wasting their time: they were pioneering a major expansion in the power of the individual human being.

## *The networked revolution*

In the middle of the biggest upsurge in labour protests for a decade, it seems impolite to mention the name of André Gorz. Gorz was a French Marxist who for twenty years was spat on by left commentators for writing a book entitled *Farewell to the Working Class* (1980).

Gorz asserted that the old proletariat had been dissolved by modern technology and that the class struggle would be replaced by individual personal politics. He was wrong: the world economy has created 1.5 billion extra workers since his book was written. He was also wrong to claim that capitalism was destroying skilled work. And yet parts of the book now bear rereading, in particular Gorz's definition of revolution:

> Taking power implies taking it away from its holders, not by occupying their posts but by making it permanently impossible for them to keep their machinery of domination running. Revolution is first and foremost the irreversible destruction of this machinery. It implies a form of collective practice capable of bypassing and superseding it through the development of an alternative network of relations.[14]

By this definition we are in the middle of a revolution: something wider than a pure political overthrow and narrower than the classic social revolutions of the twentieth century. Out of the very values and practices of free-market capitalism—individualism, choice, respect for human rights, the network, the flattened hierarchy—the masses have developed a new collective practice. They can bypass and supersede the machinery of power via, as Gorz predicted, an 'alternative network of relations'.

In the space of ten years a whole new form of behaviour, consumption, culture and even human consciousness has sprung up which has changed our attitudes to hierarchies and to property. It is already possible to find, on any demonstration, self-described 'communists' for whom the idea of a Leninist party is alien. Every nightclub contains people—maybe even a majority of people—who are happy to pay the entrance fee, and for their drugs, but who find the idea of paying to own the music itself as, again, incomprehensible.

The network, in short, has begun to erode power relationships we had come to believe were permanent features of capitalism: the helplessness of the consumer, the military-style hierarchy of boss and underlings at work, the power of mainstream media empires to shape ideology, the repressive capabilities of the state and the inevitability of monopolization by large corporations.

Richard Sennett, writing in 2004, believed the destruction of hierarchical work and its replacement by consumption as the main source of self-esteem had been wholly negative:

> The insurgents of my youth believed that by dismantling institutions they could produce communities: face-to-face relations of truth and solidarity ... This certainly has not happened. The fragmenting of big institutions has left many people's lives in a fragmented state. Taking institutions apart has not produced more community.[15]

80

But what we've seen since then, above all in the events of 2009–11, are revolts led by fragmented and precarious people. They have used the very technologies that produced the atomized lifestyle in the first place to produce communities of resistance.

And here's where it becomes essential to understand what that 'third thing' is, that gift arising from network relationships. To the business gurus, it was only ever profit: but to individuals it is something else. It's been described as a 'free dose of personal well-being'.

Technically, when we participate in e-commerce, we're just nodes in a consumer network—bidding for bargains on eBay, buying stuff on iTunes or Amazon. In return we are contributing not only money but our own intellectual property for free, in the form of reviews or star ratings (or even just our behaviour, surreptitiously logged by the company's CRM systems). The raw trade-off is that if I contribute a truthful review of an item I have bought, I might find an equally truthful one of something I would like to buy. But, as everyone involved intuitively understands, you are not just in it for the raw trade-off. There is a third 'party' in the transaction and that is the network, or community, itself. The transaction leaves a residue of collaboration.

Now, this understanding of the intangible, hidden value inside the network relationship has begun to permeate not just commerce and work, but protest. When doomed graduates, precarious workers and the poor use social networks to coordinate protests, they are waging a human fight-back against the atomizing effects of the modern marketplace.

However, there is a problem. Networked protests—as Malcolm Gladwell pointed out in his famous *New Yorker* diatribe against them—have the same downside as modern work and culture: they promote only 'weak ties'.[16]

That is, they reduce the level of commitment needed to be involved in anything. They allow users to adopt multiple identities, a pick-and-mix attitude to commitment, a kind of learned mercuriality. They allow instant concentration upon a target (as with Tahrir Square, or the

81

Manet painting at London's National Gallery), but equally instant fragmentation and dispersal. They make every action the subject of negotiation between the participants: unlike with an infantry battalion or a trade union, you cannot assume the support of the same group of people who acted together before.

Gladwell's attack on social networks is an attempt to defend the old, hierarchical forms of organizing in the face of this new reality. He writes:

> The drawbacks of networks scarcely matter if the network isn't inter-ested in systemic change—if it just wants to frighten or humiliate or make a splash—or if it doesn't need to think strategically. But if you're taking on a powerful and organized establishment you have to be a hierarchy.[17]

However, some military theorists have concluded the opposite. They have noticed that even where ties are weak, individuals can come together in ways more effective than the old hierarchical models allowed. They have noted that 'swarm' tactics often defeat hierarchical structures—even where the hierarchy has greater strength and a better information system.

In Millennium Challenge 2002, a military exercise conducted by the USA, an opposing force modelled on Iran's Revolutionary Guard con-troversially 'defeated' the US Navy by using swarm tactics. It 'sank' an aircraft carrier and half of the American fleet by concentrating every single cruise missile onto a single target. It broadcast commands ver-bally from minarets, instead of using radios; it dispatched motorcycle couriers; it mounted Silkworm missiles on pleasure boats and launched suicide attacks with propeller planes. Defeat prompted the US general staff to halt the exercise, 'refloat' the fleet and change the rules. The elderly genius who'd designed the swarm attack—Lieutenant General Paul Van Riper—resigned, warning the Bush administration that it had no clue about how to deal with the modern world.[18]

If you want to defeat one hierarchy and replace it with another, Gladwell is probably right; but the revolts under discussion did not aim to do that. The 25 January revolt in Egypt used networks to paralyze the authorities and create a fluid, unstable situation; at the same time they used networks to place pressure on unreliable potential allies like the US State Department and the SCAF.

Besides networks, they used informal hierarchies. Ahmed Maher, one of the founders of the April 6th Youth Movement, describes their way of working:

> I established this 'operations room' around fifteen days before the beginning of the protests, and we would meet daily to discuss routine details. ... Two days prior to the demonstrations we implemented a new mode of operation which saw activists being split into separate groups, with each group being made up of between thirty and fifty activists who would be posted to central areas and public squares to incite protests, whilst only the leader of each group would be informed of the precise location of where the protests were scheduled to begin.[19]

And their strategy evolved on contact with the enemy. Much has been made of the reliance of Egyptian revolutionaries on Gene Sharp's *Strategy Guide* for non-violent revolutions. While certainly some had read it, many leftists believe its relevance has been overstated. What happened is that social media allowed loose coalitions of activists to make collective decisions that looked to their opponents like they were strategic: for example, understanding the precise nature of the crowd in Tahrir Square on certain days, or gauging the precise level of incredulity among the masses at the rubbish being shown on state TV.

The network is stronger than its critics think. It has proved it can, at the very least, achieve the first phase of a democratic revolution by getting inside the decision cycle of those in power. It is altering the balance between worker, student and urban poor groups within protest movements. And it is changing the balance of power between the leaders and the led.

Whatever the limitations of networked action, and however it will be forced to morph as the revolts run up against tanks, torture, cyber-repression, etc., by 2011 it had already changed the face of protest. For Gladwell's critique overlooks a third dimension: the dimension of control.

The network's usefulness is not limited to half-hearted reform struggles that aim only to shock or disturb. It can achieve those elements of instant community, solidarity, shared space and control that were at the heart of social revolutions in the early industrial age. It can be, as cooperatives were for the workers who launched the Paris Commune of 1871, a space to form the bonds that would take them through an insurrection. It can be, as German socialist Ferdinand Lassalle described co-operatives in the 1860s, 'a means absolutely imbued with the nature of the ends'.

Time and again the impulse to create areas of self-control has led, in the past two years, to an almost mystical determination by protesters to occupy a symbolic physical space and create within it an experimental, shared community. From Tahrir and Syntagma to the student 'kissing protest' in Santiago's central plaza and Occupy Wall Street, these attempts at creating instant 'liberated spaces' have become the single most important theme in the global revolt.

The reasons for this are not palatable for many trained in the structured politics of the late twentieth century. It demonstrates that, as I observed in the British student occupations, this generation has a better understanding of power. The hardcore activists have read their Chomsky, Guy Debord, Hardt-Negri and Gene Sharp, and understood the principles; but more importantly the ideas therein have become 'common-sense' to a much wider layer of people who have never read any of it. They see the various 'revolutions' in their own personal lives as central to the change they're trying to make; not— as their liberal and social-democratic parents did—as some kind of 'retreat into personal politics'.

In a famous conversation in 1972, Michel Foucault could tell the psychologist Gilles Deleuze: 'We had to wait until the nineteenth century before we began to understand the nature of exploitation, and to this day we have yet to fully comprehend the nature of power.'[20]

But Foucault and Deleuze have been on the mainstream social science curriculum for twenty years now; we comprehend power more fully as a result.

## The crunch

The revolts, then, are the result of a technological revolution driven by the deployment of digital communications at work, in social life, and now in the forms of protest. It is not necessary to be a techno-determinist to see this.

The new technology underpins our ability to be at the same time more individualistic and more collective; it shapes our consciousness and magnifies the crucial driver of all revolutions—the perceived difference between what could be and what is.

In turn, the networked protest has a better chance of achieving its basic goals because it is congruent with the economic and technological conditions of modern society—it mirrors social life, financial structures and production patterns. It speaks to the mental conceptions that flow from the networked life we live. And to an extent, as we will see, it is satisfied with the conquest of space *within* the system rather than seeking to smash the system.

But here's the next problem: the system is not in stasis, it is in crisis. After the economic meltdown of 2008 it is highly capable of smashing itself.

# 5

## Greece: The Anomic State?
## From Austerity to Social Breakdown

*Athens, 14 June 2011, 9 p.m.* You can't miss the green dancing dots: laser pens playing across the façade of the Hotel Grande Bretagne as dusk falls. The crowd surging towards the hotel's shuttered doors is chanting: 'Underneath! Underneath!'

The chant refers to an escape tunnel they believe runs beneath Syntagma Square, connecting the hotel and the Greek parliament: the protesters want the government to use it right away. The laser pens are being shone to try to blind the TV cameras positioned on the hotel roof since 25 May, when thousands of Greek youth occupied the square. Every time some hated figure from the mainstream media is spotted peering through the hotel blinds, the green dots cluster on that window.

Antonis Vradis, an activist and blogger who's been camped here since the start of the protest, explains:

> All the media in Greece is corporately owned: people here believe it's aligned to the very same forces that have ripped off the country, so there is total hostility to them. We've even had the anchormen of mainstream networks calling for a military coup—so there is zero sympathy for the media.

In one corner of the square there is a 'pre-meet' of the politics sub-group—about a hundred people standing in a quiet circle to discuss, as

Vradis puts it, 'the fifty answers you will get if you ask fifty people here what they want'. Above, by the perimeter railings of parliament, are clustered the right-wing nationalists with their blue-and-white flags. Next to them some anti-capitalists have draped an orange banner depicting a helicopter: another invitation for Prime Minister George Papandreou to leave office. Within twenty-four hours he will, in his own way, give it a try.

In the centre of the square, under the ornamental trees, there is a campsite where around 400 people have pitched tents, including Vradis. Various stalls have sprouted among the tents, some organizing a petition, some selling literature or food. At one, people are logging the meeting times and contact numbers for the local assemblies that have formed across Athens.

Once you're inside the encampment, the sky becomes stars and banners; makeshift sheets and posters are everywhere. 'We're building real democracy'; 'One solution, revolution'; 'The dictatorship never died in '73 but we will finish it off in this square' …

These are the *indignados*—the 'indignant ones', a name borrowed from the Spanish youth who occupied their squares in May 2011—and what's new about this protest is that most of those involved were never politically active before. The Greek Communist Party, the KKE, has boycotted the camp; the far-left parliamentary alliance SYRIZA has people here, as do the anarchists, but they are not the majority. Mainly the protesters are just ordinary people. And it's the same elsewhere, in Iraklio, Thessaloniki, Patras and many smaller towns.

'It's regime change,' says Vradis. Whatever happens in parliament, whatever happens with the new austerity budget due to be introduced tomorrow, whatever happens on the streets, he thinks the rash of protest camps in town squares across Greece signals a big switch-off from traditional politics: 'In the people's minds the regime is already gone—not just Papandreou, but the whole corrupt mainstream party system.'

Vradis is one of those activists I keep bumping into who've been central to the global upsurge. He started his blog, OccupiedLondon, during the UK student riots in November 2010; now he is back in his homeland, following the trail of mayhem. He also turns out to be one of the horizontalists who are critiquing my 'Twenty Reasons' blog. 'I am working on number thirteen,' he warns me: 'your claim that this generation is picking and choosing its causes.'

As we talk outside the gates of parliament, the government is struggling to survive. Vradis gets an SMS telling him that two more MPs have just resigned from the ruling PASOK parliamentary group. A cheer goes up. Noticing my camera, people shine green lasers into it.

Now three thousand people sit down cross-legged on the stones of Syntagma—which at this point have not yet been broken up for missiles —and begin a polite mass meeting. There is little rhetoric from the platform; they're beyond the rhetoric stage. It's about the precise tactics and problems of being an unled mass movement in the post-ideological age.

Sitting among the protesters, I am struck by the meeting's atmosphere—similar to that of a music festival, and completely unlike that of, say, a big trade union march or even the UK Uncut groups. One of the Cairo tweeters said Tahrir was 'like Glastonbury without Bono', and so, in its own way, is Syntagma in June. Rena Dourou, an activist from SYRIZA who, like Vradis, has been camped here since the first night, confirms that for the vast majority of the demonstrators, it's their first protest:

> It's attracted young people, and especially young single mothers, who realize that this crisis is going to hit them very hard; also elderly people whose pensions are shrinking. I don't say they're apolitical, though. They're all well aware that only their presence in this symbolic place can change things.

It's not just Greece, either. By the summer of 2011, youth all across Europe were rapidly disengaging from the political mainstream. Maybe it's just a phase—or maybe this is what democracy is going to look like in an age in which politicians have come to be seen as corrupt, technocratic, characterless and inept: repeated standoffs between the masses and the policymakers, with very little left in the way of 'grassroots' or party command structures.

In Brussels, as the Syntagma meeting begins, Europe's finance ministers have assembled to thrash out their differences over the near-inevitable Greek debt default. But nobody in Syntagma cares. They are busy drawing lots for places on the podium—a practice copied from the *agora* of classical Greek democracy, designed to avoid, or dissolve, fixed power relationships.

Despite the calm, there is a simmering anger across Greece. Many people have lost a third of their income due to tax rises and wage cuts; many young adults have no job and no prospect of one. The green dots of laser light convey a chilling message to the rulers of Europe: we don't want to be on your TV news bulletins; we would rather bust your cameras than accept your austerity.

### On the brink of mayhem

*15 June 2011, 8 a.m.* The following morning, on a wide, deserted thoroughfare, taxi drivers have parked their cabs in a phalanx and are taping Communist posters to the hoods. Bank workers are standing around in groups, chatting, fingers wrapped around the traditional iced Nescafé that is all you can stomach in this heat. Hospital workers begin to assemble around the banners of the Communist-led trade union PAME. This is one of many assemblies in a city that's rapidly shutting down. Though they stay away from the camp, and later the rioting, the KKE are a massive force. And there is a new urgency for the workers who adhere to the party and its allied unions: they are fighting for their lives. The whole system they've worked within is falling apart.

'I'm a cardiologist,' Dr. Ilias Sioras tells me. 'I see every day, in the public hospitals, more and more poor people needing treatment. And they are asking for money, under the counter, to admit people. I believe people will die because of the austerity.'

After the hospital workers, the hotel porters and domestics form up in ranks, wearing their uniforms and name badges. They chant the deep, throaty slogan that has become the song of Greece's revolt: 'Don't bow your heads, resist!' What they're here to resist is the so-called Medium Term Fiscal Strategy, about to be imposed by PASOK—which began as a left-wing social-democratic party but is now trying to impose one of the harshest austerity programmes ever conceived.

PASOK's misfortune was to win the Greek general election of October 2009. On entering government, they discovered that the outgoing right-wing administration had lied systematically about the state of the country's public finances—despite regular visits from the EU monitoring body, Eurostat, which did not seem to notice. Instead of 4 per cent of GDP, as had been reported, the country's budget deficit turned out to be 12 per cent. Its debt was on course to spiral to 150 per cent of GDP.

In a country with a viable tax system, this would be a major problem, but it would be solvable through tax rises, spending cuts and a swift devaluation of the currency to boost its export industry. But Greece could not devalue: it was trapped within the eurozone. Nor did it have an export industry, let alone a viable tax system. The previous year PASOK's finance minister, George Papaconstantinou, had told me: 'the country is essentially corrupt. We went to the upmarket district of Kolonaki and found doctors and dentists with a claimed annual income of €30,000, driving cars worth €30,000 alone.'

Papaconstantinou, educated at the LSE and NYU, seemed like the right man to implement the solution: accepting a bailout from the European Union on harsh terms, forcing through tax reforms and cuts to public sector pay, but protecting services for the needy and protecting the jobs of state employees, most of whom traditionally vote PASOK. The problem was the EU's politicians: trapped in a time warp of their own creation, they would spend an astonishing eighteen months struggling to comprehend the scale of the crisis.

By 4 May 2010, the eurozone was on the brink of chaos. It took French President Nicolas Sarkozy's threat to quit the euro, and urgent calls both from the White House and the International Monetary Fund, to convince Europe's leaders to launch the first Greek bailout, of €110 billion. A few days later, together with the IMF, the EU created the European Financial Stability Facility, armed with €700 billion—more than enough to prevent crisis in Greece and to revive Portugal and Ireland, whose fiscal lungs had been punctured in the post-Lehman decompression.

But things spiraled out of control. By May 2011, Portugal was bust, Ireland bust several times over, with its banking system on life support —and Greece was in need of a second bailout. The reason for failure was obvious to all except the pallid bureaucrats who run the European Union and the European Central Bank: the medicine was killing the patient.

Free-market economics, written into the constitution of the European Central Bank and hard-wired into the brain of every mainstream politician, demanded that countries embark on a programme of self-imposed austerity in return for financial bailouts. It prescribed what neoliberalism always prescribes: privatization, wage cuts, pension cuts; cuts in benefits, the minimum wage and social services.

The problem is, if you impose austerity on a country already in the grip of recession and which cannot devalue its currency, that recession merely gets worse. The country's tax revenues do not rise and soon it needs another bailout—on even harsher terms.

That's what had brought such huge numbers of Greeks onto the streets in June 2011. The terms of the proposed second bailout, as dictated by the EU, would reduce the size of the state from 53 per cent of GDP to 44 per cent in just six years. The austerity programme would take one euro in eight out of Greek spending power, in the form of tax rises and public-spending cuts. It would cut the public wage bill by a third. And it would sell off every state-owned national asset that it could: airports, ports, the motorways built with EU subsidy, even some of the smaller Greek islands were mooted for sale—all at knockdown prices, at the bottom of the market.

The potential consequences were clear to anybody who has studied the 1930s: the austerity programme would suppress growth for half a decade, sink the prospects of an entire generation of young people—already facing youth unemployment of 26 per cent—and in the end could only lead to a third bailout. Except there could be no third bailout: the country would default on its debts—the only question being, in the end, by how much and how chaotically.

On the streets of Athens, in the hot dawn of 15 June 2011, they had decided not to wait. If Greece was to be forced into self-imposed recession as a prelude to default, better to default now: better to reject austerity and impose another solution, from below.

'I am sixty-seven years old and have sailed the world,' said a man with white stubble, clutching a plastic bottle full of home-made hooch. 'Once I was poor and broke: I would rather be poor and broke again than take another bailout from the EU.' His spindly arms were shaking, his body tense inside his shabby t-shirt. He sounded like a man trying to warn of imminent disaster: 'You must let me make these points: if Greece dies, Europe dies, America dies, we all die.'

At that, another old man leaned over and blocked my camera lens. 'Don't you want the world to hear your story?' I asked. 'No,' he said quite calmly as he waved his hand in my face. 'It's too late for that.'

### A taste of tear gas

Not long after, the tear gas started. There was no warning—though standing close to a bunch of protesters who were throwing bottles at the riot police should, I guess, have been warning enough.

When a tear-gas canister explodes in mid-air it spews a thick cloud the colour of 1970s furniture. Those nearest to it run; everybody clutches their t-shirt to their face. Then, like a football crowd leaving a game in the days of terracing, we crush together, shoulder to shoulder, everyone in their little bubble—fighting that little bit of panic that starts inside when you cannot breathe.

Then you daub Maalox on your face, a milky balm that staunches the burning, which as it dries gives the whole crowd the air of a troupe of clowns who have been disturbed while putting on whiteface.

After the first tear-gas canister is launched, another tribe emerges from the side-streets: hundreds—later swelling to maybe thousands—of Black Bloc youth. Their body language, dress and demeanour are completely different from those of the communists. As in London, they go in for bare midriffs, black fabric, dreadlocks and jerky movements. They make a simultaneous surge towards parliament from three assembly points, coordinated by SMS. Riot police—clad in plastic and Kevlar armour from shin to collar-bone, wearing gas masks and armed with tear gas projectors, stun grenades and metre-long batons—go into action.

Around 1 p.m. the whole of Syntagma Square becomes a battle zone. The protesters—not just the Bloc now, but also the socialist youth from the leftist groups, the horizontalists, the nationalists and the *indignados*—make repeated charges up the steps of parliament towards the phalanx of visored riot police, to be repulsed by stun grenades and thick gobbets of gas.

In the lulls there are mini-confrontations between trade unions and the Black Bloc; the Communists shout that the anarchists are provocateurs. At no point do the Communists and trade union stewards join in the fighting: eventually they form up and march away. As in London, there are rivers of antagonism flowing between the anarchists and the organized labour movement. The difference here is that this forbearance, and the organization imposed by the workers' movement, is all that stands between order and chaos.

Now, in mid-afternoon, things become eerily quiet. With the famous riot-dog Loukanikos leaping around joyfully at their head, the youth form up behind anarchist banners and try, once again, to march on parliament. The streets are littered with the debris of missiles. By now everyone is masked against the tear gas—the journos, the rioters, the police—and there is a weird silence, except for the occasional pop of tear gas or smashing of glass.

In the side-streets—abandoned by police, shops shuttered—you see isolated individuals, masked, texting; some people are hammering at a piece of marble, breaking it up to make rocks. A few yards away, couples who have been protesting walk hand in hand, everybody shambling wearily in different directions. It's like a scene from a Lowry painting, but imbued with menace.

I decide to walk back to my hotel, down the wide thoroughfare that links Syntagma with Omonia Square. Usually clogged with cars, it's completely clear. Crossing a side-street, I pass a group of youth protesters occupying the street corner; it's the same on the next corner, and the one after that. Central Athens is under the control of the protesters—not that they are trying to exert control, but, nevertheless, they are in charge. Every shop is shuttered; some proprietors have closed out of fear, others because the shopkeepers' association declared a three-hour shutdown as part of the general strike. There are no bystanders.

Two young lads take their shirts off, wrap them around their heads and dance in front of a fire they've lit across one of the side-streets, just out of projectile range—they hope—from a platoon of police. The police tactic is to make regular incursions into this eerie mayhem. They are gradually breaking it up, restoring uncertainty and danger for the rioters but not exactly 'order'.

Glued to my iPhone, I wander into a Henry Miller novel. I'm in a neighbourhood with transvestite prostitutes on the street corners; a barefoot drunk is slumped on the ground, his face deathly white; a woman hops mechanically from foot to foot, hair matted, eyes flickering; a junkie couple argue in the doorway of a shop; migrant beggars sit on the sidewalk, one holding a cardboard placard scrawled with the words: 'I am hungry.' A group of African street-sellers wanders along, smiling; there's nobody to buy their wares, but nobody to hassle them either. There are no police, no ordinary people, no traffic. Just silence.

For a few hours the protesters more or less control central Athens. They don't smash many banks—but they do break the resolve of

German Chancellor Angela Merkel. And, technically, they bring down Papandreou's government.

At 9 p.m., just as the last Molotovs are being thrown, Merkel abandons the idea that banks should lose money as a result of giving Greece leeway on its debt repayments. Shortly afterwards, the EU and IMF agree to waive conditions on the €12 billion tranche of bailout money that will tide Greece over until September 2011.

Papandreou, meanwhile, is in a panic. First, he attempts to create a government of national unity. He invites the centre-right opposition party, New Democracy, into a coalition and even offers to stand down as prime minister. But who would want to govern Greece? New Democracy spurns Papandreou's offer, so he declares the formation of a 'new government', reshuffling the cabinet. For hours, one insider tells me, he fails to achieve even this: 'nobody will pick up the phone'. The politicians are safely shuttered away with their bodyguards in their private offices, unable to communicate face-to-face.

As Papandreou goes on TV to announce the reshuffle, car horns begin blaring across Athens. In Syntagma, where their camp has been razed and trampled by the police, the *indignados* move slowly back, knocking tent pegs in and dressing head wounds. Loukanikos the riot dog has become world-famous thanks to a YouTube montage of his exploits, and somebody has created a Twitter account for him (@rebeldog_ath). He lolls exhausted on the pavement, with a look that seems to say, like Arnie, 'I'll be back.'

### The tax collectors

The next morning, just around the corner from the Greek finance ministry, I spot a group of fashionable young women sitting around a trestle table in the middle of the street, beside the tents where they spent the night. They are fresh-faced, devoid of the tattoos and nose-studs you see among the *indignados*. They could pass as young civil servants, accountants or lawyers—and that's exactly what they are.

They are part of a group of 100 graduates who, eighteen months before, had passed the exams to become tax collectors and customs officials in the finance ministry. But there is no money to employ them. Most are now living with their parents, eking out a living on benefits.

Once the *indignados* had taken Syntagma, these quietly angry young women decided to set up camp right on the doorstep of the ministry they'd hoped to work in. Anna Palamiotou, in her early twenties, has the composure and perfect English of a ballet tutor or an upmarket ski coach:

> The whole problem is: our future is unpredictable. Even our short-term future. In three to six months' time we don't know what will happen. We hope, of course: that's the best we can do. We try to keep hoping, personally, as a nation, as a community.

The irony is that more tax collectors and customs officers are exactly what Greece needs. It was the culture of 'respectable'—and therefore acceptable—tax evasion that helped sink the country's finances in the first place. Now, all parties claim to want it fixed. But with the deficit so high, the Greek state has been ordered to shrink, not grow: so, despite their educational qualifications, Anna and her friends are stuck here on the street.

During the riots, they were shocked to see masked anarchists and Kevlar-clad riot police rampaging down the street they are camped in. 'They crushed our chairs,' Anna says, arching her eyebrows at a pile of plastic shards, like a schoolteacher might tut-tut about an untidy classroom. But they've found some new chairs, where they sit texting, iPodding, chatting and sipping coffee. What would it take to make them leave? 'We have no plans to,' she says.

Following the cabinet reshuffle, Papaconstantinou is out of the finance ministry. He has been replaced by Evangelos Venizelos, a big-bellied party operator who has never run a finance ministry in his life. Anna's message to Venizelos is stark: 'He has to take some measures, of course. But he has also to know the people have made many sacrifices and we have a limit beneath which we can't live. He has to respect us.'

It was against this deep, calm intransigence that the strategy of both the EU and PASOK would begin to founder.

## Who pays?

Since their summit at Deauville in October 2010, Merkel and Sarkozy had been haggling over a crucial detail of their euro-wide bailout scheme: when and how to impose losses on the banks and pension funds exposed to Greek bad debt. Sarkozy, backed by the ECB, insisted that the private sector should not be forced to take losses; Merkel, under electoral pressure, favoured imposing losses on the banks, but only after 2013. Now, though, 2013 was looming, as was the need to design a permanent European bailout mechanism to replace the one improvised in 2010.

As the riots raged, extensive briefings were quietly given to the press, warning that any private-sector losses arising from a Greek default would trigger a Lehman-style event that could start a second global recession.

Bank analysts frantically began trying to calculate the impact of a Greek default—but it was impossible. Even now, three years after Lehman, the opacity and complexity of the financial system stood in the way. Greece, by this time, had debts of €340 billion. One half of these debts were held by Greek banks and pension funds, which meant that if the country defaulted, the entire Greek (and Greek Cypriot) banking system would go bust. Because the Greek state, too, would be bust, it would be unable to bail out its own banks. In case of an uncontrolled default, there was a high likelihood that ATMs would close and people would lose their savings.

The other half of Greece's debts were held by northern European banks and states, and by the ECB; they, too, would be dragged into fiscal crisis by a Greek default. But there was even more to worry about.

On top of the actual debt, the global derivatives market had facilitated the erection of default insurance positions worth an estimated $1 trillion. These 'credit default swaps' would act like an accumulator bet, and significant losses on Greek debt would explode like an anti-tank missile, straight through the armour of the entire global system.

It would, said one bond market contact, be a 'Credit-Anstalt moment': he was referring to the Austrian banking collapse in 1931 that turned the Wall Street Crash into a global slump. Syntagma Square had become the front line of the global financial system.

Merkel told journalists: 'We wouldn't be able to control an insolvency. We all lived through Lehman Brothers. I don't want another such threat to emanate from Europe.'[1]

So for the second time in three years, banks and hedge funds who had lent money speculatively to a basket-case entity would be indemnified by the state, in this case the EU. But the EU—it turned out—would not be strong enough to cope. And meanwhile the problems of social order and legitimacy—in Greece and across the eurozone—were only just beginning. Two weeks later they would erupt, spectacularly, in Syntagma.

### One thousand rounds of tear gas

*29 June 2011*. The Greek parliament is due to vote on the EU's austerity plan at 4 p.m. A general strike is under way, causing energy brownouts and paralyzing Greece's airports and ports. The union marches are, as always, uncoordinated. In central Athens, the Communists are blocking one entire four-lane avenue, headed by stewarding groups toting chunky banner poles and crash helmets; the PASOK unions are doing the same a few streets down. The nationalists are still clustered around the iron fences and makeshift barricades in front of parliament. The mood is gloomy.

'We're facing two routes to bankruptcy,' one leftist protester tells me. 'There is no positive outcome. I shouldn't be saying this, because I am supposed to be against it—but we need a Chirac, a de Gaulle.

Where is Chirac? Where is the leadership going to come from to sort this out?'

Like many on the left, she fears a nationalist or authoritarian outcome to the crisis. But the Greek left—pitifully weakened by its divisions—seems unable to go beyond oppositional slogans. Faced with this, many horizontalists have undergone a kind of 'regime change of the mind'—switching off from mainstream politics, living haunted lifestyles among the oil paint stores and graffiti-encrusted walls of Exarcheia. 'Our generation,' she continues, 'that's spent their whole lives since Genoa fighting for change, feels exhausted.' A burst of explosions in Syntagma Square cuts the conversation short.

It is 2 p.m. I head for the square, but it is hard to get there. A tide of people is streaming backwards, away from the fighting: earth mothers, grandmothers, old men with their shoulders hunched to their ears, gasping for breath, fleeing the violence and the tear gas.

Suddenly there are only thirty metres of empty street between me and a melee of anarchists and riot cops. A man grabs me, his face white-caked, finger stabbing towards the parliament building: 'These cops,' he says,

> paid for by the Greek people, defending the Greek parliament so it can sell the country to the international banks! I'm a salesman in a furniture company: we lost 80 per cent of our turnover in a single year. What am I supposed to do?

The *indignados* regroup inside the square. At the back are those who are prepared to resist, but not attack. Young women run up to you and squirt you in the face with Maalox as a kind of gesture of solidarity. Some people are singing. We're all under the trees, densely packed, tense: everybody's eyes are glued to the few hundred protestors who are slugging it out toe-to-toe at the top of the square, near the Parliament. Tear gas and stun grenades rain down. Now, to the beat of alter-mondialiste bongo music, a few hundred *indignados* surge up the steps towards the parliament. I go with them, filming on a tiny stills camera to avoid the attentions of the police and some protesters, both of whom have taken to attacking mainstream TV crews.

All over the square there is the incessant clatter of people breaking up the marble balustrades and steps to make missiles. A tear-gas canister spirals down and lands at my feet; a guy in a hoodie tries to boot it, but he slips on something and does a parkour-style backflip. Another guy kicks it but it spins into another group of rioters, who kick it back, and it becomes—for one of those fleeting moments that lasts a flickering hour amid the violence—an extreme-sports version of five-a-side football.

I reach the top of the steps just in time to see a group of twenty policemen converging on one guy. As he disappears beneath the steel-tipped batons a man beside me, his friend, lets out a howl of fear and despair. As we retreat, I realize the liquid we're slipping around on is blood.

On the shuttered frontage of the Hotel Grande Bretagne somebody has spray-painted: 'Fuck May 68, Fight Now'.

Now a very dense crowd, maybe 10,000 people, gets crushed into a side-street. Alongside me is a man sweating in a gas mask. 'I'm a classical pianist and I run an NGO documenting the oral history of the Cyclades,' he tells me. 'This is not a democracy, man, it's a dictatorship. There is no way Greece can take the austerity: just look!'

This crowd is the salariat: not the fifty-something manual workers, and not the Black Bloc. A model-thin woman with carrot-blonde highlights tells me she's a bank worker on strike. 'They just keep trying to do this every time we protest: hospitalize us. Always the same: violence. But we will stop them. We will strike, protest, occupy.'

A Maalox-caked man interrupts her, yelling manically: 'There's a group of riot cops spraying us with chemicals when all we came here to do is protest and tell this fascist government to go!' Then, realizing my nationality, he adds: 'You British? I lived in your country for ten years. I am an interior designer.'

Later, it will be reported that the police fired one thousand rounds of tear gas during the Syntagma protests. I am lifted off my feet in the crush. A crowd numbering tens of thousands is being collectively punished for the actions of a few hundred—and, if you think about it, for a decade of venality among the bankers and political elite.

The scene in Syntagma degenerates into the familiar choreography: running battles between cops and anarchists. In the side-streets, though, there is a different kind of resistance. People are lighting fires, dragging wheelie bins across the road, breaking pavements to make projectiles. Again, it is apparent that the vast majority are not anarchists: most are not masked, most are not even young. This is the Greek middle class: the bank clerk, the designer, the concert pianist, the shop owner, the woman with the Gucci sunglasses and Radley handbag.

And what's really burning is consent. The side-streets of Syntagma are where the Plaka district begins, the age-old urban playground of the Greek petite-bourgeoisie, with its quaint family-owned shops: one selling only maps, another only books on coin collecting, another only vegan food. They proclaim the Greek model of capitalism: civilized, small-scale, old-fashioned and now—as parliament votes to destroy what's left of economic growth—doomed.

As the vote goes through, people cluster around TV screens in the cafés around Syntagma, which do not stop serving even while rocks and grenades are being hurled twenty yards away. One TV shows the vote in parliament split-screened with the riot itself; if you look in the other direction, you can see the same riot in real life just behind you.

As the socialist MPs vote one by one for the austerity programme, people thrust their open palms at the TV screen, a traditional Greek gesture of disgust. Many are zoned out from so much tear gas and anger. As they watch the vote unfold, you can see in their eyes that intensity of people watching penalty shootouts at football finals. To see those arms and hands outstretched, those contorted faces, is like seeing legitimacy drain away from Greek democracy.

### The danger of 'anomic' breakdown

By the summer of 2011, there was a social crisis under way in Greece —one very different from those found in history books. It was not the smashing of the state, nor even a political revolution. Rather, the Greek state—which had never reached very far into civil society— had simply begun to lose its grip on the actual functions a state should perform.

It could not determine its own economic policy. It could not convince its own people it was acting with good intent. The rule of law was being imposed with draconian force in one place only to break down somewhere else, as consumers pledged non-payment of bills for their privatized utilities, drivers flouted road tolls, restaurants voted to defy tax increases and youth disappeared into the grey economy.

Borrowing a term from the early twentieth-century sociologist Emile Durkheim, commentators started to speak of 'anomie' and 'anomic breakdown'—a situation where instead of anarchy (lack of government), you find mass refusals to cooperate with the system, amid the collapse of social norms. As veteran journalist Takis Michas put it, pleading with the political class to get a grip: 'Greece is slowly becoming a society where "low-intensity conflict" dominates, the legal order is breaking down and appeals to universal values become meaningless.'[2]

Political commentator Antonis Papayiannidis told me why it was becoming impossible for the politicians to save the situation:

> The Greek political class was always floating above the people, for decades. And the people didn't care. It was win-win. They floated above us and got rich; and we got rich. Now they have lost all connection to the Greek people. They have no legitimacy.

To the youth, amid this real-life movie trailer of fire, adrenaline and blood, it had begun to feel like war. 'The social war encompasses the totality of everyday life,' one wrote; 'to be alive today is to be at war, to never sleep properly, to awaken at odd hours to work, to be constantly surrounded by surveillance and police …'[3]

On 21 July 2011, faced with runs on the sovereign debt of Italy and Spain, the EU would soften the financial terms imposed on Greece. Further austerity was called for; the result was faster economic collapse and—as the EU leaders found out in late October—imminent bankruptcy. Faced with new evidence showing that austerity had no hope of saving Greece, and the first outbreak of open violence between communists and anarchists in Syntagma, the big powers of Europe climbed down. On 25 October they forced the banks to accept the 'voluntary' writedown of Greek debt—a controlled default—in return for the installation of permanent foreign control over Greek economic policy. To prevent a second Lehman event, they pumped €100 billion into the banking system and a trillion into the EFSF, the mega-bailout fund designed to end the crisis. But the crisis did not end.

Meanwhile the legitimacy of the Greek state was fatally eroded in the eyes of its people. And it is in this that Greece—though an outlier economically, representing just 6 per cent of the eurozone—becomes a signifier in the year it all kicked off.

Greece is the modern case study of what happens when the political elite of a developed country allows its legitimacy to go up in flames. Democracy and globalization itself are challenged. The minds of a whole generation begin to switch off from the dreams that had sustained them. And there is reason to fear that Greece might not be unique.

# 6

## 'Error de Sistema':
## Economic Causes of the Present Unrest

The youths who swarmed into squares all over Spain on 15 May 2011 were an unlikely bunch. Journalists mocked them for their naivety; the socialists, communists and seasoned anarchos, meanwhile, were politely amazed. Was this not the generation that had smooched its way through a thousand mornings of *café con leche* and cigarettes, seemingly unconcerned about the serious business of politics?

What mystified both pundits and hardened activists most of all was the vehemence of the protesters' anti-capitalism. 'Error de Sistema', said one placard, brandished by three girls straight off the fashion pages of some upmarket magazine—adding, for instant Twitter relevance, '#spanishrevolution'. 'La Crisis Es El Capitalismo' said the banner in Madrid's Puerta del Sol, big as a tennis court, held up by similarly good-looking youths.

But once you see Spain's unemployment figures, there is no mystery to the anger: by mid-2011 youth unemployment was running at 46 per cent. As in Cairo, Athens and beyond, it's economic disruption— joblessness, price rises, austerity—that has driven the unrest. To most people it may feel as though this period of disruption started with the collapse of Lehman Brothers. But the real disruption began much earlier, with the onset of globalization, and in particular after 2001. Once you grasp this, you can grasp the scale of the challenge facing those in power.

## *How we came to the crisis*

The first decade of the twenty-first century saw an uncontrolled expansion of credit, during which the major financial actors' understanding of the risks involved in lending became—and was encouraged by governments to become—detached from reality. The credit boom, in turn, was caused by a mismatch between the savings generated in the export-oriented countries—China, Japan and Germany—and the debt-fuelled consumption of the Anglo-Saxon world.

The excess credit fuelled asset price inflation in technology stocks, housing, commodities and finally financial assets themselves. On top of this a new market in complex debt vehicles was created, and on the back of that a credit derivatives system whose notional value, at the time of the crash, was about the same as global GDP: $68 trillion.

As the housing bubble began to deflate, the increasingly toxic debts were found stored inside a system of off-balance-sheet financial entities, which became known—only after it collapsed—as the 'shadow banking system'. Very few mainstream financial journalists had noticed its existence.

Once the first phase of the crisis was over, parts of the business elite began to breathe easy and tell themselves they'd seen it all before. 'No one has yet dis-invented the business cycle,' Rupert Murdoch chuckled, quoting Margaret Thatcher to an invited audience in London in 2010, including numerous beaming members of the Coalition Cabinet. 'The "gales of creative destruction" still roar mightily from time to time.'[1]

But this is no mere business cycle, and no ordinary cycle of boom and bust. As the data clearly illustrate, the seeds of the crisis were sown by structural changes.

Exhibit One: the average US house price at the peak, in 2006, was double what the historic trend line said it should be, even when compared to every other boom–bust cycle since the war. This was no ordinary housing bubble.

Exhibit Two: the value of mortgage-backed securities issued (that is, of complex debt products designed to mask the risks involved in riding the house-price bubble) increased fivefold between 2000 and 2003, to $3.2 trillion. Credit default swaps, where unknown actors in the market can bet on the future failure of another's investment, had grown from zero to $68 trillion in eight years. This was no ordinary credit cycle.

Exhibit Three: there was a massive rise in so-called global imbalances. China's foreign currency reserves grew from $150 billion in 1999 to $2.85 trillion in 2010. The US current-account deficit (the difference between goods, services and capital flowing in and out) grew from $99 billion in 1989 to $800 billion by 2007. Before the crisis, these imbalances had been conceptualized as a kind of yin–yang pictogram of perfect harmony: China exports, America imports; China lends, America borrows; Chinese consumers save, American consumers borrow— it's just a new form of the division of labour. But in the ten years after 1999, the imbalances unleashed chaos. This was no ordinary division of labour.

Exhibit Four, probably the most signal disruption of them all: the trend for global capital flows. In 1980, the economists Feldstein and Horioka observed that since the dawn of industrial capitalism, there had been a high correlation between saving and investment within countries, at a ratio hovering just below 1:1.[2] This was the famous Feldstein–Horioka paradox: why, given that capitalism had become so global, did we continue to invest our savings in our own 'home' markets?

But after the year 2000 the paradox collapses: the ratio inverts. In a reversal unparalleled in the history of capitalism, the ratio of domestic savings to domestic investment fell to zero: capital had begun washing around the globe at speed, as savings in the west dried up and, in the east, piled high.[3] This was no ordinary decade.

The scale of the property bubble, the scale of global capital flows, the scale of speculation and of the mismatch between consuming and producing countries was unprecedented—all of it. Right now, mainstream economics remains confused about the ultimate source of the disruption. Is it our greed? Are these the growing pains of the Chinese century? Was it all down to testosterone on the trading floors of major banks?

Actually, the answer is staring us in the face, but it's unpalatable. The root cause, simply put, is globalization, and the resulting monopolization of wealth by a global elite.

In the two decades after 1989 the world's labour force grew from 1.5 billion people to 3 billion and, through migration and outsourcing, the labour market itself became global. Harvard economist Richard Freeman has called this phenomenon 'The Great Doubling'. The move from farm to factory in China and the developing world, combined with the entry of the former Soviet bloc into the global economy, effectively doubled the amount of labour available to capital, and halved the ratio of capital to labour.[4]

The impact on wages was startling. In the USA, real hourly wages for men were, by 2005, the same as they had been in 1973.[5] In Japan, the real wage index fell by 11.2% in the decade to 2007, and fell a further 2% in each of the following years.[6] In the former West Germany, gross wages per employee have slipped by about 6 per cent from their post-unification high of 1991. For former East German employees, the same measure leapt by 25 per cent after unification—only to stagnate after 1999, and fall back by around 2.5 per cent between 2003 and today.[7]

Of course, there are places where real wages are rising—notably, peripheral Europe and the emerging markets. But the figures show real wages falling in the 2000s across many of the West's heartland countries and in a variety of different economies: in deflationary Japan; in the highly socialized economy of Germany; in the free-market USA. And the shortfall between stagnating wages and consumption growth is met by credit.

The results of all this look benign—until, that is, they turn bad. There is a 'heroic' period of globalization, beginning in 1989 and ending around 1999, during which China's entry into the world market helps suppress inflation; where falling wages are offset by a seemingly sustainable expansion of credit; where house prices rise, allowing the credit to be paid off and a whole bunch of innovations are suddenly deployed—above all mobile telephony and broadband Internet.

Then there is a second phase in which the disruption overwhelms the innovations: China's increased consumption of raw materials creates world-wide inflationary pressure; the house-price boom ends, because the banks run out of poverty-stricken workers to lend to; mass migration begins to exert a downward pressure on the wages of unskilled workers in Europe and the USA; the financial dynamic overtakes, dominates and ultimately chokes off the dynamics of production, trade and innovation.

The rise of finance, wage stagnation, the capture of regulation and politics by a financial elite, consumption fuelled by credit rather than wages: it all blew up spectacularly. If this process had been accompanied by dire warnings from economists and politicians; if Madonna and Fifty Cent had wagged their diamond-encrusted fingers at us and rapped, 'Hey kids, be careful, it won't last'—then maybe the ideological shock would have been smaller. But the 2000s boom was accompanied only by yelps of glee. In Britain, the then chancellor in the Labour government, Gordon Brown, told us he'd achieved 'an end to boom and bust', adding that the era would be seen as 'the beginning of a new golden age for the City of London'.[8]

Even the diehard opponents of the system seemed cowed. Some of those who had organized the anti-capitalist revolts in Genoa and Prague moved to the West Bank to stand in front of Israeli bulldozers, others moved into concept art; the gritty eco-protesters who had mobilized against Shell and Japanese whaling fleets became sustainability experts for the newly greenwashed corporations. Aid charities that had flayed Bill Gates now gratefully received billions of dollars from Bill Gates, and toned down their criticisms accordingly.

But then it all exploded. The system, the conceits, the ideology. In fact, you need something better than the word 'explosion' to do it justice.

## The alien and its toxic blood

There is a scene from the movie *Alien* (1986) that offers a perfect metaphor for what's happened since the Lehman crisis.

In the spaceship's medical bay, the alien is sitting on John Hurt's face, breathing on his behalf: a perfect parasite. The surgeon tries to cut it off with a laser scalpel. But the alien's blood turns out to be acid. The blood splashes on the floor of the operating theatre and burns through. The crew rush down to the next level of the spaceship, but it's already dripping through the ceiling and fizzing through the floor. On the next level down it's the same. Horror-struck, they realize that if it burns through to the hull, the spaceship will explode. Luckily, after burning through several decks, it stops.

In this metaphor, the banks are the alien; the acid blood is the toxic debt; the scalpel incision is made by US Treasury Secretary Hank Paulson on 15 September 2008, as he attempts to amputate Lehman Brothers. And the unleashed toxic debt then burns through layer after layer of the global economic system.

The first layer it burned through was the credit system. The next layer was the real economy, whose output, trade and stock market valuations collapsed at a rate completely in line with post-1929: there was a 20 per cent fall in trade, a 50 per cent fall in global stock market valuations and an annualized 40 per cent fall in merchandise exports.[9]

But then it hit a deck that did not burn. In the spring of 2009, a slump on the scale of the 1930s was halted by the intervention of the state.

By spending taxpayers' money and reducing taxes; slashing interest rates and then printing money; quarantining trillions of dollars of bad loans inside the balance sheets of governments—the state became the barrier that contained the acid blood of toxic debt.

The ideological implications of the state's intervention are always avoided in conversations at Davos or Jackson Hole, or on the yachts of the super-rich. Because among the wealthy, the default theory of our age still rules: that the state is dysfunctional to capitalism; that (as free-market economic guru Milton Friedman taught) the regulator can never know more than the two parties in the deal and therefore should not, ideally, exist.

The dominant economic theory states that individual self-interest is the great driver of progress. According to this dogma, any attempt to impose rationality on economic life leads not just to inefficiency but—as another free-market economist, Friedrich Hayek, put it—to 'serfdom'.

But even while mainstream economics struggled to understand the new effectiveness of the state, another problem arose. The state could not hold. That is to say, not all states, or state formations, were strong enough to absorb the acid bath of bad debt they were being asked to take.

It has now become obvious that four globally strategic institutions were corroded to the point of failure by the attempt to contain the crisis. These are: the eurozone, British social democracy, bipartisanship in American politics, and the network of Western-backed dictatorships that ran the Middle East.

That is nice work for one small alien over the space of three years, and its mission is not over yet.

### The euro crisis

Ireland was bankrupted by its banks, which had become the conduit for hot money operations out of London during the boom. As they went bust, progressively, so did the Irish state, bailed out to the tune of €85 billion after a month of protesting there was no need to, on 29 November 2010.

Greece was bankrupted by ten years of co-existence with Germany inside a single currency. Southern Europe became a market for German loans and German cars: already boosted by the low Deutschmark exchange rate fixed on entry into the single currency, the German economy simply reaped the rewards of its institutional dominance. Meanwhile stagnant wages in Germany, alongside galloping unit labour costs in the periphery meant, as economist Costas Lapavistas put it: 'Monetary union is a "beggar-thy-neighbour" policy for Germany, on condition that it beggars its own workers first.'[10] Allowing Greece to join the euro with a detrimental real exchange rate, a dysfunctional tax system and rising labour costs practically guaranteed its future penury.

Portugal, meanwhile, was bankrupted by its failure to compete—not just with Germany but with China and developing Asia, as offshoring quickly sucked the life out of the country's traditional timber and leather industries. In a factory outside Porto early in 2011, I saw first-hand a whole shed full of equipment for making softwood Venetian blinds. It was deserted, the machinery laced with fine cobwebs; two years before, thirty people had worked there. Next door, an unbuilt speculative property development—no more than a deserted sales office and some tattered corporate flags—completed the narrative of broken dreams.

Greece, Portugal and Ireland could have been saved by early intervention. In the end they were saved too late, and therefore not saved at all. In May 2010 and again in July and September 2011, the entire euro currency was taken to the brink of breakup and collapse by the indecision of the eurozone's leaders, above all Merkel and ECB boss Jean-Claude Trichet. The three bailed-out countries are now destined to remain on life support for several years. But by August 2011 inaction had dragged Italy and Spain into the danger zone, so that the European Central Bank was forced to break its own rules and start buying up the debt of these two massive, un-bailable economies.

The dilemma throughout the euro crisis has been clear: whether to impose losses from south European bad debts onto north European taxpayers, or onto the bankers who had actually lent the money to these bankrupt countries in the first place. The outcome was always a function of the level of class struggle. By hitting the streets, Greek people were able to force Europe to impose losses on the bankers; where opposition remained within its traditional boundaries—the one-day strike, the passive demo—it was the workers, youth and pensioners who took the pain. Meanwhile Europe itself was plunged into institutional crisis. At summit after summit, the fiction at the heart of the Maastricht Treaty was exposed. Monetary union without fiscal union had failed; not as in a 'failed aspiration', but as in a concrete girder tested to failure.

There are only two logical outcomes to the euro crisis. Either northern Europe, whose taxpayers will bail out the south, takes control of eurozone economic policy, issuing 'Eurobonds' or some proxy vehicle to cement an effective fiscal union; or, the eurozone breaks up. Whichever happens, north–south solidarity in the eurozone is corroded beyond repair. From Helsinki to Milan, the far right is gaining ground on opposition to bailouts for the 'feckless south'. This means that, even if the eurozone's leaders summon up the courage to attempt fiscal union, they can hardly sell it to their electorates. Logically—though in practice its demise may take some time—the eurozone in its present form is doomed.

### British Labour's 'third way' collapses

For the thirteen years Labour ruled Britain it relied on an implicit deal: taxes from the bloated financial services sector were placed at the disposal of a welfare system that allowed 9 million people to become dependent on state handouts. Benefits and tax credits, together with neighbourhood policing and CCTV systems, made life tolerable in towns where there would never be high-paid work again.

For those who had bought their homes, including council-estate dwelling workers, the Blair years would see 'equity withdrawal'—borrowing against rising house prices—equivalent to a stunning 103 per cent of GDP growth.[11]

Crime fell, and the feel-good factor increased with credit-fuelled spending power, especially for the poor; analysts noted that the main drivers of equity withdrawal were people 'with low credit scores and high credit card utilisation rates, who are most likely to have been credit-constrained in the past'[12]. But the fundamental lack of productive industry—indeed, in great swathes of the country the lack of any vibrant private sector beyond aerospace and military hardware—was never addressed.

Labour's then Business Secretary Peter Mandelson had summed up the party's strategy when he announced it was 'intensely relaxed about people becoming filthy rich as long as they pay their taxes'; his Cabinet colleague Geoff Hoon is said to have told Labour MPs worried about the decline of shipbuilding that: 'metal bashing is no longer a vital national asset'. Under Labour, Britain lost 1.3 million manufacturing jobs.

But this was social democracy. There had to be a palliative. The scale and persistence of poverty in Britain prompted Labour to extend the benefit system into the lives of those at work, in the form of tax credits. As a result, by 2010, 9.2 million adults out of a working-age population of 37 million were receiving state tax credits, while 5.4 million people were dependent on out-of-work benefits.[13] By the end of the Labour government, former Labour minister Alan Milburn would admit: 'We still live in a country where, invariably, if you're born poor, you die poor, just as if you go to a low-achieving school, you tend to end up in a low-achieving job.'[14]

Redistribution through welfare was never overtly sold as compensation for the destruction of the 'old' working-class lifestyle, but that's how it was widely understood. When I interviewed ex-miners in Leigh, my home town, in September 2009, in a pub at lunchtime, it was the Conservative threat to their benefits that worried them most. 'They closed the mines, but at least they allowed you to draw your "sick",' one told me, meaning the Incapacity Benefit that large numbers of former manual workers were entitled to. 'Now they're going to take away the sick.'

But by then, whatever deal Labour thought it had with this older, male, manual demographic had begun to erode. In 2003 Labour enthusiastically opened its labour market to workers from Eastern Europe; by 2010, the Office for National Statistics released figures that showed 81 per cent of all jobs created under Labour had been filled by non-UK-born workers.[15] The influx placed a downward pressure, not so much on unskilled wages (which were pegged at the national minimum), but on the layers just above. Anecdotally, time and again, it was this that proved the deal-breaker for many of Labour's traditional supporters. In that same Leigh pub, numerous old miners quietly told me, off-camera, that though they were lifelong Labour voters, they had voted for the British National Party in the European elections of 2009. They were not alone.

In May 2009, 2.5 million people in Britain voted for the right-wing-conservative, anti-Europe party UKIP, and just under a million for the fascist BNP. A year later, in the British general election the BNP still gained nearly 600,000 votes, largely from among the traditionally Labour-voting 'C2DE' social groups—which is sociological double-speak for manual workers.

Once again, the financial crisis had been the crucial deal-breaker between the politicians and the electorate. As long as their homes gained value and their credit-card limits were raised, people on low incomes could tolerate the 'filthy rich' character of Labour's friends and donors, and Labour's encouragement for the influx of cheap, unorganized labour. Now, with the economy grinding to a halt, many could not.

Today, whatever its electoral fortunes may hold, Labour's thirteen-year strategy of a high-welfare, low-industry economy paid for by a finance and housing bubble, is finished—and agreed to be so by the party's leadership. What the future may hold for its relationship with its traditional base is less clear.

### The collapse of bipartisan politics in America

*Indiana, October 2010.* The university gym at Angola, Indiana, is not quite packed, but at $20 a ticket and $10 for the t-shirt, a couple of thousand people is a decent payday for Glenn Beck, the Fox News presenter who's to be the star attraction.

But Beck comes later. The day starts with a very fat man in a very tight polo-neck sweater singing 'God Bless the USA' in an excruciating tenor voice. Everyone except me stands erect, many with fists clenched against their chests. Some put their hands in the air and close their eyes in an expression of quasi-religious rapture.

The crowd is 99 per cent white and 100 per cent Christian. Of those I speak to at the interval, many believe President Obama is neither American nor Christian. One is offering for sale a set of playing cards modeled on the famous Saddam Hussein deck, with Obama's picture captioned as a 'Kenyan born, lying, arrogant Muslim communist that hates America'. 'We had to print 'em abroad because no American printing house would handle 'em,' he tells me proudly.

Now Jackie Walorski takes the stage, as the warm-up act for Beck. The forty-seven-year-old Congressional candidate points to the American flag and yells at the audience that they have just days 'to fight for who we are as Americans':

> If we don't fight for freedom, liberty, individual destiny *they* are redefining this country out from underneath us. The battle we're facing is to defend this flag on *our* turf, *our* soil. When our soldiers came out of the boats in Normandy they literally walked over bodies to fight for our freedom. The battle we face today, the ideological war that we're fighting, is for standing up for a constitution. The land of the free and the home of the brave is under assault today.

Walorski's speech is preceded by videos that splice footage of Omaha Beach in 1944 with scenes from 9/11 and the Iraq war: the 'they' she's referring to are Obama and the Democrat-voting Congress. America's airwaves, though, are alive with the angry voices of enraged white Christians, for whom 'they' means something else. No one on the stage in Indiana needs to assert that Obama is 'a racist' with 'a deep-seated hatred for white people or the white culture'—because Glenn Beck has already said so on TV, back in July 2009. To the American right, 'they'—subtextually—means the migrants, the black and Hispanic Americans, the newly married gay couples and, inevitably, the Muslims.

This is the Tea Party in full flow, injecting into traditional fiscal conservatism the belief that state intervention into economic life is immoral, un-Christian and unconstitutional. Walorski (who will narrowly miss getting elected in November 2010) explains the thinking to me:

> We are watching a freight-train of spending in this country. Americans don't live that way. We're the land of capitalism, we're not the land of taking people's public tax money and throwing it into a concept that isn't proven, that has not produced jobs. That's not what the key is in this country. You can continue to write checks but recovery comes from private-sector jobs and holding a line on spending.

By the autumn of 2010, what's sapping the energy of Democratic Party supporters is that Walorski's words—stripped of their rhetoric—ring true for many Americans who are worried sick about the economy.

According to his advisers Jared Bernstein and Christina Romer, Obama's fiscal stimulus—$787 billion of discretionary spending— would 'create or save' three million jobs.[16] They even produced a graph to show the before and after: fiscal stimulus, concentrated as extra government spending rather than tax cuts, would have an amplified 'bang-for-bucks' effect. Without stimulus, they predicted, unemployment might peak at 9 per cent. It was a gross under-estimate. In the end it peaked at 10 per cent, even with the stimulus.

In March 2009 a further bout of stimulus, this time monetary, was unleashed. Ben Bernanke, boss of the Federal Reserve—who just two months previously had delivered a lecture in London arguing against the classic policy of printing money to stimulate demand—decided to print $1.75 trillion.

This was Keynesianism as practiced by an elite that did not believe in it. The real Keynesians—Paul Krugman in the *New York Times*, Nobel Laureate Joseph Stiglitz in numerous books and articles—warned that the stimulus would not be enough. It was, however, enough to erode the last vestiges of bipartisan politics in America.

For during the neoliberal years the super-rich had spared no effort or expense to create a plebeian backlash against the Federal state. From the platform of Fox News, Rupert Murdoch's employees had railed against big government and high taxes. Across the Bible Belt, the holy book had been brandished by preachers warning against the combined evils of abortion, gay marriage, 'positive discrimination' for black people, illegal immigration, big government and high taxes.

By February 2009, the religious right in America had an enemy it had always dreamed of: a black president, committed to liberal social policy, big spending and a bailout of Wall Street at the expense of everyone else. In November 2010 they found the means to humiliate him, when the Republicans won a majority in the House of Representatives, including eighty-seven signed-up members of the Tea Party. And in the summer of 2011 they found the issue—America's $14 trillion national debt.

If Obama's stimulus had worked, or if Bernanke's $1.75 trillion had ever filtered through to homeowners as a supply of new credit, then the power of the conservative argument would have been blunted. It would have remained what it always was, an ideological trend; a frustrated faith in small government, co-existing with the actuality of a giant state.

But in July 2011, with the impact of the stimulus running out and unemployment once again rising, the Tea Party would take America to the brink of technical bankruptcy, forcing the end of fiscal stimulus and the beginning of a decade of austerity. President Obama, who had come to power pledging to restore bipartisan politics in Washington, would preside helplessly over its destruction—and with it the destruction of the certainties at the heart of American politics for decades.

With the approach of the next phase of the crisis, the atmosphere is defined not just by this paralysis at the level of Federal economics, but by the fractiousness, verging on outright defiance, that prevails between conservative state governors and the presidency. As we will see, this has massive implications for the rest of the world.

## The economics of the Arab Spring

The social and political roots of the Arab Spring, and the Western myopia towards them, have been well documented. But the economic roots were, at first sight, a mystery. The experts were blindsided, in part, because the economics of the region looked positive. In 2009, growth in Tunisia bottomed out at 3 per cent; in Libya it was 6 per cent and in Egypt, 4.7 per cent. Thereafter, the economies of all three countries bounced back strongly.

On top of this, lots of other indicators looked good. Egypt had managed to pull 9 per cent of its population out of absolute poverty in the 2000s; in terms of corruption, according to Transparency International, Mubarak's regime was on a par with Berlusconi and Hu Jin Tao's—and certainly nowhere near the top of the global league of crookedness. On the Gini Index, which measures levels of inequality, Egypt stood level with France, Tunisia with the USA.[17]

But the positives masked severe structural imbalances, the most obvious symptom of which was youth unemployment. In Egypt, even before the crisis hit, 92 per cent of the unemployed were first-time job-seekers. As growth slackened, unemployment in the twenty-to-twenty-five age range rose to 28 per cent. In Tunisia it stood at 30 per cent; in Yemen, estimates put the figure at 50 per cent.[18]

As Arab dictators have now learned to their cost, youth unemployment is not just any old statistic to be offset by high growth, high oil prices, or a pat on the back from the IMF. It destroys human capital and spreads bitterness across society.

What was more, when the recovery came, youth unemployment did not fall back. The reasons were, again, structural: the International Labour Organization found that, in Egypt, patronage was causing three-quarters of school-leavers to wait five years to get their first job. Meanwhile, massive underinvestment in education had left 44 per cent of the workforce illiterate and more than 75 per cent lacking anything higher than middle-school qualifications. The ILO found, in other words, what you find if you hang around the edges of Tahrir Square: a smattering of graduates and a mass of chirpy, uneducated teenagers with nothing better to do than sit on somebody's parked motor-scooter, crack jokes or join in revolutions.

When the global recovery got under way in 2010, the poor were hit by price rises, occurring in the first place because, since 2000, all global recoveries have sparked commodity price inflation; and secondly, because the USA had decided to unleash inflation onto the developing world.

As the effects of Obama's stimulus faded, in November 2010 Ben Bernanke began a second round of money printing—$600 billions' worth—known as 'Quantitative Easing II'. QEII, it was recognized even at the design stage, would not increase demand directly in America. By reducing the value of the dollar, and the attractiveness of dollar investments, it would create an international 'wall of money' flowing out of the USA towards its emerging rivals: Russia, Brazil, India and other dynamos of the global south. Those countries' currencies would have to rise against the dollar, or they would have to tolerate rampant inflation, or both.

Some countries resisted. Brazil responded to a 40 per cent rise of the real against the dollar with a tax designed to suppress the flow of capital into Brazil. It spent tens of billions of dollars in the foreign exchange markets buying its own currency to depress the exchange rate, and slapped a ban on short-selling the dollar inside Brazil.

But other countries could not, or would not, use capital controls. The outcome speaks for itself: the UN's global Food Price Index, which had been set at 100 in 2004, rocketed from 180 in July 2010 to an all-time high of 234 in February 2011. In spring 2011, after Bernanke vigorously denied that QEII had had the slightest impact on the Arab Spring, UK economist Andrew Lilico produced a graph showing the almost exact correlation between Federal Reserve money-printing operations and global commodity prices. Noting the revolutions that followed, he observed drily that 'the Fed seems very clearly to have achieved more in the Arab world in six months than the Pentagon achieved in decades'.[19]

In Egypt the impact of QEII was particularly acute: food prices rose 19 per cent in the year to February 2011. Over the same period in Syria, the price of dairy products and cooking oil went up by 27 per cent.[20]

In an intriguing historical comparison, bond analysts at Barings Asset Management took food price data from the revolutions of 1848 and superimposed them onto wheat price movements in the Arab world in 2010. The results were remarkable. In 1848, inflation correlated closely with revolt: the higher the cost of bread, the more revolutionary the outcome. In 2011, Tunisia, Yemen and Lebanon experienced price hikes which, in 1848, would have been prompted expectations of violent revolution; Egypt, Jordan and Palestine, meanwhile, were off the scale. Saudi Arabia stood exactly where England had stood as Europe raged 150 years ago: with food price stability and minimal unrest.[21]

Commodity price inflation, as all global agencies agree, hammers the poor. It turns the 'acceptable' poverty of $2 a day into utter destitution. And the problem is that it has become endemic. Every economic recovery now sparks a commodity boom, mainly because of structural factors which currency manipulation by rich countries only exacerbates: population growth, rising demand in India and China, resource scarcity and the impact of climate change.

As the experts bicker over the precise role of poverty and food inflation in the Arab Spring, they do so to the sound of unrest across the
developing world. Fragile dictatorships that have not yet fallen wonder
how long they would survive in any second financial crisis, or any third
commodity spike.

## The economic fault lines

Watching Obama fail, the UK's Labour government crash and
burn, the eurozone's technocrats stagger from one catastrophe to the
next and Arab dictators wilt in the glare of revolt has not been pretty.
This bonfire of ideologies has left a trail of broken-hearted believers:
diehard Mubarak supporters clustered outside the great man's trial;
the German Green Party pleading for the EU's leaders to ignore the
anti-euro sentiments of their own voters; Obama himself, wearing his
trademark puzzled frown as his ratings lurch from bad to worse.

But this is not the end of the process. Returning to the *Alien* metaphor, if the 'floor' represented by the state burns through, then it is clear
where the acid will start corroding next: the hull of the spaceship itself,
that is, globalization. For if the state can't contain the crisis, the crisis
will move on to relationships between states and classes.

Brazil's finance minister has already fired the warning shots. At the
World Trade Organization in January 2011, exasperated by the
impact of QEII, he threatened to sanction the USA for currency
manipulation: 'This', he affirmed, 'is a currency war that is turning
into a trade war.'[22]

As monetary stimulus becomes currency manipulation and G20
summit agreements give way to summits that end inconclusively (as in
Seoul in 2010), the possibility looms of trade wars, outright competitive
devaluations and the nuclear option of debt default. As one bond
market participant put it to me, we are no longer dealing with market
forces: 'all market risk is now political risk'.

Now, throughout the world, there will be austerity on an

unprecedented scale. From California to Cairo, it is certain that the rising generation will be materially poorer than those that came before. Even if we do not have a deflationary slump, 1930s-style, countries like Greece will experience 1930s levels of austerity.

But the mainstream political and economic decision-makers seem unable to rethink. Their mental framework was shaped in a world in which Lehman Brothers was on Seventh Avenue and house values always rose. And this, in turn, creates a crisis of legitimacy: non-centrist parties of the right and left are advancing electorally across Europe, while the Muslim Brotherhood is making steady gains in Egypt; and these are just the tip of a deeper disaffection.

Domestic discontent and inter-state rivalry feed off each other. It was Ben Bernanke's book on the Great Depression that taught us the monetarist truism: 'To an overwhelming degree the evidence shows that countries that left the Gold Standard recovered from the Depression more quickly than countries that remained on gold.'[23]

The lesson is this: he who devalues his currency first escapes the crisis first. In the 1930s, tight monetary policy, driven by adherence to gold, exacerbated the depression.

This time there is no Gold Standard, but a system of free-floating exchange rates. Britain was first out of the blocks to devalue—the governor of the Bank of England, Mervyn King, told colleagues privately that he was proud of his contribution to the 20 per cent slide of sterling after 2008. America launched an effective devaluation strategy with QEII, despite simultaneously claiming to be for 'a strong dollar'. Then, during the desperate flight to safety in August 2011, when both America and the eurozone toyed with default, others piled into the currency game: Switzerland and Japan sold mountains of money to try and depreciate their own currencies. China's policy is, of course, permanent undervaluation of the renminbi.

So we are already into a new phase, in which one country offloads the costs of crisis onto another, the rich offload the costs onto the poor and the old onto the young. As the pain increases, ideologies of resistance will get stronger, and there is a danger that they will become magnetized towards nationalism and protectionism. The blue-and-white flags on the steps of the Greek parliament, the Gadsden flags waved by the US Tea Party (a 1776-era rattlesnake logo and the motto 'Don't Tread On Me'), and the anti-migrant sentiment flaring from Arizona to Athens, all attest to this.

But these are just advance warnings. If the acid eats through the hull of the spaceship and globalization is replaced by competing economic blocs, as it was in the 1930s, then all bets are off in terms of the diplomatic and military certainties that have prevailed since 1989.

So much of the fabric of our lives is woven into the system based on globalization that there is, in many respects, more at stake than there was in the collapse of 1929. Because we in the West have experienced real and rising personal freedom during the last twenty years, the end of it might feel rather more like the end of the belle époque in 1914.

The most dangerous thing is that, even now, it becomes rational for politicians, strategists, global corporations and military planners to prepare for a fragmented world. It becomes rational for policymakers of both left and right to ask: what shall we do if the currency war turns into a trade war? How would we rebalance our economy unilaterally if world conditions turn against us? It becomes absolutely logical—as the UK's Strategic Security and Defence Review did—to ask: how many aircraft carriers would we need if globalization breaks down?

That is the real problem with the 'error de sistema'. It poses, for all shades of old-school political opinion, a very stark alternative: either fight for a new, more equitable and sustainable form of globalization—with new treaties, new transnational organizations, a new deal on global currencies; or retreat behind national barriers and stage the battle between the classes over social justice and redistribution there.

Sources of support for the latter course of action are strong, albeit screened out of the mainstream. When I met steelworkers in Gary, Indiana—skilled and educated left-wing Democrats, determined to force Obama to take on the banks and deliver union rights—they told me: 'If it means trade war with China, bring it on.' Probably the only thing they could agree on with the Tea Party was that.

But trade wars, whether driven by left, right or centre, have a negative logic that can escape the intentions of the participants. As Charles Kindleberger's masterly account of the Depression showed, 'by advancing its own economic good by a tariff, currency depreciation or foreign exchange control, a country may worsen the welfare of its partners by more than its own gain ... so that each country ends up in a worse position'.[24] Kindleberger concluded that only a hegemonic power could hold things together in this situation; a country prepared to absorb unwanted produce, accept IOUs from everybody and maintain the flow of investment capital as it dried up elsewhere. It was the fall of Britain and the delayed emergence of America that ultimately accounted for the prolonged Depression of 1929–39, Kindleberger said: the parallels with the decline of America and the non-emergence of China as a world power are very clear.

But the stakes go higher than even this. Globalization and the techno-revolution have created new forms of human behaviour, culture and even consciousness that would be unlikely to survive another breakup of the world economy.

Any repeat of the 1930s economically could provoke a culture war just as bitter as the one that turned Berlin from a tolerant, jazz-age metropolis into a racially pure Wagnerian wasteland in the space of five years—but this time on a global scale.

These are the risks the world is running with every month that the economic causes of discontent go unaddressed.

# 7

## 'I Tweet in My Dreams':
## The Rise of the Networked Individual

In 1910 the composer Frederick Delius wrote an opera so revolutionary that nobody noticed. The plot was thin: a few static scenes from an obscure Danish novel—'pictures', Delius called them. The premiere, four years later, was cancelled because the First World War broke out. On its first performance, in 1919, it flopped.

Nobody liked *Fennimore and Gerda*. Even Delius's biggest fan, the conductor Thomas Beecham, described it as a story about 'three rather dreary people who have nothing to sing'. But if you listen to the music you can hear what was revolutionary. *Fennimore and Gerda* is the first opera written directly about modern, liberated sexual relationships, dispensing with the pretexts of historical or exotic settings. It is, above all, about being free.

And it is a product of an age very much like ours. The decade before 1914 saw an unprecedented surge in human freedom, a freedom that found expression in all kinds of literature and art: the early D. H. Lawrence, André Gide, Klimt's *Beethoven Frieze* with its lesbian orgy, painted in 1902 and immediately covered up. There's C. P. Cavafy in Alexandria daring to write, by 1904, his ultra-sensuous gay love lyrics, and of course Picasso, whose *Demoiselles d'Avignon* changed everything.

John Maynard Keynes would eulogize that age as an 'extraordinary episode in the economic progress of man'.[1] In his memoir *The World of*

*Yesterday*, published in 1943, the Austrian writer Stefan Zweig summed up the zeitgeist of globalized trade, technological progress and sexual liberation:

> There was progress everywhere... There was more freedom as well as more beauty in the world... I feel sorry for all those who did not live through these last years of European confidence when they were still young themselves. For the air around us is not a dead and empty void, it has in it the rhythm and vibration of the time.[2]

But the decade before 1914 turned out to be a giant false start as far as freedom was concerned. It was followed by a century scarred by economic crisis, militarism, genocide and totalitarian rule.

After the First World War, of course, the cultural elevation of the self took off in earnest. Controversial stories of sexual adventure, psychological rebirth and revolt became ten-a-penny. But by now these artists and writers were out of sync with the 'rhythm and vibration of the time'. With eighteen million war dead and the world in the grip of revolutions, the zeitgeist had become collectivist, not individualist. Individual human freedom was on hold—except for the rich, or those prepared to flout accepted social norms.

It's hard to remember, given the status we now accord writers like Joyce, Fitzgerald, Miller, the Lawrence of *Lady Chatterley's Lover*, and artists like Klimt and Picasso, that such status eluded them in the collectivist decades. Henry Miller's work was banned in the USA as late as 1964; *Lady Chatterley* in the UK, famously, until 1960; Klimt's frieze was not publicly exhibited again until 1986; even Picasso himself did not dare exhibit the *Demoiselles* until 1916. *Fennimore and Gerda*, by no means challenging compared to the atonal music of the 1910s, would not be revived until—you guessed it—1968, and then only by a group of amateurs.

In the depths of the twentieth century, even the rebels began to accept the impossibility of breaking free. Koestler's *Darkness at Noon*,

Orwell's *Nineteen Eighty-Four*, Sartre's *Roads to Freedom*, Vasily Grossman's *Life and Fate* all speak to the same problem: that in a time where the great forces of progress and reaction are totalitarian, only the dedicated 'party soldier' is really free.

In the 1960s, however, individual freedom attempts to make a comeback. It begins in late 1950s America, with the Beat Generation, as personal wealth rises, education becomes liberal and disillusion sets in at the apartheid and militarism of the USA during the Cold War. It's not just the ker-rang of the electric guitar that fragments the old order but an outburst of reportage journalism, which tears apart the long-peddled illusions about policing, race and, above all, the Vietnam War.

The students who wrote the iconic Port Huron Statement, in 1962, summed up the nature of the break which young radicals of the day were attempting with the collectivist past:

> We regard men as infinitely precious and possessed of unfulfilled capacities for reason, freedom, and love. In affirming these principles we are aware of countering perhaps the dominant conceptions of man in the twentieth century: that he is a thing to be manipulated, and that he is inherently incapable of directing his own affairs.[3]

It's become fashionable now to interpret those liberation movements of the 1960s as the doomed precursors to neoliberalism. Thus the Port Huron Statement becomes the founding text of Thatcherism, and the Hell's Angels gang-bangs a rehearsal for the financial Big Bang of the 1980s. In free-market capitalism, says this interpretation of the Sixties, the children of '68 got what they wanted, and indeed deserved: individualism, the collapse of institutions, and profound disillusion.

I propose a different reading. The Port Huron generation failed to achieve the humanist revolution they desired because: a) the level of technology was not then adequate to make personal freedom possible for the majority; and b) the forces of collectivism, nationalism and corporate power were, at that point, stronger than the forces fighting against them. Nevertheless, the 1960s laid the basis for a new model of individual freedom, which, though never fully realized, was at least clearly conceived: it's been labelled 'networked individualism'.

## *The networked individual*

If you've ever seen somebody transfixed by their BlackBerry in the middle of a riot, you've seen a networked individual. If, in a multi-player computer game, you've ever led a squad of Russian *spetsnaz* to storm a nuclear power station, then you are a networked individual. If you cannot understand how somebody can simultaneously watch TV and tweet about it on their iPad, you are struggling with the concept— but hurry up: 60 per cent of all young people use a 'second screen' while watching TV.

Social theorists observed the beginnings of 'networked individual-ism' very early in the development of information technology. Sociologist Barry Wellman identified birth control, divorce laws, women's participation in the workforce, and the zoning of cities into suburbs and business parks as preconditions to the Internet way of life. Long before Facebook came along, Wellman noticed that people preferred to live with multiple networks, flat hierarchies and weak commitments:

> Rather than relating to one group, [people] cycle through interactions with a variety of others, at work or in the community. Their work and community networks are diffuse, sparsely knit, with vague, overlap-ping, social and spatial boundaries.[4]

But the theory of 'networked individualism', pioneered primarily within sociology in the 1990s, was at first focused on patterns of interac-tion within groups. Fifteen years into the communications revolution, it's possible to see equally profound impacts on individual behaviour and even consciousness.

The sociologist Manuel Castells observed, in an oft-cited 2003 study of Catalan Internet users, that web use had begun to produce new attitudes and behaviours *away* from the computer:

> The more an individual has a project of autonomy (personal, professional, socio-political, communicative), the more she uses the Internet. And in a time sequence, the more he/she uses the Internet, the more autonomous she becomes vis-à-vis societal rules and institutions.[5]

The emergence of a new kind of individual with 'weak ties', multiple loyalties and greater autonomy is, as sociologist Richard Sennett argued, the product of big changes in the workplace and in consumption, driven by technology. Obviously, this has implications for the future. But it also affects how we might interpret the past.

One of the great contributions of historical materialism was to allow us to understand pre-industrial conflicts—for example, the German Peasants' War of 1525, or the English Civil War of 1642—as essentially class struggles, despite their religious trappings. The past could be reinterpreted from the point of view of the present, which by the mid-nineteenth century was dominated by class relations.

Now suppose—at the risk of annoying Hegelians, orthodox Marxists and mainstream sociologists—we tried to reinterpret the 'class struggles' of the industrial age from the point of view of this emergent networked individualism. If you are into 'teleology'—that is, history as progress towards an ultimate, predetermined goal—you could even rewrite the whole story of the last 200 years as the emergence and suppression of the free, networked individual. Let's try.

What's important is not that there are a few isolated rebels determined to live a full, untrammelled human life. What's important is whether technology, and the social structures we use to manage it, can make individual freedom possible for the masses of people who do ordinary jobs at the heart of the industrial machine.

Up to the late nineteenth century, it clearly could not. If you worked in a factory you barely had time to sleep, let alone socialize or create art. Your only hope was in solidarity and structure. In fact, attacks on the self-organized world of the nineteenth-century labour movement were often condemned as promoting 'egoism'.

It was only during revolutions—1830, 1848 and above all 1871—that the poor got an accidental glimpse of human freedom. In the Paris Commune, working-class women rushed to the pulpits of churches converted into 'revolution clubs' to proclaim marriage illegal, confession immoral, freedom to love essential. A sixteen-year-old gay youth hiked 150 miles from Alsace to see it all. It blew his mind: he declared himself a new type of human being, and wrote some of the greatest poetry of the century. But the world was not ready for Arthur Rimbaud's idea of freedom. After a few chaotic 'seasons in hell', he moved to Ethiopia to become a coffee trader and wrote nothing more until death.[6]

Not till the Edwardian period—known in France as the belle époque, in America as the 'Progressive Era'—did experiments with individual freedom become widespread among the middle and lower classes. Women's liberation and even gay rights came onto the agenda of mainstream politics; and the general health, education and leisure time of the workers began to rise to the level where they could participate in mass consumption and sport.

This is the atmosphere that Zweig describes, that Picasso and Klimt luxuriated in, that Delius brings to life in the score of *Fennimore*: and it's no accident that this surge of individualism coincided with the high point of the first era of globalization. The pre-1914 era was, like our own, one in which the most innovative technologies were those that produced greater freedom of action and thought: the motor car, the cinema, the phonogram and the telephone.

Zweig summed up how it felt to be young before 1914, and what was lost when war, revolution and the swing towards totalitarianism ended it all: 'Before those wars,' he recalled, 'I saw individual freedom at its zenith and after them I saw liberty at its lowest point in hundreds of years.'[7]

Looked at this way, the real precedent for the past twenty years of ecstasy-fuelled, iPod-engrossed, latte-sipping individualism is not the 1960s but the years before 1914. The radicals of the Sixties were able to conceive the possibility of a new mode of human existence, but technology and the balance of global forces—class, race, inter-state rivalry— militated against achieving it. In the pre-1914 period, the freedom zeitgeist, technological progress and globalization were aligned. Now they are aligned again.

The past ten years have seen disruptions in the pattern of social life that mirror what happened in that era. But this time, it's happening at high velocity and across the canvas of all humanity.

What the new zeitgeist clashes with are the power relations of the old hierarchical world. And this is the materialist explanation for 2011: it is as much about individuals versus hierarchies as it is about rich against poor.

## The Masai with a mobile

The driver of behavioural change has been technology. There's been a revolution in the recording, storing and searchability of information; in the networked availability of information; in the digitization and globalization of commercial transactions; and finally, through social networking, in the ability to form connections away from the old hierarchical channels of the past. In each technology, the 'node'—or individual—has been empowered at the expense of the hierarchical central core, which is the state or corporation—or even the tribe.

When I travelled across Kenya in 2007, following the cellphone signal from Mombasa into the Rift Valley, it was clear that mobile telephony was causing a micro-level social upheaval. I met minibus drivers suddenly able to contact their bosses when pulled over by corrupt police in search of bribes; hairdressers who, by simply collecting the cellphone numbers of their clients, had freed themselves from the decades-old tyranny of the 'madam' who owns the parlour; slum dwellers mobilizing by text message to fight evictions; villagers able to receive cash remittances at the touch of a button through a cellphone money-transfer system.

Even in the red dust of Masai country, tribespeople living in mud and grass huts had been able to procure cheap Chinese cellphones, which they charged using solar power. One woman explained how life had changed:

> You can phone up your cowhand to see how your cattle are doing. If somebody is sick you can phone an ambulance. But the biggest change is that the husbands have learned how to use that button which tells you who has called. Now they get jealous: they go through the list and say: 'Who is that person, and who is that?'

The 'Masai with a mobile' has become one of the iconic marketing clichés of the early twenty-first century, but the change it describes is real: a revolution in property relations, sexual relations and even language itself. After I'd finished the report, I met a Masai lawyer and asked him whether I might make a documentary about the effect of mobile telecoms on the Masai language. 'Be quick,' he said; 'some dialects will be gone within three years.'

Technology—through the web browser, the cellphone, the GPS device, the iPod, the instant messaging service, the digital camera and above all the smartphone, which contains each of these things—has accelerated what the contraceptive pill and divorce laws started: it has expanded the power and space of the individual.

At the same time, it has allowed the creation of virtual 'societies' just as real as the cramped analog social networks we created for ourselves in the pre-digital era.

If this had happened at any time in history, it would have felt like a cultural revolution. But coming as it did amid the collapse of what sociologist Robert Putnam called 'social capital'—the atrophy of voluntary organizations, from village fetes to trade unions[8]—it has felt like a handbrake turn for humanity.

And it has happened fast. In fact, the real rush forward took place in the years of imminent crisis. Launching in 2004, Facebook achieved its 100 millionth user in 2008, and at the time of writing has 750 million users. In other words, Facebook has put on six-sevenths of its user base in the three years after Lehman Brothers went bust.[9] Twitter was launched in 2006; it took until 2008 for its users to send one billion tweets; by 2011 there were 250 million users, sending one billion tweets a week.[10]

The rush was particularly acute in the Arab world. In the three years before the crisis, Internet access in the region mushroomed, from 33 to 48 per cent of the population. Facebook opened an Arabic-language facility in mid-2009; within a year it had 3.5 million Arabic-language users, and at time of writing has 9 million. The English-language usage of Facebook in the Middle East North Africa (MENA) region is even more startling: there are 56 million Facebook members, totaling 16 per cent of the region's population. Nineteen million of them joined in 2010.[11]

How has it affected the lives of ordinary people? Listen to @sarrahsworld, the twenty-two-year-old Egyptian drama student whose video blog became a cult after the fall of Mubarak:

> I think my morale, my general mood is so connected and parallel to how Egypt is doing. I wake up to check Twitter. In fact this is how I get myself to wake up. Before 25 January I had 200 followers on Twitter; now, I have 13,000. It took off because of my video blog on YouTube. Most of the viewers are male, aged 18–23 and from Egypt, but you'd be surprised at the people that see this: some people just get it on their phone. A doorman ran up to me and said, I recognize you from YouTube. But he's illiterate and I'm going: how? He said, someone sent it to my cellphone via Bluetooth.

And listen to @littlemisswilde, aged twenty-one, who ran the occupation Twitter feed at University College London. She could write the story of her life through social media, she tells me: Bebo as a kid, MySpace as a teenager. Her sisters know nothing else but Facebook, and move around it frighteningly unconscious that it's new: 'For me it's second nature—I tweet in my dreams. I can't imagine where it's going next, but it's completely inseparable from my personality. In the future, when a child is born it will just be given a Twitter account.'

## A social laboratory of the self

The power of social networks to alter consciousness was noticed first among those who took part in, and studied, computer games in the 1980s. Gamers, together with hackers, were the first cohort of people who used information technology to form 'affinity groups'. And the most perceptive among them were able to capture early on the changes in behaviour and thought-patterns that we now see as mass phenomena. Psychoanalyst Sherry Turkle used the metaphor of 'windows' and the experience of Multi-User Dungeons (MUDs—the early text-based online games) to propose that the Internet had become a 'social laboratory of the self', allowing users to live parallel and multiple lives:

> The self is no longer simply playing different roles in different settings at different times ... [There is] a de-centred self that exists in many worlds and plays many roles at the same time ... The experience of this parallelism encourages treating on-screen and off-screen lives with a surprising degree of equality.[12]

Science writer Margaret Wertheim proposed that this parallel self could be just as 'real' as the physical self, arguing that in the creation of online communities, humanity has begun to create 'a collective mental arena':

> We are witnessing here the birth of a new domain, a space that simply did not exist before ... If the self 'continues' into cyberspace ... it becomes almost like a fluid, leaking out around us all the time and joining each of us into a vast ocean, or web, of relationships with other leaky selves.[13]

In the 1990s, these early sociologists of Internet consciousness documented nearly every behaviour pattern we now see in social networks: multiple personalities, masquerading, stalking, community formation, intense personal relationships, seeing the online world as real, or hyper-real, and the prevalence of utopian schemes. But theirs was a niche world inhabited by the techno-elite; it seems prehistoric now.

For social media has moved the 'collective mental arena', with its intense interpersonal bonds, from the realm of gaming and fantasy into the world of everyday interaction.

The woman tweeting at work or from the front line of a demonstration is experiencing the same shared consciousness, role-play, multifaceted personality and intense bonding that you get in *World of Warcraft*—only now it's from within real life. Though the old multi-user games still hold their attraction for millions of geeky people, the newest, most satisfying and most immersive user experience is reality.

As I write this, for example, at 23:00 BST on 20 August 2011, my own Twitter feed is exploding with accounts, from people on the ground, of the final offensive of the insurgents against Gaddafi in Tripoli:

'Never forget Mohamed Bouazizi'

'Do you guys realize #Libya is right on the verge of being the FIRST, REAL DEMOCRACY in the MiddleEast!!!'

'Its about time #Eygpt recognizes the NTC as a representative of the Libyan people ! #Libya ...'

'Late night celebrations in #zawiya at the news of uprisings in #tripoli. huge booms from poss. NATO strikes audible from the east ...'

'#AlJazeera and #PressTV report #Gaddafi en route to Italy by air. #NATO "lying" about Tripoli fall to gain extension to military attacks'

'Dear world: This is REAL for us, no war game, our families/neighbors r getting shot while we tweet their stories!'

'AJA reporter: Nato is bombing some areas in #Tripoli ...'

'BREAKING: Israeli gunboats shooting at Al Sudaniya area to the north of #Gaza'

'I have to take a short break, and a cup of coffee. God bless #Libya and
the Freedom Fighters.'

I would say that the above—pinging onto TweetDeck in the space of
ten minutes, and about twelve hours in advance of the mainstream
media reporting of any of it—beats any ten minutes of Counter-Strike
ever played.

The power of social networks, then, is not only that they alter consciousness. They bring this altered and networked consciousness into
real life in a way that the old hacker/gamer, stuck to their PCs, never
experienced. As London student @littlemisswilde describes it: 'I can be
hanging out in the same room as another activist, tweeting, and other
people will see us and say: you're being antisocial. But in fact we're
being ultra-social.'

### The impact on activism

The rise of online social networks has happened so fast that there is
almost no quantitative research into their impact on politics and political campaigns. However, two social theorists—Clay Shirky and Manuel
Castells—have helped to predict what the impact could be.

Shirky's seminal 2009 book, *Here Comes Everybody*, describes the
basic dynamic of activism in socially networked societies. It becomes,
Shirky says, 'ridiculously easy' to form groups with shared beliefs who
can coordinate action and choose targets much faster than hierarchical
states or corporations can react: 'Most of the barriers to group action
have collapsed, and without those barriers we are free to explore new
ways of gathering together and getting things done.'

USC professor Manuel Castells foresaw that the combined impact of
the social network and the individualistic self would facilitate a clear
break with the old forms of organization, including parties, unions and
permanent campaigns: 'The emergence of mass self-communication
offers an extraordinary medium for social movements and rebellious

individuals to build their autonomy and confront the institutions of society in their own terms and around their own projects.'[14]

Castells realized that the new technology has changed the relationship between the collective and the individual within protest movements. It allows activists to assemble fast and zap the enemy, without any greater commitment to each other than doing this.

But it also propels people into long-term occupations of physical spaces—from Bahrain's Pearl Roundabout to Tahrir, Syntagma and the Occupy Wall Street protests. And it focuses their struggle on the creation of new meanings and narratives, beyond the head-to-head confrontations with the old order on its own terrain.

However, changing the method of struggle is only one impact of network technology. Equally important are the new modes of economic activity it has thrown up—methods that were born amid the altruistic hacking and eco-communities that grew out of the 1960s, but which have now become deployed into the mainstream economy.

The key concept here, says Shirky, is 'collaborative production': people working together on a shared project, with no managers, and sometimes no direct intent to produce profit. It was pioneered in the Open Source software and hacking movements.

At one level, this is just the same as what keeps a Sunday league soccer team going—the voluntary contribution of skill and time to something bigger than the participants. But what open-source programmers did was to move this kind of collaboration into space formerly occupied by profit-seeking corporations. In 1994, when version 1.0 of Linux was released, the most successful company on earth was Microsoft. Microsoft's business model was based on providing—at an eye-watering markup—what the Linux community was to provide for free: an operating system to run your computer. Now, Linux runs every computer in the Google empire and half of all Internet servers. And although people make money out of it, they do not do so in the same way as Microsoft did.

Linux, and other open-source software projects such as the Perl programming language, were created using 'distributed collaboration' —hundreds of people correcting, improving and documenting other people's work, voluntarily, for the greater good of mankind (and, of course, to annoy Bill Gates). Linux's only condition was that nobody was allowed to commercialize the product.

Out of the Open Source movement came the 'wiki': a user-editable website which leaves an audit trail of changes, designed to facilitate collaborative work among groups without any prior role-designation or command hierarchy. As a tool it looks like nothing special. But its first two global uses were to prove revolutionary: Wikipedia and WikiLeaks. Wikipedia was not only a commercial challenge to the encyclopaedia business: it expanded the supply of in-depth and dependable knowledge, and reduced the price to zero.

And not just knowledge of stable and finished episodes. Shirky points out—and I have personal experience of this—that the Wikipedia page devoted to the London bombings of 7 July 2005 was at all times during the first twenty-four hours more reliable and comprehensive than reports from the mainstream media. I can attest to the fact that the mainstream media noticed this immediately: it was a talking point among my colleagues in press and broadcasting that the "new" version of news was the dispassionate assembly of the facts, easily eclipsing confused rewrites of online "articles" as the detailed events filtered out.

The second big wiki—WikiLeaks—has yet to finish exploding in the faces of dictators, spies, torturers, crooks and politicians. But leaving aside its political impact, what's important here is the creation process itself: what Shirky calls the 'unmanaged division of labour'.

This process did not appear out of the blue; it can trace a direct lineage to the liberation movements of the hippy Sixties. In her brilliant cyber-memoir, technology writer Becky Hogge describes how survivors of the LSD fraternity in California 'quit drugs for software', seeding a techno-revolution that would create the mouse, the pixel, the Apple Mac, the Internet, hacking and free software.[15] Their goals were made explicit in two famous statements by Stewart Brand, the visionary founder of the Whole Earth Catalog: 'Like it or not, computers are coming to the masses'; and 'Information wants to be free'. This would open up a forty-year battle, still ongoing, between those trying to monopolize, censor and commercialize information technology and those who want it to be open, uncensored and free.

And it's a battle over fundamentals. The rise of the profitless enterprise, of unmanaged collective labour, of free information and the massive scalability of collaborative work: each of these issues challenges a core belief in management theory. Likewise the rise of the networked individual, the multiple self, the 'leaky self' and the collective consciousness may challenge some basic assumptions of liberalism, which has assumed the self to be singular and self-contained.

However—and this is the crucial point—none of this should be challenging for those who dream of creating a more equal and just society.

But it seems that it is. First, because networked activism challenges the old methods—parties, trade unions, leaders, hierarchies. Second, because open-source technologies and collaborative production raise an even more fundamental question: what *type* of economy is to be the starting point for the transition to sustainable and equitable growth, and on what timetable?

## Marx, technology and freedom

Karl Marx dominated the radical agenda of the late nineteenth century for good reason: he was the most modern and most pro-capitalist of the revolutionaries of the age.

His polemics with rival nineteenth-century leftists don't get so much attention these days—but they have become relevant. Both on the issue of networked individualism, and the role of stored knowledge might play in human freedom, Marx had already asked the pertinent questions.

On individual freedom, Marx's argument amounts to this: any project to deliver a classless society, with wealth distributed according to need, must be based on the most advanced technologies and organizational forms created by capitalism itself. It can't be based on schemes originating in the heads of philanthropic bosses or philosophers. And you can't return to the past.

So in the 1840s, as the workers' movement became obsessed with model factory settlements set up by utopian visionaries like Robert Owen, Marx laid into the utopians. In the 1860s, when workers all over the world tried to set up cooperative shops and factories, Marx became a robust critic of cooperation. And he never ceased to pour scorn on the back-to-the-land socialists who wanted to return to rural communes and low growth.

Capitalism, Marx argued, was headed in the direction of big enterprises, which the capitalists would own collectively via the stock markets. Co-ops and utopian villages were a distraction. You had to find a way to take control of this big stuff—finance, industry and agribusiness—and create enough wealth so that, when you redistributed it, it would eliminate human need. Only then, said Marx, could you begin to address the alienation and unfreedom at the heart of human existence.

Capitalism itself, he believed, had created a social group whose material interests would force them to seize the means of production: the proletariat, owning nothing but their own capacity to work. However, there was nothing in the lifestyle of the workers themselves that could foreshadow the freedom they would create.

It is often forgotten that Marx's goal was not 'class solidarity' or 'proletarian power' but the liberation of individual human beings. In 1843 he wrote a passage that has become newly relevant in the context of social networks:

> Every emancipation is a *restoration* of the human world and of human relationships to man himself. Human emancipation will only be complete when the real individual man has absorbed into himself the abstract citizen; when as an individual man, in his everyday life, in his work, and in his relationships, he has become a species-being.[16]

Marx believed this truly social life—'species-being'—could not be attained without abolishing capitalism. Indeed, the whole thrust of the book this passage comes from (*On the Jewish Question*, 1843) was that the nineteenth-century goal of political and civil rights was really a form of self-enslavement: the individual with his 'human rights' alone against the world.[17]

Because Marx believed capitalism could only atomize, only alienate, he concluded that this ultimate 'human emancipation', in which people would express their freedom through communal interaction, could only happen after it was gone.

The actual history of organized labour was to be one long refutation of this theory. First, from the late nineteenth century, workers did develop highly sophisticated subcultures in which they attempted to develop civilized and communal lifestyles. Second, the most skilled gained possessions and a material stake in the survival of the system itself. On top of this Marx himself moved away from this initial, humanistic version of communism, settling on a theory that stressed the clash of technology against social relations, rather than humanity versus alienation, as the dynamo of the coming revolution. Finally, after the 1960s, the old manual workforce began to decline and frag-ment, leading theorists like André Gorz to propose its disappearance as any kind of revolutionary force.

What none of the critics dared suggest, however, was that it might be possible to achieve this 'species-being' under capitalism.

The technological and inter-personal revolutions of the early twenty-first century pose precisely this question. Namely, is it now possible to conceive of living this 'emancipated' life as a fully connected 'species-being' on the terrain of capitalism itself—indeed on the terrain of a highly marketized form of capitalism, albeit in conflict with it?

I don't know the answer, but merely to pose the question is exhilarating.

Strangely, it turns out, Marx himself posed the very same question. In a notebook known as the 'Fragment on Machines' (1858), he

143

explored the potential impact of automation. What if, Marx asked, you took 'labour' out of the process of making things and did it all through intelligent machines? The machines, he speculated, would become repositories of a 'general intellect', calling into question an economic system based on wages and profits, since neither could be properly allocated through market mechanisms.[18]

Those who want to turn Marx into an anti-humanist detest this fragment, just as they detest his pre-1845 writings about alienation. The reason is clear: it opens up a whole new dynamic of social change based on the clash between free information and economic systems. It creates the possibility that the real 'contradiction' in society is not so much about economics but about shared human knowledge versus 'intellectual property rights'. It opens the possibility that the new society can be created within the old, in a struggle over information and power.

For orthodox Marxism, of course, these debates were marginal— and who knows what substance the man himself was on the night he scribbled these thoughts down. But the political theory that influenced the events of 2009–11—'autonomism'—had theorized very clearly the idea of a struggle between the 'general intellect', the suppressed human being and capitalist legal norms.[19] Its figurehead, Franco Berardi, put it like this, in a manifesto issued at the height of the Occupy Wall Street movement:

> There is only one way to awake the lover that is hidden in our paralyzed, frightened and frail virtualized bodies. There is only one way to awake the human being that is hidden in the miserable daily life of the softwarist: take to the streets and fight.[20]

And that is the significance of 2011. It was the year people realized that instant collaboration could extend out of Facebook groups and wikis and into the public squares of major cities; that amateur news could be more reliable than the professionally produced propaganda of TV networks. And they rediscovered what the Berkeley rebels of 1964 had found out before them, that the act of taking a space and forming a community within it might be just as important as the objective of the struggle itself.

And if all this challenges orthodox Marxism, it also challenges social democracy, which in the late nineteenth century embraced a watered-down version of Marxism. In social democracy, of course, the working class is not the 'subject' of history, but it nevertheless remains the 'object' of politics: to be delivered to in return for votes. For social democracy it's the capitalist state that does the delivering; but it shares with Marxism the essential premise that conditions predominate over consciousness. Since capitalism can only produce the alienated, helpless human being, social conditions have to be changed from above, by benign state intervention.

For both social democracy and Marxism, the challenge amounts to this. If you are an anti-utopian and want to build a socially just society starting from the most modern and advanced forms of capitalism, what exactly is that most advanced form? What if it turns out not to be Microsoft, or Toyota, or another highly profitable corporation, but instead this emerging, semi-communal form of capitalism exemplified by open-source software and based on collaboration, management-free enterprise, profit-free projects and open-access information?

What if—instead of waiting for the collapse of capitalism—the emancipated human being were beginning to emerge spontaneously from within this breakdown of the old order? What if all the dreams of human solidarity and participatory democracy contained in the maligned Port Huron Statement of 1962 were realizable right now? Yeah: what then?

## The general intellect has expanded

Economists and business gurus have for two decades been grappling with the concept of 'information capitalism': what it means if the most valuable commodities in the market are ideas, rather than physical objects.

145

One fact is clear: *people know more than they used to*. That's to say, they have greater and more instant access to knowledge, and reliable ways of counteracting disinformation.

Though academia has become obsessed with firewalling and commercializing the products of research, the info-revolution has massively expanded the primary sources of knowledge. Since 1665, when the first two scientific journals were started, researchers estimate that about 50 million scholarly papers have been published. Of these, 10 million were published in the last ten years, and 20 million in the last twenty-five years.[21] But even here, the open-access revolution is corroding commerce: a 2006 study found that useable copies of 11 per cent of all papers published that year could be found for free, through self-archiving on academics' personal websites.[22]

It's now possible to conceive of a situation where the great bulk of academic research will be free, open to all, and transparently cross-referenced. This will destroy the business models of media empires like Reed Elsevier but, arguably, they have already been destroyed.

Meanwhile the nature of learning has been transformed. There are huge numbers of facts available to me now about the subjects I studied at university which were not known when I was there in the 1980s. Back then, whole academic terms would be spent disputing basic facts, or trying to research them. Today the plane of reasoning can be more complex, because people have an instant reference source for the undisputed premises of arguments. I am not referring here to Wikipedia, which can be unreliable, but to sources like instantly searchable documents, scanned books, census data and digitized historic photographs and manuscripts. It's as if physics had been replaced by quantum physics, but in every discipline. Or, as Clay Shirky has argued, it's as if the impact of the calculator on school mathematics were now being replicated in every field.

And as the nature of learning changes, the nature of the individuals produced by it evolves. We are prepared to consult secondary sources less, primary sources more, and each other always. We are prepared to follow our search results across academic boundaries; we are prepared to 'load' complex information into our minds—just as a computer loads software—and then 'unload' it, once the task is complete, making room for a new upload of expertise to do something else. High-level knowledge work becomes less about 'information conquest' than 'information management', and the latter is the valued corporate skill.

It is as if, in response to the creation of digital networks, we are changing our behaviour to become not just networked individuals but 'network animals'.

This should come as no surprise: observers of the early factory system described how, within a generation, it had wrought a total change in the behaviour, thinking, body shape and life expectancy of those imprisoned within it. People grew smaller, their limbs became bent; physical movements became more regimented. Family units broke down.

Why should a revolution in knowledge and technology not be producing an equally dramatic—albeit diametrically opposite—change in human behaviour?

### The challenge to info-hierarchies

The impact of social networks on knowledge, community and individuals constitutes a challenge to three kinds of hierarchies that stood at the heart of twentieth-century reality: repressive states, corporations and hermetically sealed ideologies.

Repressive states rely not just on the manipulation of news, but on the suppression of truth and the control of narratives. Today, in the face of totalitarianism, more or less everything you need to know to make sense of the world—and explode a false narrative—is available as freely downloadable content on the Internet; and this content has not been pre-digested by teachers, parents, priests, imams or commissars.

For example, if there was a narrative that really finished off Mubarak's regime, it was not the April 6th movement but the 'We are all

Khalid Said' Facebook page: again and again you find that those who became detonators of the 25 January uprising acted through the links made over Said's murder. Though Mubarak shut down Twitter on 27 January 2011, to stop the revolution he would have had to close down the Khalid Said page, hunt down its members and round up the protest networks that sent people like @sarrahsworld, @Hennawy89 and @3arabawy into the slums of Cairo on 25 January.

But you cannot run a modern economy that way. The only defence against information-driven revolt is to de-network your society and institute Nazi or East German Communist levels of surveillance and control.

Likewise, info-capitalism makes it increasingly difficult for corporations to control their own narratives. Rupert Murdoch's News Corporation empire was plunged into crisis not just because *Guardian* journalist Nick Davies discovered it had hacked the phone of a teenage murder victim. It was also because, by day three of the furore, one in every four tweets mentioning the *News of the World* hashtag (#notw) also mentioned the brand name of a company advertising in the paper. The marketing agency We Are Social, which produced these metrics, reported:

> Every brand involved was dealing with its own social-media crisis last week. The sheer volume of this protest will have been a shock for many brands and drowned out any normal marketing activity. This cannot have failed to influence their decisions about whether to pull advertising from the *News of the World*. It was a mass outpouring of public opinion which hit at the right time and had its desired effect.[23]

Manuel Castells had put his finger on the source of Rupert Murdoch's power: News Corp acted as a 'switch' within the political elite systems of the world. It created valuable niche groups of right-wing voters around particular media outlets, and then traded influence over those voters for political influence pursuant to the growth of News Corp.

Backing up this unspoken deal was always the hidden sanction of scandal or opprobrium, ready to be unleashed on anyone who did not cooperate.[24]

But News Corp's position as a 'switch' within the system was over-whelmed by these decentralized attacks. Faced with a massive pull-out of brand advertising, and in an attempt to stop the crisis spreading through the whole corporation, Murdoch pulled the plug on the *News of the World*, a massively profitable Sunday newspaper. In other words, social media killed it, once more demonstrating the truism that the network defeats the hierarchy.

As for hermetically sealed ideologies—Christian fundamentalism, fascism, clunking Leninist orthodoxy—the info-revolution simply reinforces the choice globalization had already forced on them: isolate yourself from reality inside a closed community, or unseal the ideology, exposing it to critical dialogue and difference.

For the traditional left, the info-revolution presents an additional problem: it loses its monopoly on critical narratives about capitalism. From the 1960s, the left and progressive liberalism were jointly engaged in a struggle against the censorship of news and the suppression of information about the past. It was from radical journalists that we learned the truth about Vietnam, or the miscarriages of justice in Northern Ireland, or the hidden secrets of the Cold War 'Gladio' network that ran Italian politics. And it was the left that dug through history to discover the hidden and forgotten struggles of workers, women, racial minorities, lesbians and gays.

For activists, the moment of political commitment often coincided with a moment of revelation. Anybody, in theory, could have rediscovered the story of Toussaint L'Ouverture, the slave who led the Haitian revolution in 1789; but in practice, only the Trinidadian Marxist historian C. L. R. James took the trouble to do so. James's book *The Black Jacobins*, produced in 1938, shaped the outlook of black activists in the 1960s and 1980s because—even forty years after publication—it was the definitive account, influencing two generations of anti-racists.

Today the left is no longer the gatekeeper to subversive knowledge (although it can aspire to remain a 'preferred provider'). Those seeking a narrative critical of the world order, and evidence of corporate or state wrongdoing, are free to cut out the middleman.

It is worth here exploring the role played by 'memes'. Richard Dawkins invented the concept in 1976, speculating the existence of core ideas within human societies that had survived, and mutated, like genes:

> Examples of memes are tunes, ideas, catch-phrases, clothes fashions, ways of making pots or of building arches. Just as genes propagate themselves in the gene pool by leaping from body to body via sperms or eggs, so memes propagate themselves in the meme pool by leaping from brain to brain via a process which, in the broad sense, can be called imitation. If a scientist hears, or reads about, a good idea, he passes it on to his colleagues and students. He mentions it in his articles and his lectures. If the idea catches on, it can be said to propagate itself, spreading from brain to brain.[25]

Before the Internet, the 'meme' idea would have been useful as a speculative tool for understanding the prevalence of certain themes and patterns in human culture. Dawkins himself was quite negative about memes, tending to see them as autonomous entities, as selfish as genes, replicating themselves in their own interest. Meanwhile the study of memes got sidetracked into an academic debate between anthropologists and neuroscientists who purported to describe their laws of motion.

With the Internet, however, and above all with the advent of social media, it's become possible to observe the development of memes at an accelerated pace (much as fruit flies, with their short life cycles, help geneticists study mutation).

What happens is that ideas arise, are immediately 'market tested', and then are seen to either take off, bubble under, insinuate themselves into the mainstream, or, if they are deemed no good, disappear. While this process is observable in mass culture generally, activists in the horizontalist and hacker movements believe memes are tools for creating direct democracy. Ideas replicate, or do not replicate, through social media according to whether they hit the right buttons within the collective consciousness.

Examples are legion: the 'Uninstalling dictator: 99% complete' tweets that spun across the world as Ben Ali and Mubarak fell; the decision by thousands of activists worldwide to change their Twitter location to 'Tehran' in June 2009, in a bid to mask the location of the real Iranian activists. Above all, the occupation of physical space with tents: begun in Tahrir, spreading to Madrid and then Athens, and bursting out again in the autumn of 2011 in the Occupy Wall Street movement, which on 15 October inspired space-occupations in 962 cities, in 85 countries.

For activists, memes create a kind of rough alternative to representative democracy. Methods of protests, slogans, beliefs—like the repeated insistence that 'Black Bloc is a tactic, not a lifestyle' among British students after the debacle of 26 March 2011—spread in a seemingly autonomous way.

I am not certain whether memes are anything more than small cultural portions of the zeitgeist. That they move and replicate faster than they used to seems pretty obvious. Yet it is important to understand that, for the activists themselves, memes are seen as facilitating decentralized action. One of those critiquing my original 'Twenty Reasons Why It's Kicking Off Everywhere' blog post, an activist aligned with the hacker group LulzSec, wrote:

We don't see this decentralisation of power and authority in determining the direction of actions to be a negative impact of technology. Memetics offer an opportunity for the instigation of autonomous actions, delivering death by a thousand cuts to our enemy.[26]

Ultimately, whether real or illusory, memes are felt to be real by the participants. If the idea reflects anything fundamental it is that networked individuals are free to choose, rank and reject ideas or forms of expression. At the height of the collectivist century such options were not available: modes of resistance were dictated, and usually hierarchical. Type into YouTube the words 'Ernst Busch' (German Communism's star singer of agitprop anthems) to see just how hierarchical.

## The meaning of 2011

If the economic situation turns strategically bad, and if—as in the 1930s—globalization gets replaced by competing economic blocs, much of what I've described here could be reversed. It might seem inconceivable but so, to the Zweig and Delius generation, did bookburning ceremonies or the outlawing of scientific theories as politically unacceptable (as the USSR did with Einstein's theory).

Another caveat, of course, is that to the deprived half of humanity the 'Internet way of life' is out of reach. People struggling to live on $2 a day cannot get worked up about memes. However, what I've observed is that wherever the technology penetrates, so do the social and psychological changes.

A third caveat is, of course, that 'teleology is bunk': there is no predestined outcome to human development, whether we see it as the development of 'world spirit', class struggle or individual freedom.

Despite all this, I cannot help believing that in the revolutions of 2011 we've begun to see the human archetypes that will shape the twenty-first century. They effortlessly multitask, they are ironic, androgynous sometimes, seemingly engrossed in their bubble of music—but they are sometimes prepared to sacrifice their lives and freedom for the future. By the middle of the second decade of this century it will be clear whether that is enough: whether hope, solidarity and ironic slogans can prevail against austerity, nationalism and religious fundamentalism. Right now the future hangs in the balance.

# 8

## In the Tracks of Tom Joad:
## A Journey through Jobless America

'To the red country and part of the gray country of Oklahoma, the last rains came gently, and they did not cut the scarred earth.' So begins John Steinbeck's *The Grapes of Wrath*, in which a poor Oklahoma family journeys to California in search of work.[1] The events it describes happened eighty years ago, when America was in the grip of recession and Oklahoma in the grip of drought.

In July 2011, as Congress took America to the brink of a debt default, I decided to drive from Oklahoma to Los Angeles following the route described in Steinbeck's book, in order to take a snapshot of Recession America. It was a snapshot alright—but it turned out to be of something else.

### *Farmers don't quit*

*Kiowa County, Oklahoma*. It's a wide, flat country with only the Wichita Mountains to give the skyline any kind of edge. The sky is cloudless, the grass is white and crunches under your feet as if covered in deep frost. If you look closely at the redbud, the state tree of Oklahoma, the leaves are brown and curled, as if they too are about to drop with frostbite. But it's 110 degrees Fahrenheit. Oklahoma, like much of the American south, is in the middle of its deepest drought for sixty years.

153

In the field where what's left of his herd of cows huddles beneath the skeleton of a mesquite tree, Brett Porter slashes the netting on a bale of hay; it too is on the white side of green, but moist enough for the cows, who jostle into a feeding line. They are sleek, muscular, prime Angus beef. Brett has spent twelve years working on the DNA.

But this DNA is doomed. The Porter ranch is down to just eighteen bales of hay, which will last a week. He has already sold twenty out of 100 cows for hamburger meat. Once the hay runs out, it will cost $200 a bale, or $3,600 a week, to feed the herd. And he doesn't have that kind of money.

> I can't control it. You can't control a drought. There's a lot of nights I don't sleep—I stay awake thinking how I'm going to make this out, and that out.

That July, across western Oklahoma, they are starting to scuff the grass under their feet, look at the sky, look at the temperature gauge—which hovers way above 100°F even at dusk—and talk in their cracked, gravelly voices about the Dust Bowl years of the 1930s.

'It's the worst it's been in sixty years, and we're actually drier today than in the 1930s,' says Terry Detrick, who runs the American Farmers and Ranchers union here:

> Right now, though the farms are bigger than the 1930s, 90 per cent are still family owned. Our winter wheat failed; we tried to put in a summer crop and now the summer crop's not going to make it. Double the input costs and zero income. They have crop insurance—but they can only afford to insure 65 per cent of the value. We owe retailers, can't pay our bills; so they're going to go as well.

We remember the Dust Bowl primarily through two stark sets of imagery: Dorothea Lange's photographs of displaced Oklahoma farmers, staring vacantly as their hopes and children die; and

Steinbeck's novel, made into a haunting movie by John Ford in 1940. *The Grapes of Wrath* begins with the Joad family losing their land to drought and debt; it follows their journey southwest to California, where, like 350,000 others, they end up as exploited farm labourers living in squatter camps.

Today's situation looks different. The Porter ranch is not small—Brett farms 3,500 acres. And the problems of land misuse that caused the Dust Bowl have been solved by sixty years of applied agronomy: Brett's generation no longer tills the land, but uses crop rotation—cattle, wheat, alfalfa, barley and cotton—to keep the soil nourished. For there is no river water here, only rainfall. And now the rain has stopped.

As for debt, though Brett borrows half a million dollars a year to run the farm, the Federal government underwrites his loans, so instead of 5 per cent interest he's paying 2 per cent. On top of that there are direct state loans. In good years he breaks even; in bad years he relies on disaster payments and crop insurance—again from Federal money.

But as the relentless summer of 2011 hammers the earth solid, the strain is beginning to show. Brett and his fellow-farmers are worried that Steinbeck's 'red country' might again be the stage for another one-sided fight between nature and a broken economic model.

For the Joads' penury was partly the product of the economic model small farmers had fought for during the Civil War: the right to claim and farm 'homesteads' no bigger than 160 acres. They had wrested these rights from the cattle drivers and the southern cotton barons. But, sinking deeper into debt as the rains dried up, they could not defeat the banks. It's a cycle as old as capitalism: finance capital screws the farmer.

Now, right here on these vast lands, the cycle is being played out again. Detrick, in a low voice, tells me:

We don't quit. What the banker managers say to me is, the first people to come to them asking to be foreclosed are the wives. She says: 'There's no way we're gonna make it and he won't quit, you gotta wind us up'—the women! Always the women, because the men don't quit.

By 9 a.m. each day at the stockyard in El Reno, just outside Oklahoma City, there is a queue of trucks and trailers as the farmers come in to sell their cattle. Always, in the driving seats, the same demographic: a grey-haired farmer and his grey-haired wife. Brett Porter, in Oakleys and baseball cap, is untypically young; the average age of an Oklahoma farmer is fifty-eight. Instead of a 1930s-style geographic exodus, there's been a quiet, generational one, even during the boom years—and the boom years are over.

You can read the worry on the faces of the men on horseback too, beneath their crisp, white Stetsons. Most of them are farmers working the sale to make an extra buck. Grim-faced behind their sunglasses, they consult clipboards, spit tobacco. There are only three big buyers, each of them specializing in the hamburger trade: the occasional magnificent bull goes for a decent price, but most of the animals sell for around $52 per 100 pounds, down on last week and just two-thirds of the price they were getting six months before.

On top of climate change and the credit crunch, the farmers now face yet another problem. In Washington the newly installed Republican majority in the House of Representatives is blocking the Federal budget. Though everybody is sure that it's political manoeuvring and that a deal will finally be done, the Republicans' price for their approval of the budget is a $4 trillion cut in Federal spending. In the firing line are the Federal direct state farm loans—worth a billion dollars in Oklahoma alone—and the disaster payments. Detrick says:

I think we're going to see some drastic cuts. Some programmes will survive, but they won't be sufficient. The young will look at farming and say: I can't do this. The elderlings can liquidate and sell out—but without the incentives, nobody young's going to do this.

## Route 66

At Hertz they fix me up with a Mercury Grand Marquis, an old beige Zimmer frame of a car with white leather seats. Plus a GPS, which I will barely need because the road to California is simply the Interstate 40 for 1,800 miles. But Route 66 runs beside it, the route the real-life migrants took in the Thirties. I dip on and off Route 66 along the way: a single-lane highway whose edges now are crumbly, invaded by sunflowers and alfalfa.

The geography changes dramatically as I tank westwards, but the human geography along Interstate 40 is forlornly uniform: low-rent motels, high-carb food outlets, the occasional roadside porn cinema and a vast sky. For company there is always the radio, which favours homilies from Christian country-music singers before switching to Spanish oom-pah music somewhere around the Texas–New Mexico border.

Then there are the shock jocks: Glenn Beck, Rush Limbaugh and their local imitators. Actually, Beck is inimitable:

> There was this guy, remind me, an advisor to Putin who said in the nineties America would break up into five separate countries. You think that's not happening? Well, take a look at who's buying land in California! The Chinese! I'm sure the Mexicans would want to take New Mexico and Arizona. [*Doomy voice*] It's happening.

All the way along, the jocks and news bulletins will riff endlessly on the same theme: the unsustainability of Federal spending, its evil, un-Christian nature, and the sinful character of 'pork-barrel' politics—which signifies that some special interest is being disproportionately served in Washington.

At the motels they advertise 'hot breakfast'. Day after day I am con-fronted with 'biscuits and gravy'—a combo of buttermilk scone and white reconstituted sludge, with a microwaved hamburger and a slab of yellow gloop they call scrambled egg; washed down with coffee so weak, you can read the minuscule type of the *Wall Street Journal* markets columns through it.

On the TV, as you struggle to get breakfast down, it's always Fox News: no longer starring Beck, who's been relegated to the radio after one outrageous claim too many, but folks indistinguishable from him. Presenters obsessed with the debt and deficit, determined to cut the healthcare of the poor, the pensions of the elderly, the farm payments of the Oklahoma ranchers, and the minimum wage.

If you're up early in a motel, you meet the people who earn the minimum wage. They are nearly always women. And these jobs are not full-shift jobs. They are low-skill, part-time jobs for people who, in the era of globalization, cannot find anything better than microwaving burgers and cleaning greying bedsheets for $7.50 an hour.

One motel blends into another. There's a whiteboard in the reception: *Welcome Brad and Stacey*, *'thanks for choseing us'* and a bunch of other misspelt words announce a party for the newly graduated Brad. Which college? 'Ha, no sir, infantry basic training.'

In the morning, an elderly woman shuffles out of the kitchen with a tray of reheated burgers and slides them—painfully slowly because she is fatter than she is tall—onto a plastic tray, then tidies the plastic knives in a plastic cup, and is she in my way? Yes she is, but, 'No, ma'am, you go right ahead,' for America has become the land of polite, meaningless conversation.

The bed is soft; the sheets are old; the towels have been laundered a hundred times too many and are stiff. The soap does not lather. There is nothing whatsoever organic in the room as you arrive: no bottle of water, no flower—not even a plastic one. Yet someone has individually hand-wrapped each of the four plastic cups available, in cling film, so that you cannot sue them if you catch a mouth infection.

Outside the traffic swirls and hums. There are, from the looks of the car park, maybe twenty guests staying. Some drive shiny station wagons or ride the classic menopausal boy's toy of the American Midwest, a Harley-Davidson. But there are also battered repossessed cars—and the people who own them, playing with their kids in the motel's swimming pool, look local, downtrodden and poor. Could they really have come to the motel pool, completely unsheltered from the glaring sun, to spend a Sunday afternoon?

I cross the Canadian River on Route 66: the riverbed is pure dry white sand. I cross the Texas panhandle and then the little Steinbeck-era towns flash past, just as the writer lists them: Shamrock, McLean, Wildorado, Amarillo, 'and there's an end of Texas'. In New Mexico, the farmland ends and the mesas begin: arid scrubland with canyons and island plateaus.

As I turn off the Interstate and into Albuquerque, I'm about to experience something that will never again leave me feeling unlucky to be sleeping in a motel.

## Joy Junction

> The families learned what rights must be observed—the right of privacy in the tent; the right to keep the past black hidden in the heart; the right to talk and to listen ...

That's how Steinbeck describes the camp for homeless migrants that awaited the Joads in California. Joy Junction is its modern equivalent: 300 people bed down each night in the barrack blocks and gymnasiums of this abandoned school by the railroad tracks in Albuquerque.

Jeremy Reynalds set the place up twenty years ago. With his white smoking jacket, dyed ginger hair, crucifix earrings and sparkly nail-job including tiny pictures of the face of Jesus Christ, he has a distinctly non-Steinbeckian air. 'There are two Albuquerques,' he tells me: 'the one that queues for lattes in the morning, and the one that queues for mattresses at night.'

Joy Junction is, he admits frankly, mainly used by people who've had alcohol, drug or domestic violence issues, including some of the staff. The routine is to do a religious version of the twelve-step programme, some literacy and some praying. But now, Reynalds says, there's a new kind of clientele, the American middle class: folks whose problem is not drink or drugs, but debt.

Sandra and Tim live in one of the barracks at Joy Junction, which means they get a single room and a shared bathroom. She worked in Subway, but they cut her shifts; he managed a branch of McDonald's, but it closed. They lost their house and downsized to a small apartment, and then the unemployment benefit ran out and they lost the apartment. 'We slept in our car for four weeks. It was scary,' says Sandra. 'We'd buy fast food. Take a wash in a gas station.'

On the floor of the reception centre, a gym strewn with about eighty mattresses, I meet Larry Antista and his daughter Michelle, aged fourteen: 'We're here because of the economic times: my spouse split on us and that halved our income so we lost our place.'

With a grey ponytail, grey moustache and dreamy eyes, Larry, maybe in his fifties, looks like a character out of Pynchon rather than Steinbeck. He's been a driver and worked in adult care, but has lately been trying to write a screenplay. They stayed on the floors and sofas of friends—'sofa surfing', Reynalds calls it—until their friends got sick of it. Now they sleep, dad and daughter, side by side with eighty people they do not know.

'It's not bad,' says Michelle. 'It's safe; I stay at school till six o'clock to get my homework done.' Do they know she's homeless? 'I didn't tell them.' Why not? 'They didn't ask.' This means she does not show up on New Mexico's register of homeless children, which already numbers 5,500.

She's trying to keep her Latin dance class going; Larry is still working on his screenplay 'about a biker who gets accused of doing something he didn't do'. His eyes drift towards some inner memory, and Michelle smiles. Larry says:

The job market was supposed to make progress a little in May, but it levelled off and now it's dropped back. The government needs to stimulate this somehow: they're not very imaginative—they need to look at how Franklin Delano Roosevelt did it. It's a lack of vision. We managed to keep our apartment for an extra twelve months because of the stimulus money, so I don't know what they are talking about when they say cut the Federal budget!

It's from Larry that I hear the beginnings of what Steinbeck heard sixty years ago: the simmering wrath of Americans who regard themselves as 'middle-class' but have been thrown into penury. They express thoughts you never hear on the holy-rolling radio stations. Larry says:

How much does it cost for one fighter plane or one bomb? And we're not doing anything to stop terrorism—just blowing people up and pissing off the rest of the world. They're getting stronger and we're getting tired of it: and there's some money that could be cut loose instead of wasting it on that. One multi-million aircraft could sure feed and house a lot of people.

A few mattresses away are Maurice Henderson, Roseangel Ortiz and their three children, including Maurice Jr, four months old. Maurice Sr, who's African American and built like a football player, begins the answer to every question with a three-second silence, during which he takes a deep breath, stares intently and eventually manages to stem his inner rage:

I was an auto fleet maintenance mechanic; I've been unemployed about eight months. I was living in a motel. Nice motel with a full kitchen. And my unemployment ran out: I couldn't certify Sunday, so Monday I had to be out by 12 a.m. We called everybody, but ...

He does an awkward grimace to indicate the end of the story. He's just managed to sign on again for benefits, and expects $200 in the next few days. But this will barely cover nappies and juice for the kids, certainly not re-entry into the 'nice motel' sector. How come somebody like him ended up here?

'I could go get a job, but the kind of jobs I could get right away are not going to pay me as much as I get on welfare: eight dollars an hour.'

Where would you start to put things right? He stares over my shoulder, searching for a way to put this nicely. 'Needs to start with President Obama.' What does he need to do? 'Help! Start helping, and he *is* helping—but people gotta help too—stop playing games.' He is bitter about the war spending:

'They say they're spending too much Federal money, but on what? Too much money on that war they got over there. Sure, they created jobs, but …'—and Maurice heaves another deep sigh—'if you're not the first layer to get there, you're not getting the job.'

Hostility to war spending and bitter disillusion with President Obama run through this dormitory like a grassfire, and there is more. A man crawls over to me across two mattresses crowded with his own large contingent of children:

> I'm a Native American, we're Navajo. What I want you to report is: where is all the money going from the casinos? Our nation has a casino but they keep all the money. It's the same everywhere. Why don't they use the money to help their own people?

In the morning Reynalds takes me to a street corner, right by the Interstate, where the poorest motels are clustered. Outside one stands a drunken woman in tears: her sister is about to be evicted, together with her sister's boyfriend, who's in a wheelchair. 'He's disabled, but they don' even have a shower.' Reynalds and his co-worker go into the Evangelical spiel that will soon bring three more people to sit around the table and hear Bible stories, repent and put their heads down on a clean mattress.

He tells me: 'The motels fill up at the beginning of every month, when the social security checks get paid; and then about two weeks later they migrate over to Joy Junction, as the money runs out.'

He's not against these cheap motels, because, while they will sometimes ask the unemployed to work in return for their keep, they extend unofficial credit, and if they didn't exist there'd be thousands more on the streets. There are at least fifteen motels like this in Albuquerque, he says, and, of course, 'It's like this at the edge of every American city.'

This is what the automobile stupor and the bluegrass music and the Glenn Beck monologues numb you to as you speed along America's highways. Those vintage motel signs, which summon up the era of Elvis and full employment, are in reality flagstaffs for the hidden homeless. They are right next to you, on every highway in America.

And, just like in the 1930s, there is a president in the White House elected on a platform of hope, radicalism and concern for the working poor. And like in the 1930s, Congress is determined to stop him—insofar as he has not stopped himself.

As I leave Albuquerque the landscape becomes drier. The spectacular red canyon walls of the Mogollon Rim dwarf the mobile homes of the Pueblo nation, whose land this once was. There are no Native American shacks in Steinbeck, and no red canyons; no giant cacti, no endless days of blue sky, no vast gulches and ravines. That's because Steinbeck himself never made the whole journey. *The Grapes of Wrath* gives little sense of the vastness, the emptiness, the distances of the south-west. To real-life Okies, this land must have seemed like a different planet.

But Steinbeck's book isn't really about the journey. It is about the conflict and injustice that the Joads find at their journey's end: the strikes, vigilante squads, roadblocks and anti-migrant prejudices that greeted them in California. Today, you don't have to get to the end of the journey to find all that.

*They call you Alien*

They were hungry, they were fierce, and they had hoped to find a home. And they found only hatred.

Steinbeck, *The Grapes of Wrath*

*Phoenix, Arizona.* It's a world of pink and green: the tent awnings are olive drab army-issue, 'from the Korean War', says the prison guard proudly. Pink is the colour of the inmates' socks, towels, pillowcases and underpants: it's been chosen to humiliate them. Their overalls are, of course, striped black and white. Their skin, in the ICE wing, is usually a shade of brown.

This is Arizona's notorious Tent City jail. The ICE wing is where those arrested for migration crimes are segregated: about 100 men out of 500 in the jail. They live in the tents twenty-four hours a day, the side-awnings open to the elements. As they crunch across the gravel in the harsh sunlight to fetch water, they sling their towels around their necks: the guard yells at them if they try to cover their heads. On the day I was there the temperature reached 114 degrees Fahrenheit, but it's been known to hit 122.

In heat like this you mostly sleep; numerous young men are stretched out on the close-packed bunk beds. Others read: there is a high level of literacy in Tent City, and a low level of menace and craziness compared to other jails. That is because most of these men are not hardened criminals: their crime is being Mexican.

In May 2010, the state of Arizona passed a law called SB1070. This required migrants to present proof of their legal status on demand: if stopped for speeding, if questioned at work, if questioned as a witness to a grocery-store heist, if noticed existing by a bored cop. It's a crime if you cannot prove you are American.

That's a problem: officially there are 11 million undocumented migrants in America. Unofficially, it could be as high as 20 million. In any case, around a million live in Phoenix, Arizona. You can see them

164

hanging out for work on the corners of the car parks at big hardware stores; their hands wash the linen at hotels and make the burritos and the tacos in fast-food joints.

Migrant children already had poverty, dislocation and the language issue to contend with (Arizona declared itself an English-language-only state in 1986). Now they have something else: the skin-crawling fear that if your mother goes to the corner store she will not come back. Leticia Ramírez, mother of three and an activist in the migrant group Puente, tells me:

> We are living in a state of fear. We can't even go to the store—can't even go out to the park, the zoo, the mall—because the kids fear the police might stop their parents. So we just stay home. They say: 'If you go out, you may not come back.' One family bought three months of groceries so they don't have to leave the home.

To enforce SB1070 and the other laws that criminalize Hispanic migrants, Phoenix has Sheriff Joe Arpaio. And Sheriff Joe has Tent City, and boy, is Joe keen for the media to see Tent City.

My guide, John, a prison guard, is dressed in Iraq-style combat gear and carries a Taser on his belt. As we pass the row of blue telephones, positioned in full sunshine on an outside wall, John tells me proudly:

'The phone calls are at a premium price; we make 'em pay over, to help fund the cost of their own detention.'

In fact, much of Sheriff Joe's operation here is designed to keep costs down. The tents themselves are sixty years old; there are only two meals a day, 'to minimize catering costs'; the guards drink out-of-date Gatorade. There are no heating expenses in winter (on the coldest desert nights the inmates steal plastic refuse sacks to stuff between the sheets); and the a/c in the prisoners' mess room comes cheap—as one prisoner says, sotto voce: 'They only turned the a/c on for you.'

The average sentence they're serving is twenty-six days, the maximum a year. After that they'll be processed by ICE, the Federal deportation service.

Fernando López's mistake was to drive without a licence: he couldn't get one because he has no documents to prove he is a legal migrant, and that's because—though he does not say the words to me himself—he did not come here legally. In June 2011 he got stopped for speeding.

> They took me to Fourth Avenue Jail, Arpaio's jail. They questioned me for four days. I won't lie to you—in the first twelve hours they must have had me in eight to ten different cells. It's a psychological game, the way they talk to you, even look at you. You don't see the sun; you don't know what time it is. And they're always telling you: sign this and you'll be deported immediately. But it's not true. I refused to answer questions and didn't sign, so they made my process even longer. They took me to the ICE department—eight hours; then Florence, a Federal clearing jail, for three days; then detention. I was there for a month—for a traffic violation. When you're there you don't have a name: you're just a number—and they call you Alien, like you're from another planet.

López is slight and soft spoken: he leans forward to explain in a semi-whisper the effect of Arizona's 'attrition' law: 'They cannot deport eleven million people, so they play this game. They are trying to scare them, so they don't have any other option than to leave—they are going to make us self-deport.'

When I ask if the strategy is working, he answers with a question: 'I don't know if you've heard about NAFTA?' He says the trade deal between the USA and Mexico, together with other bilateral deals, is making poverty south of the border worse:

> When I was in jail I met guys from El Salvador, Ecuador, Honduras—conditions are really hard—they cannot live there; they got no option but to go to other countries. It's not that they want to be here, but they just don't have any other option. SB1070 won't stop them coming.

Arpaio made videos of prisoners in the chain gang under the sun: people see this, but they still come.

Latino migrants work, but for precious little: it is a certainty that the impact of illegal immigration is to reduce wages for people like Maurice and Larry in New Mexico, who are US citizens. Fernando tells me that some of his friends are working a 100-hour week, for below the minimum wage: housekeeping, landscaping, kitchen work.

'They should be creating jobs instead of jails, building schools instead of jails.'

But as Fernando and I sit there in the sweltering heat of the migrant centre, beneath posters with the slogan 'We Are Human' and a grimly humorous bumper sticker saying 'I'm Mexican, Pull Me Over'— President Obama is getting ready to sign away two trillion dollars' worth of money for building schools and creating jobs. His only beef with the majority in the House is whether it should go to $2.5 trillion.

'I don't trust him,' López says, pointing out that Obama also promised a law to offer illegal migrants 'earned amnesty'. But that did not happen.

In fact, by the summer of 2011 Obama was in trouble: healthcare reform got whittled down to a minimum and was now gridlocked at state level; a law to lift obstacles to trade union organization never got to first base; the promised pullout from Afghanistan turned into a surge of troops; and the Dodd–Frank Act, aimed at curtailing the power of Wall Street, had become a toothless object of derision on Wall Street.

But Obama was so determined to stick at two trillion dollars' worth of cuts for the needy—instead of $2.5 trillion—that, at one point, he walked out of negotiations with the Republicans. 'I'd rather see my presidency destroyed than give in on this,' he's reported to have said. And this rancour, this left–right stand-off, is now buzzing and twanging on every radio station as I head out of Phoenix, west, for California.

## A museum of the twentieth century

As I leave Phoenix the radio sings out adverts for repossessed ranches in the desert: 'You can hunt there, ride—anything you want: it's your ranch!' urges the disc jockey. It's a reminder of the basic problem: America had a house-price boom that is now bust—and twenty years of credit-fuelled growth are over, so even the mild recovery in 2010–11 is failing to create jobs. Meanwhile, the money that fuelled the recovery has pushed America into deep and unsustainable debt.

The gas stations are far apart and the Mojave desert is wide, so I've timed my refills rigorously against the distances on the GPS. But the GPS does not agree with the Grand Marquis's fuel gauge, so I glide into the desert truck-stop at Cedar Hills, in neutral gear, having coasted eight miles downhill on empty.

The store in the gas station is full of stuff that's by now emblematic of the Interstate's economy: the stimulant drinks in yellow bottles that keep truck drivers going all night, the Confederate-flag-themed bandannas to wear, defiantly, instead of a helmet as you cruise along on your Harley. Plus those Route 66 stickers, baseball caps and t-shirts. As with so much of today's American culture, the subtext—if you dare admit it—is 'We were great once'.

I cross the Mojave Desert in the dark and get to Bakersfield, California at midnight: this is the town where the Joads planned to find work in the orange groves. The bar at the hotel is full of oilmen and military guys: the economy of Kern County is no longer dominated by agriculture. The main employers are the Air Force, a naval weaponry base, big oil and private healthcare. Despite that there is still 15 per cent unemployment here—17 per cent at the height of the crisis.

The town is, like so many in the southern USA, a boomtown suburb that's been busted. Its population grew 25 per cent in the 2000s decade, but since the bust, one in seventy homes is in repossession.

But, like I say, the bar is heaving with clean-shaven, loud young guys with lantern jaws: their ladies are kitted out in that regulation designer

IN THE TRACKS OF TOM JOAD

bling you see wherever easy money flows. This is Obama's fiscal
and monetary stimulus in action: it has engorged the military and—
by boosting the global price of everything—made the oilman's life
sweet too.

But the parking valet, a Mexican who casts a disgusted eye over the
Red Bull cans and trail mix strewn all over the car, tells the other side of
the story:

'You can't get work here anymore: $8 an hour for picking fruit. Why
bother? A lot of the farmers sold their fields to build homes on. My
family, my Mom picked fruit here for thirty years but, well ...' He lets
his hands drop to his sides and looks shamefacedly at his uniform.

In the morning I go in search of the spot where Steinbeck must have
seen this: 'They drove through Tehachapi in the morning glow, and the
sun came up behind them and then suddenly they saw the great valley
below them ...'

In the John Ford film there's a great top shot of the San Joaquin
valley, but the Interstate highway obliterates the old road now. I drive
into a vineyard to find the view that must have greeted the real-life
Okies as they crossed the mountains. It's still beautiful. But like the rest
of America, hidden from your gaze by the mainstream media, it's a
story of poverty for some, work for others; and widespread denial of
where much of the work comes from, and what averted the disaster
back in 2008: the state.

Steinbeck, who had lived most of his life in California, was among
the first to publicize conditions for the Dust Bowl migrants, and to
pillory the near-racist attitudes of those who hounded them. Though he
faced resistance from the cheap-labour bosses and the police, by the
time he wrote the novel Steinbeck was cutting with the grain in terms of
Federal policy. For the book is not just about a journey: it is about the
search for a new economic model based on state intervention to guarantee full employment, and about a new social model based on solidarity
and tolerance.

This was Roosevelt's New Deal, which would, between 1933 and

1937, create twelve million jobs, power America out of double-dip recession and—in the teeth of opposition from corporations—redistribute wealth. Roosevelt would, within days of taking office, abolish speculation in the finance system. Within two years he would pass pro-union legislation, which led to the biggest one-time uplift in wages and conditions in US history. He would raise taxes on the rich and spend Federal money, unashamedly, not just on social programmes but in creating art and theatre for the people: 40,000 actors and directors and scene painters were employed in the first year.

The Joads, then, had Roosevelt. People like Larry Antista and Fernando López have Barack Obama. And on Sunday night, 31 July 2011, those tuning into the radio on Interstate 40 would hear the news: President Obama had agreed to make $2.5 trillion in spending cuts, mostly on infrastructure and welfare payments to the poor. 'An about-face', as the *New York Times* described it, 'in the federal government's role from outsize spending in the immediate aftermath of recession to outsize cuts in the future.'

The boss of Pimco, one of America's biggest investment firms, summarized the impact of the debt-ceiling deal: 'Unemployment will be higher than it would have been otherwise. Growth will be lower than it would be otherwise. And inequality will be worse than it would be otherwise.'[2]

That summer, key indicators of US economic growth began to flatten off. The Federal Reserve responded with a third tweak to its money-printing operation, and Obama published a job creation plan. But the US recovery was, by now, intertwined with the fate of the global economy, and this—because of the euro crisis—was looking grim.

My trip from Oklahoma to LA was conceived as a snapshot of America struggling with the depths of its jobs and housing drought. If we are very unlucky, the depths may lie ahead of us.

# 9

# 1848 Redux: What We Can Learn from the Last Global Wave

*Paris, December 1847.* One winter morning Frédéric Moreau, the archetypal 'graduate with no future', left his student hovel on the Parisian Left Bank, his mind, as always, on his forlorn romance. But history intervened:

> Youths in groups of anything from five to twelve were strolling around arm in arm, occasionally going up to larger groups which were standing here and there; at the far end of the square, against the iron railings, men in smocks were holding forth ... policemen were walking up and down ... Everybody wore a mysterious, anxious expression; clearly there was something in the air, and on each person's lips there was an unspoken question.[1]

This is how Moreau, the hero of Flaubert's novel *Sentimental Education*, collided with the revolution of 1848, and like his romance it did not end well.

On 22 February 1848 the 'men in smocks'—the Parisian workers—overthrew the monarchy and forced the middle class to declare a republic. It was a shock because, like Saif Gaddafi and Gamal Mubarak long afterwards, King Louis-Philippe had counted himself something of a democrat.

In 1848 a wave of revolutions swept Europe: by March, Austria, Hungary, Poland and many states of the future Germany were facing insurrections, often led by students and the radicalized middle class, with the small, mainly craft-based, working class in support. Elsewhere —as in Jordan and Morocco in 2011—riots and demonstrations forced beleaguered monarchs into constitutional reform.

Within months, however, class conflict tore the revolutionary alliance apart. In Paris, the newly elected assembly was dominated not by the radicals who'd made the revolution, but by social conservatives. They hired a general to crack down on unrest; that June, he crushed the working class in four days of intense barricade fighting. The first newspaper photograph in history captures the moment: three forlorn barricades, made of cobblestones and carts, stand deserted on the rue Saint-Maur: four thousand people have just been killed. The scene's eerie modernity is reinforced by an advertisement on the wall for a chocolate factory.[2]

Elsewhere in Europe, there was open warfare. Revolutionary armies manoeuvred through Hungary, Poland, Italy, Austria and along the Rhine. Fourteen years later many of the defeated insurgents would turn up on the battlefields of the American Civil War, from Shiloh to Chattanooga, led by the same radical officers and singing the same socialist songs.

But by 1851 the revolutionary wave in Europe was over, its leaders exiled or dead. A military coup ended the French revolution, the president rebranding himself as Emperor Napoleon III. The Prussian army crushed the German states that had voted for radical democracy. Austria defeated the Hungarian uprising, put down its own and enlisted Napoleon III to suppress the republic that had sprung up in Rome.

In each case, the survivors observed a similar pattern of events. Once the workers began to fight for social justice, the businessmen and radical journalists who had led the fight for democracy turned against them, rebuilding the old, dictatorial forms of repression to put them down. Conversely, where the working class was weak or non-existent, the radical middle classes would die on the barricades, often committed to a left-wing programme themselves.

Eighteen forty-eight, then, forms the last complete example of a year when it all kicked off. As with 2011, it was preceded by an economic crisis. As today, there was a level of contagion inexplicable to governments. But in hindsight, it was actually a wave of revolution and reaction, followed pretty swiftly by a wave of war. Even if today's situation defies parallel, the events of 1848 provide the most extensive case study on which to base our expectations of the present revolts.

When the next global wave of revolutions broke, in February 1917, the uprisings were led by hardened revolutionary socialists and involved a large, industrial working class. They featured a similar cast of characters to 1848, but the plot was attenuated.

By contrast, May 1968 looks less like a wave of revolutions and more like a surge of protest: students in the lead, workers and the urban poor taking it to the verge of insurrection only in France, Czechoslovakia and America's ghettoes. Nineteen eighty-nine was—with the exception of Romania—achieved by demonstrations, passive resistance and a large amount of diplomacy.

In each of these global spasms, issues of class were crucial. The key questions were always: what do the workers do? Do they lead? What is their ideology? How fast do they move from a democratic to a social agenda? How does the middle class react?

But these worldwide protests were not only about class. With the rise of social micro-history, we've begun to understand that these events were also about 'the personal': about relationships, freedom of action, culture, the creation of small islands of autonomy and control. In this respect, the demographics of 2011 resemble those of 1848 more than any other event. There is an expanded layer of 'graduates with no future', a working class weakened by the collapse of the organizations and lifestyle that blossomed in the Fordist era, and a large mass of slum-dwelling urban poor.

As today, 1848 was preceded by a communications revolution: the telegraph, the railway and the steam boat formed part of an emerging transport and communications network clustered around the cities that became centres of the social revolution.

As today, 1848 was preceded by the rapid formation of networks—in this case, clubs and secret societies. The students, worker-intellectuals and radical lawyers who led them were indeed part of an international network of activists. Marx and Engels had holed up in London's Soho to write *The Communist Manifesto*; they were in Brussels by February, Paris by March, and soon after sneaked across the border to join the revolution in Cologne. They were not unique in their globetrotting. Nor was the opening line of their manifesto—'A spectre is haunting Europe, the spectre of communism'—mere rhetoric.

As today, 1848 was a revolution in social life as well as politics. In a pioneering micro-study of the Languedoc region of France during that year, historian Leo Loubere explored how social-republicanism spread among the workers and farm labourers of the wine-producing district. Cafés became hubs of political discussion, driven by the newly published radical newspapers; farmhands would gather to hear doctors and lawyers spread the word. At the core of the movement were town-based artisans. Albeit driven by the economic downturn of 1847, the character of the revolution, once unleashed, went beyond economics:

> Most of the active militants were relatively young, in their twenties and thirties ... Often their wives and even their children participated in the more festive programs, such as planting liberty trees and crowning them with Phrygian caps, or serenading a local hero, or dancing the farandole in long serpentine columns, or just plain mischief which the police reports refer to as 'tapage nocturne'.[3]

Basically, the radical workers of Languedoc turned the region into one giant festival until the military coup of 1851 ended the revolution.

We know from newspaper and police reports what their mass meetings advocated: nationalization of the railways, insurance and finance; a publicly funded urban infrastructure; cheap credit for workers' and farmers' cooperatives; the breakup of large landholdings; and free, secular education for all.

They resisted the 1851 coup by force of arms: after their rising was crushed, 5,000 people were arrested, of which 2,000 were deported to Algeria. These had been identified as 'decurions'—organizers—of something we can recognize all too easily now: a network.

To anticipate where today's revolts may lead, we need to avoid two mistakes. The first would be to ignore the classic dynamics of revolution—to imagine that material antagonism between the democratic business class and the workers can remain suppressed forever. The second mistake would be to think there is nothing new, seeing only the parallels with what came before and ignoring the changes in personal identity, knowledge and behaviour described above.

Today the chaotic, interpersonal and cultural character of the revolution is front and centre. This makes the 'democratic' aspect of the uprisings more complex, and the line between politics and economics harder to draw. As it happens there is a glaring historical parallel for this, too, but it's one of the least recognized.

## The Great Unrest 2.0?

In 1913 America's leading business magazine warned the world of a new social movement. Although the name of this movement was not in any dictionary, it threatened 'to bring the world face to face with the greatest crisis of modern civilization—perhaps of any civilization'.[4]

The name of this movement was 'syndicalism': a new kind of unskilled trade-unionism that sparked an upsurge of strikes, unionization drives and sit-ins across Europe, the Americas and the Pacific between 1909 and 1913. It had no leaders and no centralized programme, but it inspired a global fight-back by the working poor and a general feeling of defiance aimed at the rich, the media and conservative religions.

Syndicalism was also a mass cultural movement, creating free social spaces such as secular schools, from Barcelona to Buenos Aires; an Oxbridge college run by workers in the UK; popular community centres in Italy—and, through the 'Wobblies', a whole underground network of camps and canteens for America's itinerant workers.

Syndicalist methods of struggle went far beyond the strike. They encompassed general strikes, store boycotts, and the boycott of newspapers that took adverts from boycotted stores. Other innovations were industrial sabotage, the 'union-made' label on clothing, the school kids' strike, the rent strike, the occupation of factories, mutiny and sedition in the army, the dynamiting of non-union mines and the unionization of the most downtrodden people on earth.

Syndicalism was not the product of a grand plan, but of a new mass culture and new methods of managing work. Its ideas were nurtured in the vaudeville theatres and dancehalls of the early twentieth century. Its organizers travelled in railway box-cars and in the steerage class of migrant ships. The message went viral because it was spread using popular culture. One of syndicalism's iconic activists and martyrs—Joe Hill, executed in Utah in 1916—became famous for writing radical cover versions of hit songs. If you've ever heard 'You'll get pie in the sky when you die', that's one of Joe's.

Above all, the syndicalists showed a determination to live *despite* capitalism; to achieve something better than reform, but less than a full-blown revolution. Journalists christened their heyday—the strike-torn period before 1914—the Great Unrest.

If the political aspect of the 2011 revolts shows parallels with 1848, the social aspect has echoes of the original Great Unrest. The movement is unled; it is the result of changes deep in the organization of work and leisure; it's inseparable from popular culture and mass technology. And it coincides with a wider cultural embrace of human freedom, just as the era of Joe Hill coincided with the era of Delius and Stefan Zweig. But where does it go next?

## *The class issues will surface*

From every previous democratic revolution, we can infer the certainty of an attempt at 'democratic counter-revolution' in countries where despots have been overthrown. That is, a moment where the liberal middle classes start to separate from, and oppose, the demands of the workers and urban poor.

The first stages of it are already clear in Egypt, where evidence of a backroom deal between the army and the Muslim Brotherhood indicates that radical democrats and secularists, let alone the unions, are likely to face tight constraints after the November 2011 elections. The arrest of Asmaa Mahfouz, the Egyptian video blogger, by a military court—after she was accused of calling the regime 'dogs' on Facebook —was a straw in the wind.

The greater the success of an agenda based explicitly on social justice, the more likely will be the retreat from democratic goals by the new Arab governments. Nevertheless, for now, the labour movements in North Africa remain at a basic stage, concentrating on economic goals, sporadically inspired by modern techno-radicalism but not yet imbued with it. They are not, of their own volition, going to provoke a clash with the liberal middle class that led the revolutions.

More likely, in Egypt at least, is a clash between the secular youth and conservative Islam. The harbingers of this are clear in the repeated attempts by the SCAF regime to stir up Muslim gangs against Coptic Christian churches, leading in October 2011 to the deaths of at least twenty-five Copts at the hands of the army at Maspero.

In light of the 1848 experience we can further expect the rise of new 'strongmen' from within the ranks of the revolutionaries. The events of 1989, meanwhile, taught us to anticipate the rapid rise of the corporate gangster with strong influence inside the fragile new democracies: Ukraine currently offers the best example of how to kill a democratic revolution with corruption.

The strongman threat is especially significant because, during the

Arab Spring, standing national armies proved quite resilient: both in Tunisia and Egypt the army took part, or acquiesced, in the revolution. In Libya, the National Transitional Council's incorporation of defectors from the Gaddafi regime, together with former Islamist insurgents, provides plenty of candidates should the country need a new dictator. And across the region, while the US State Department will encourage the creation of civil-society counterweights to authoritarianism, it will also search for a new Saif Gaddafi, a younger version of General Tantawi, an Assad with more brain cells, a moderate mullah in Tehran.

A third development which we cannot rule out is war. 'Once Syria goes, the next on the list is Iran,' predicted former Blair aide Jonathan Powell in August 2011. But Iran is the lynchpin of the Middle East balance of power. It contains, alongside the discontented rural poor, a modern urban economy that takes in 71 per cent of the population— with automobile plants, barely suppressed radical trade unions, gay nightclubs and tens of thousands of secular youth whose hearts and minds are still on the rooftops of 2009.

If the failure of 2009 is explained by the revolution's lack of social depth, then any successful revolution in Iran would have to be both deep and social. It would involve civil war with the Basij militia and the Islamic Revolutionary Guard Corps, whose status rests not just on its access to military hardware and exotic uniforms, but on an economic empire of Guard-owned factories and energy businesses.

Long before it would allow itself to be dispossessed, Iran's power elite would most probably attempt to provoke war with Israel or the Gulf states, or both, fomenting maximum strife in Iraq and Syria.

The potential for class conflict, authoritarian backlash and war in the Middle East is overlaid by the danger of anomic breakdown and depression in southern Europe. What the diplomats call euphemistically 'a crisis of democracy' is still possible in the peripheral arc that stretches from Dublin to Athens.

## *Culture wars are colliding with the crisis*

On top of this, a further crack in the world order has appeared, involving the domestic politics of two states at its very core: Israel and the USA. In both of these countries, for different reasons, we are seeing unprecedented culture wars.

The July 14 or #j14 protest movement in Israel, in the summer of 2011, instantly disproved any idea that the country was immune to the new unrest.

Those who began the tent-camp protests—modelled more on Syntagma than Tahrir—were mainly young, Westernized and from the Ashkenazi middle class. They had organized, inevitably, through social media. Triggered by the soaring cost of housing in Israel, the protests quickly expanded to embrace a series of grievances: disability rights, freedom for POW Gilad Shalit, more care for the elderly.

The first protesters were explicitly hostile to Israel's anti-Zionist left—and the feeling was mutual. The left-wing blogosphere excoriated them when, almost on cue, they declared their willingess to suspend the protest if called up to fight with the Israeli Defense Forces in Gaza.

Despite the fact that #j14 went out of its way to avoid the issue of Palestine, as the protests gained momentum the movement began to tolerate those raising the issue, even drawing in members of Israel's Arab population. Dimi Reider, a journalist and activist in Tel Aviv, described how on 3 August 2011 the residents of a poverty-stricken, Likud-voting Jewish neighbourhood signed an agreement to campaign jointly with supporters of a pro-Palestinian party, including Arabs:

> They agreed they had more in common with each other than with the middle-class national leadership of the protest, and that while not wishing to break apart from the J14 movement, they thought their unique demands would be better heard if they acted together. At the rally, they marched together, arguing bitterly at times but sticking to each other, eventually even chanting mixed Hebrew and Arabic renditions of slogans from Tahrir.[5]

On 3 September 2011 the #j14 movement brought 450,000 Israelis onto the streets, calling for more public housing, public education and an expansion of public spending. Head for head, this had been the biggest demonstration of the year so far.

Whatever its limitations, #j14 proved the portability of the new kind of protest to Israel, going beyond traditional left–right constraints in the fight for social justice. But even as it flowered, #j14 exposed a cultural fault line that no social media can overcome.

Spending on public services in Israel is low because so much public money is spent supporting the ultra-Orthodox settler movement, and on the Israeli military. The ultra-Orthodox right has built itself a role as power-broker in politics which many in the #j14 movement resent. As one protester put it:

> Every few years we vote in the elections, and after the elections we discover that the interests of the ultra-Orthodox, the settlers and the tycoons are always represented, but we, the middle class, the ones that work, pay the taxes, carry the load, have nobody to speak for us.[6]

However briefly, and however hampered by its avoidance of the issue of Palestine, Israel experienced the same kind of protest as those in Madrid or Wall Street, led by the same type of people. Three months before #j14, Prime Minister Binyamin Netanyahu said: 'The world is shaking, but there are no tremors or protests in Israel.' Not anymore.

In America, the dynamic of culture war is more advanced. It is paralyzing national political institutions, and in danger of creating two hostile camps which no longer want to exist inside the same polity. The outcome, obviously, will affect the way the whole world exits the crisis.

The passage of Obama's healthcare bill in March 2010 proved a turning point for the American right. The Tea Party movement, formed in opposition to the $700 billion 'Troubled Asset Relief Program' bailout of banks and automakers, found itself in an undeclared formal alliance with healthcare corporations, the Republican right, some libertarian millionaires and Fox News. This laid the basis for a state-level offensive against organized labour, employment conditions, migration and abortion rights.

The defeat of the right over healthcare was accompanied by a rise in violent imagery in political speech. Sarah Palin's website famously 'targeted' Democrat election candidates, using rifle cross hairs super-imposed on a map. When Democrats condemned this as incitement to violence, the right laughed off their response as over-sensitive political correctness.

The Tea Party movement itself then went through something of an internal split. Sensing its grassroots power, mainstream conservative politicians scrambled to realign themselves, seeking Tea Party endorsement in the 2010 midterm elections. While this would pull the GOP in Congress significantly to the right, its impact on the Tea Party was to force the most committed libertarians to split or form parallel organizations.

After the healthcare bill, former Alabama militiaman Mike Vanderboegh posted on his blog: 'To all modern Sons of Liberty: THIS is your time. Break their windows. Break them NOW.' Democratic Party office windows were broken in several states. Ten House Democrats were offered police protection.[7]

Now Glenn Beck weighed in. In a tone more in sorrowful than angry, Beck speculated:

> Why are the Tea Parties always being labeled as terrorist? Why is it? 'They're extremists, they're terrorists, they're hatemongers, they're dangerous!' What is it that these evolutionaries want? You'd pick up a gun? You ever thought of that? These people have. Because possibly, maybe, the question should be asked: maybe they're tired of evolution, and they are waiting for revolution.[8]

At the end of the broadcast Beck called for a return to civilized discourse. But he had just accused the liberal wing of US politics of contemplating armed struggle.

The problem is, as Chekhov once said, if a gun appears in Act One, then before the end of the play somebody is going to get shot. On 8 January 2011, a gunman in Tucson, Arizona, maimed the Democratic senator Gabrielle Giffords and killed six bystanders. Giffords had been targeted in one of Palin's cross hairs.

The event, though essentially the action of a lunatic, was a wake-up call.

Because, in America, the gun has appeared before. Every serious history of the American Civil War (1861–65) reminds us that it was preceded by a long and complex political breakdown in the 1850s, the result of demographic change and economic modernization. The war was not just 'about slavery'. It was about the emergence of a new political model of industrial capitalism and the rise of a political party which, though it represented that new system, had no support whatever in the slave-owning south. That, at the time, was the Republican Party.

As the situation degenerated in the late 1850s, the habitually rowdy electoral process gave rise to sporadic violent acts, from the outbreak of political violence in Kansas, to John Brown's guerrilla raid on Harper's Ferry, to a fight on the floor of the Senate that left the anti-slavery senator Charles Sumner maimed for life.

The historian Allan Nevins argued that by the late 1850s America contained no longer just two political factions, or parallel economic systems, but 'two peoples' who were culturally, socially and ethnically different (by this time 90 per cent of all European migrants were headed for the north). Another historian, James McPherson, explained why, to the white slave-ocracy and its plebeian supporters, the rise of industrial capitalism and its liberal values did look like a revolution:

> The ascension to power of the Republican Party, with its ideology of competitive, egalitarian, free-labor capitalism, was a signal to the South that the Northern majority had turned irrevocably towards this frightening, revolutionary future.[9]

While it would be wrong to force an analogy, there are worrying echoes of 1850s America in today's USA.

First is the combination of violent political rhetoric with the prevalence of weapons, something that led one despairing critic to tell me: 'America is the Weimar Republic with 250 million guns.' Secondly, there is the transformation of TV news and talk radio into a zone of culture war: thanks to Fox and MSNBC, the conservative and liberal halves of America can now live in completely separate media bubbles, never hearing ideas they don't like or seeing news that contradicts them.

Third, all this is building up into an argument about the assertion of 'states' rights' in the face of Federal government, with individual states attempting to impose, for example, Arizona-style anti-migrant laws or to resist the healthcare legislation. Following Obama's healthcare bill, indeed, seventeen states passed legislation attempting to nullify it; twenty-nine states have mounted a constitutional legal challenge.

Finally, the culture war has spilled over into the fiscal management of the biggest economy on earth. In August 2011 the Republican majority in Congress took the USA to the brink of technical bankruptcy in order to impose on President Obama their desired mixture of tax cuts and lower spending. Though essentially a piece of political theatre, the debt-ceiling crisis of 2011 sent a strategic signal to global markets, to the effect that the USA lacks a solid institutional framework to deal with economic crisis.

If this were just a case of ideological warfare over the same old issues—abortion, gay marriage, race and so on—it would remain pretty much what it's been since the 1970s: something for the political strategists to manoeuvre around as they fight for control of essentially stable institutions.

But America is facing a big new issue—economic decline. This is not a temporary blip. Before 2050, it will have to deal with an energy crisis and numerous resource rivalries, as well as the impacts of an ageing population and climate change. The danger is not that civil conflict

breaks out because of one egregious rant by Glenn Beck or Al Sharpton
—but that at a certain point the apparatus of government becomes
paralyzed, as it was in August 2011, and the mechanisms for resolving
conflict break down.

### Tahrir comes to America

It is in this context that we have to consider the Madison, Wisconsin
revolt, which began on 14 February 2011. Madison was sparked when
Republican Governor Scott Walker attacked public sector workers'
collective bargaining rights and pensions. As tens of thousands of
teachers, firefighters and students protested outside the state capitol,
four days after the fall of Mubarak, Lin Weeks (@weeks89) tweeted:
'Weirdly high number of signs ref'ing egypt. And now chanting:
"From Egypt/ to wisconsin/ power to the people".'[10]

The demonstrations continued on successive days, swelling from
30,000 to 75,000 protesters in the first week and becoming a national
media spectacle. On 17 February, fourteen Democratic senators left the
state in order to prevent Walker's budget vote getting a quorum.

While the hearings were in progress the protesters, who were entitled to sleep on the floor during this time, carried out a mass occupation
of the building. By now the #wiunion tag on Twitter was appearing in
so many posts that they were scrolling, impossible to read, across the
laptops of the activists, huddled in their sleeping bags on the Capitol
floor.

Anna Ogden-Nussbaum (@eponymousthing), who describes
herself as a theoretical—i.e. unemployed—librarian, went into the
Capitol on the second day. 'We set up a library,' she tells me. 'Mainly
stuff about Madison, because there were people who just didn't know
about the city and its history. There was stuff about Egypt everywhere:
posters about Mubarak.'

Soon, not only was there 'stuff about Egypt', there were direct links
with the protesters there—one of which came in unexpected fashion.

From the start of the Capitol occupation in Madison, a local pizzeria, Ian's Pizza, had been sending in pizzas to the protesters. Soon, as news of the demonstrations spread, supporters from all fifty states began ordering pizzas on the protesters' behalf. Then, Ian's Pizza started to get orders from Cairo. Finally they got so many paid orders from all over the world, they simply opened the doors of the restaurant and served everybody for free.

The social-media resonance of Wisconsin was amplified by America's radical blogosphere. This has grown to include numerous commercially run blogs with paid correspondents, alongside NGO and trade union blogs who use trained, accredited journalists. Ben Brandzel of *HuffPo* wrote a widely read account that captured the atmosphere:

> Everything is donated. The community survives because people from Madison to Cairo have chipped in for Ian's Pizza, endless bagels, or breakfast burritos from an organic café … I saw masseuses drive for hours and haul their chairs up three flights of stairs just to give free massages (before, of course, the chairs were banned). I saw people who had slept on cold marble for weeks gladly share or give away camping mats and pillows … And when the pizza supply was cut off, I saw people who hadn't eaten all day gladly share their only slice.[11]

If these had been just the usual consumers of organic burritos, the students or the radical left, the occupation could have been easily cleared, or coerced into clearing itself. But trade unions organized 100-strong delegations to sleep in the Capitol in shifts: plumbers, electricians, firefighters. Though it was to be defeated, the #wiunion protest was one of the clearest examples in 2011 of explicit 'role-allocation' and division of labour between workers and students. The workers understood that their role was to provide the protection of respectability to the youth activists who'd initiated the sleep-in. But there was also crossover. One protester told me:

The way the firefighters reacted was interesting. On the first day they arrived, they spread their sleeping bags out in a solid group as if to say: hey everyone, stand back, we the firefighters are here now to lead the movement. But then, after a couple of days of joining in with the washing up, and talking to people, they just dissolved into the mass. They loosened up.

And they were not the only ones. Brandzel describes how even the police detailed to guard the Capitol were sympathetic: 'Many of the same officers who guarded us during the day would take their uniforms off at night and join us in protest, often bringing large *Cops for Labor* signs with them.'[12]

The Wisconsin sit-in exhibited all the symptoms of the new kind of protest, and the new social mix: workers alongside students and community activists; the occupation of physical space for a prolonged period; a determination to be non-ideological; awareness of the power of social media.

Though it was ultimately contained within mainstream, constitutional politics, Wisconsin located the economic policy struggles firmly within the culture wars. The Capitol's occupiers included students, unions, farmers and community groups; their opponents were the local Tea Party, the billionaire libertarians who own Koch Industries, agribusiness and—of course—Glenn Beck. On his televised show, GBTV.com, Beck played a video of an allegedly 'substance-fuelled rave of anarchists, communists and socialists' in the Wisconsin Capitol. Taunting the leader of the Democrats in the Senate, he said:

> These are revolutionaries. If you think, Nancy Pelosi, that you're going to control these people? ... Since 2005 I've been talking about the coming insurrection, I called it the perfect storm where all of our enemies say, 'Now! Go, go, go!' This is it. And you are looking at something that will build stronger and stronger and stronger. If we lose Bahrain, that's our Fifth Fleet, man. Bahrain is on the edge ...

With Libya melting down, if Gaddafi can't stop it do you think Nancy Pelosi can?[13]

Within months it would be clear that—though it was well short of insurrection—nobody could stop it. On 17 September the Occupy Wall Street protest began. By 15 October it had spread to tens of American cities. As I write, it is filling my computer screen with livestreamed images of joy, solidarity, and repression.

With America confronting huge, painful economic choices in the next twenty years, it is not ideal for politics to be so polarized along ethnic, demographic, social and cultural lines. Yet in less than a generation US politics has become riven in a way that the mainstream media and academia are still struggling to understand. Its political institutions are coming under severe strain. And there is a feedback loop between institutional crisis, cultural conflict and the economy.

## The absence of a coherent left

When the Languedoc workers of 1848 demanded the nationalization of monopolies and the provision of cheap credit, these were not random wishes. The ideology of social-republicanism had been coherently expressed in the works of Louis Blanc, whose book *The Organization of Labour* had been published eight years previously. If the workers of the Rhineland tended towards the same demands in 1849, it was because a newspaper edited by Karl Marx had sudden freedom to advocate them in dense columns of 9-point Gothic type.

What is striking about the revolutions of 2009–11, however, is the absence of a coherent left. Leninism is looking shrunken and disoriented; horizontalism can stage a great demo, but does not know what it wants. Meanwhile, the mainstream left—Labourism, social democracy, the US Democrats and left-liberalism generally—appears politically confused.

President Obama is the prisoner of a right-wing Congress; Ed

Miliband's Labour Party has spent its first year out of office casting around for an ideological alternative to Blairism; French socialism's expected saviour, Dominique Strauss-Kahn, spent his first night out of jail at a $600-a-head dinner in Manhattan. In Portugal, Spain and Greece, the politicians leading the socialist party were the ones who initiated the austerity. In Ireland, fearing it might win the election and find itself presiding over an economically crippled country, Labour was accused of sabotaging its own campaign.

If you were to summarize the problem for the mainstream left in the present crisis, it comes down to three points: free-market capitalism has failed; there's a wave of resistance to wage cuts and austerity; the political leaders of social democracy cannot accept points one and two.

These, then, are the sources of incoherence for the left. But its weakness impacts on the dynamics of unrest in a paradoxical way. By removing the danger of social revolution—or even systematic social reform—it undermines the rationale for a 'democratic counter-revolution' of the June 1848 type.

The incoherence of the left has emboldened the liberals, the Facebook youth, the urban poor, and so on, to speak of social justice and to fight for it, secure in the knowledge that they cannot be accused of being communists (except on the Glenn Beck show). In this sense, across much of the Arab world but also in parts of Europe, the situation resembles Germany in 1849, not France in 1848. The weakness of the left has allowed the radical middle classes to retain their radicalism—for now.

## What is the spectre?

Marx and Engels wrote their *Communist Manifesto* at around the same time as Frédéric Moreau ran into the student demo at the Panthéon. The authors sent their manuscript to London for publication, in German, on 21 February 1848, one day before the uprising in Paris. It therefore had no impact whatsoever in France that year, and no mass circulation in Germany.

By contrast, the modern equivalent of *The Communist Manifesto* has enjoyed widespread circulation—and been widely vilified. It is titled *The Coming Insurrection*, published in French, in 2007, by a collective called 'The Invisible Committee'. Later, nine French anarchists—the Tarnac Nine—were arrested for allegedly trying to sabotage France's TGV railway network; they were also accused of being the authors of the tract.

*The Coming Insurrection* is a remarkable document. Couched in the language of contempt for capitalism, alienation, advertising and the modern city, it seemed to me—on reading it in the middle of the Lehman crisis—designed to remain esoteric, gestural and largely unread.

It captures vividly the frustrations of the youth and urban poor:

> We can no longer even see how an insurrection might begin. Sixty years of pacification and containment of historical upheavals, sixty years of democratic anesthesia and the management of events, have dulled our perception of the real, our sense of the war in progress. We need to start by recovering this perception.[14]

The authors' solution is spelled out in a series of exhortations to act: alone, clandestinely or in small groups, with fluidity, through symbolic gestures. 'Get going ... find each other ... start from what's political in friendship'. Expect nothing from established organizations. Above all, 'form communes'—that is, form autonomous groups to do sporadic things: 'Becoming autonomous could just as easily mean learning to fight in the street, to occupy empty houses, to cease working, to love each other madly, and to shoplift.'

In 2007, this was indeed the height of activity for most anti-globalization activists: a series of fluid gestures, an alternative lifestyle in close-knit small groups, the occasional 'day out' outside a conference or nuclear power site.

But the authors of *The Coming Insurrection* were thinking much bigger than the milieu from which they came. Two years in advance of the first networked insurrection, they described how it might come about. The disconnected youth of the urban wasteland, they predicted, would play the role of the new revolutionary subject:

> The pioneers of the workers' movement were able to find each other in the workshop, then in the factory. They had the strike to show their numbers and unmask the scabs. They had the wage relation, pitting the party of capital against the party of labor, on which they could draw the lines of solidarity and of battle on a global scale. We have the whole of social space in which to find each other. We have everyday insubordination for showing our numbers and unmasking cowards. We have our hostility to this civilization for drawing lines of solidarity and of battle on a global scale.

In Athens, Tehran and then spectacularly across North Africa and the Middle East, people who had never heard of *The Coming Insurrection* 'found each other' and acted in ways that conformed to its imperatives. They formed 'communes' of a type many anarchists might find difficult to imagine: 'communes' of Google executives, rebel army officers, off-duty cops, Obama campaign staffers; communes of the non-political and the unschooled. Strangest of all, communes of people who had no intention of fighting for communism.

It is something of a paradox that the only mainstream media figure in the US to notice the book—and to understand the importance of its message—was Glenn Beck. In July 2009, Beck warned viewers of Fox News:

> The Invisible Committee ... want to bring down capitalism and the Western way of life. This started in France and started to spread to countries like Greece and Iceland, where people are out of work, out of money and out of patience. Now, it's about to come here to America.

That is the spectre: that the insurrectionary wave becomes linked to mass disillusion with the economic system and leads to an inchoate struggle for something different. As with Marx and Engels, the bohemian desperadoes who first imagined it stand way to the left of what the mass of people actually want; but they have still captured what's in the air.

## *The endgame is dictated by economics*

The revolutionary wave of 1848 ended in defeat: all the monarchies under threat survived, except the French, which upgraded to Empire status. But it nevertheless ushered in modernity. Napoleon III industrialized France; Prussia unified Germany. In Italy the republican radicals of 1848 would go on to refight the war of independence, unifying Italy as a kingdom by 1861. The age of Balzac gave way to the age of Zola, the age of secret societies to the age of trade unions.

But it is not clear what, even if defeated, 2011 will leave behind. The masses in Tahrir chanted: 'Bread, Freedom, Social Justice'—and the 'social justice agenda' seems pervasive. So too does democracy: it will be difficult in future for any Western policymaker to argue that a certain race, culture or religion makes authoritarianism 'durable'.

Everything depends on the outcome of the economic crisis. Before 2008, globalization 'delivered' in a rough-and-ready way to the poor of the developing world. It dragged one billion people out of rural poverty and into urban slums, and created an extra 1.5 billion waged workers. It provided access to life-changing technology. And it offset the decline in prosperity and status for the manual workers of the rich world with unlimited access to credit. At the same time it made the rich of every country richer, and inequality greater—even in the developing world, where real incomes rose.

If the West's economy now flatlines—suffering a decade of stagnation, as Japan did in the 1990s—the whole deal is off. As HSBC economist Stephen King put it:

With the West now in economic permafrost, paper wealth is vulnerable to loss ... Any plausible resolution to the current financial crisis must involve burden-sharing on a scale not seen since the 1930s. Unemployment, defaults, inflation, currency crises, stock-market collapses, austerity: all these are consistent with the new, lower, level of economic activity and are not unique to any one country or part of the world.[15]

All of which means that the aspiration for social justice will depend on the economy's ability deliver it.

Because 1848 delivered economic progress—almost independently of the actions of the main players—republican socialism died out, to be replaced by respectable trade unionism and social democracy. Marx went back to the library and stayed there for decades. Flaubert's Frédéric Moreau fled the barricades, travelled the world and, like many of the youth of 1848, 'resigned himself to the stagnation of his mind and the apathy of his heart'.

Industrialization delivered a rising standard of life to the masses, and, if not the democracy they had fought for, at least an element of democratization from above. And it civilized the city, replacing slums with boulevards.

What becomes of the present wave of revolts—political, social, intellectual and moral—now depends completely on what the global economy delivers. If it is nothing but heartache and penury, we are in the middle of a perfect storm.

In these postmodern times we have Glenn Beck to warn us of the dangers of contagion; in 1848 they had Alexis de Tocqueville. The speech he made to the French Assembly, just days before the insurrection, has an eerie resonance today:

> I believe right now that we are sleeping on a volcano. Can you not sense by a sort of instinctive intuition ... that the earth is trembling again in Europe? Can you not feel the wind of revolution in the air?[16]

# 10

## 'We Will Barricade':
## Slum Dwellers versus the Super-Rich

*Gapan City, Philippines, 2011.* The bridge stretches a couple of hundred metres across a river and some rice fields. Water buffalo nuzzle the vegetation. The air hangs, stifling, somewhere between humidity and rain. Occasionally, from one of the battered jeeps crossing the bridge, somebody heaves a plastic rubbish sack over the rails without changing gear.

I stand on that bridge for half an hour, watching fishermen cast their nets and bee-eaters dipping between the reeds, before I notice the squatter camp below.

I can count more than fifty homes: some are shacks, some made of breeze blocks. They are wedged beneath the bridge, forming an unofficial street. Though the shacks are topped with corrugated iron, the most effective roof is the bridge, which provides shelter during the monsoon. What doesn't help them is the river, which, says Len-len, flash-floods twice a year. She points to a mark on her porch where the water reached last time. It is three metres high.

'We bought this place for 50,000 pesos [$1,100],' Len-len tells me. 'The family that sold it to us moved on to Manila.'

Len-len is thirty-one years old, gap-toothed and striking, in a moth-eaten pink t-shirt, faded grey track-pants and ancient flip-flops. In another world—if the gap tooth issue could be solved—Len-len would be one of those women they pick to be PA to the chief exec. The reason she's talking to me—while the others hide their faces behind their hands—is that she's gutsy:

> My husband works as a farm hand. I don't have a job. We have four children. He earns 150 pesos [$3] a day, but that's on the days he gets work. We moved here because we had an argument with our relatives: my family has always worked the land but we never owned any. If we knew anybody in Manila, we would go there and look for work—but we don't.

These are the Philippines' rural poor. The kids are thin, their legs dotted with sores; the crowd that's formed around me has too many nut-brown oldsters with smiles crazed by whatever hooch they're on. And too many people snigger when Len-len tells me she has no job:

'It's hard here, sir. The local government keeps threatening to move us on. But they do nothing for us. There's no work on the land, not regular work. We can only afford rice and, if we've anything left, a bit of meat.'

Her home is clean, but with few possessions. In the kitchen there is a five-litre water container, empty, on a stand: it costs 60 pesos ($1.35) for five litres, which last three days. Fresh water alone costs Len-len's family one-seventh of their daily income—but that still gives them less than two litres per day between six people. In this heat, an adult can sweat two litres in an hour.

Despite the temporary and ramshackle nature of the camp, someone has run bare electrical wires into the shack and Len-len pays a monthly bill for it: 700 pesos, or more than four days' wages. But not all days bring wages.

Beneath the cleanliness and the proud attitude, what lingers just under the surface is shame. This camp, a couple of miles outside a bustling rural town, has a biblical bleakness. Its inhabitants are surrounded by fields which, twice a year, produce the staple rice crop. But they don't own the fields. They own their bodies, a few tattered clothes and some irrational inner hope that maybe their kids can escape this life. It is like Steinbeck without heroes—unless you count Len-len: 'I wanted to become a security guard, sir. Lady security guard. I went for one day's training. But then my money ran out so I can't complete the course.'

Do the kids eat every day? 'It's no problem, sir,' she says with an awkward smile.

What's driving them from the land is a mixture of rural poverty plus climate change. Typhoons smash trees down with increasing frequency; the rice harvest—the crop needs 110 days of sunshine—is becoming volatile.

The farmers nearby tell me they could solve the problem by planting rain-resistant GM rice. But that costs money; and, says farming folklore, once you're borrowing from a bank you're a slave. At least with the traditional seed next year's crop comes free: they scrunch the seed, dry, a desiccated handful of hope for the next harvest.

But for financial whizz-kids in the global commodity markets, failing rice crops are good: they drive the world price higher. Hedge funds have built entire strategies on the wager that food and land prices will rise inexorably. And as investors piled into commodity indexes at the height of the credit bubble, say Princeton economists Tang and Xiong, wholesale prices started to fluctuate—in response not to the supply and demand of food itself, but to the supply and demand of speculative money.[1]

Right now the supply of speculative money is high, and so is the price of rice. The wholesale price is now 32 pesos per kilo—approaching once again its 2008 high of 35 pesos. Ten years ago it was half that. So, without a government subsidy to fix the retail price, Len-len would go hungry.

Soon, she will do what tens of millions of the rural poor have done already: leave the land and move to a mega-city to live in a slum and look for work. She will live in a shack just like this, but it will be more cramped, wedged in by others like it. Instead of the viridian and lime of the paddy fields, she will live in a landscape whose colours are predominantly rust and grey.

For, horrific as they are, the slums of Manila—as in all the megacities of the world—are a makeshift solution to rural poverty.

### The tunnel dwellers of San Miguel

*Estero de San Miguel, Manila.* There is a long curve of grey water and, along both sides, as far as the eye can see, shacks, trash, washing and grey tin, bits of wood and scraps of cloth, rats and children. At the water's edge lies a flotsam of multicoloured plastic rubbish. This is the Estero de San Miguel, the front line in an undeclared war between Manila's rich and poor.

Seen from the bridge it shocks me, and everybody with me, into silence. When you enter a slum, no matter how many times you've done it, there is that doom-laden feeling of plummeting, helpless, such as you feel when somebody has just died: for what you are seeing in a slum is a form of death. Not the death of hope, but of possibility.

Mena Cinco, a community leader here, volunteers to take me in—but only about fifty yards. After that she cannot guarantee my safety. Mena is short and very determined; she wears some kind of organization logo on her polo-shirt that I am not really paying much attention to.

From the bridge there is a ladder into somewhere gloomy. At the bottom of it Mena reveals the central mystery of the Estero de San Miguel: a long tunnel four feet wide, dark except for the occasional naked bulb. It's like an old coal-mine, with rickety joists, shafts of light, puddles of water on the floor. The tunnel is lined by doorways: front doors of the homes of about 6,000 people.

We knock on the first door that's ajar. We step into a room about ten feet by six, laminated from floor to ceiling with blown-up photographs of a tulip field. There's a TV and a computer, a teddy bear hanging from the ceiling: a woman with a toddler, another woman with not many teeth, and a teenage girl whose homework we've interrupted. Off the main room, forming an L-shape, is a corridor with a one-ring gas stove and a toilet at the end. The teenager sleeps in the corridor and the toothless woman in a tiny loft above; husband, wife and toddler sleep in the tulip room. The husband, Mena explains, is a driver for a Chinese family and constantly at work. They've lived in these rooms for twenty years: 'But you see we have solidarity, social capital. They are happy, the kid is in school.'

A few feet farther along the tunnel there's another door ajar. Oliver Baldera comes blinking to it, pulling on his shirt as he wakes up. On the floor behind him are his four kids, eating ice cream; his wife, also pulling on clothes, now joins us and they all stand at the door, very chirpy. They do not invite me into the room: about eight feet by eight, it is their entire living space and appears to contain everything they own: a television, four bowls of ice cream, a light bulb, a mattress and the clothes they are wearing. 'We've been here more than ten years,' Baldera tells me:

> There's no choice. I'm a carpenter in the construction industry. We came from Mindanao. We moved because of the poverty. It's easier to get a job here, and I can earn 400 pesos a day. I can send the kids to school and they eat three times a day—but it's not enough. I need more space.

'But they're happy,' Mena chips in. 'Notice the father has bought them ice cream.'

Farther along there's a shaft of daylight and a bunch of kids splashing about in an inflatable pool, wedged between crates of old bottles and a crumbling wall. Mena makes them sing. A kid comes up to me; he's called Paul. Me too, I say. What's it like living here? Mena mutters something to him in his own language: 'Happy,' he says. And smiles.

This is a place where you cannot stride forward confidently for fear of hitting your head or bruising your elbow: people pick their way along, and creep, and shuffle. You cannot go to the toilet without standing in a queue; sex between man and wife has to take place within breathing distance of their kids, and earshot of twenty other families.

This is the classic twenty-first-century slum. Across the globe, one billion people live in slums: that is, one in seven human beings. By the year 2050, for all the same reasons that are pushing people like Len-len off the land, that number is set to double. The slum is the filthy secret of the modern mega-city, the hidden consequence of twenty years of untrammelled market forces, greed, neglect and graft.

Yet Mena, at my elbow, is feeding me this constant stream of verbal PR-copy: 'We are happy; there is social cohesion here; only we can organize it like this.'

She's all too conscious that the Estero de San Miguel has been condemned. The left-liberal government of Benigno 'NoyNoy' Aquino has decided to forcibly relocate half a million slum dwellers back to the countryside, and the Estero is at the top of the list.

'Many of our people are no longer interested in agriculture, so we need to give them the incentives to go back to the land,' says Celia Alba, who heads the Philippines Housing Development Corporation. 'If we had to rehouse the slum dwellers inside Manila, in medium-rise housing, it would cost one third of the national budget.'

But the San Miguel will not go without a fight, says Mena: 'We will barricade and we will revolt if we have to. We will resist slum clearance and we will fight to defend our community. We are happy here.'

It's not an idle threat. On 28 April 2011, residents of the Laperal slum, a few miles away across Manila, engaged demolition teams with Molotov cocktails and bricks in a riot that injured six policemen and numerous slum dwellers. An arson attack had wiped out most of their homes ten days before.

Technically, global policy is on the side of the rioters. In 2003 an influential UN report, *The Challenge of Slums*, signalled a shift away from the old slum-clearance policies and recognized that slums make a positive contribution to economic development: they house new migrants; being dense, they use land efficiently; they're culturally diverse and harbour numerous opportunities for ragged-trousered entrepreneurs.[2]

'Even ten years ago we used to dream that cities would become slum-free,' Mohammed Khadim of UN-Habitat had told me at the organization's Cairo office. 'Now the approach has changed; people see the positives. The approach now is not to clear them but improve them gradually; regularize land tenure.'

Cameron Sinclair, who runs the non-profit design firm Architecture For Humanity, goes further:

> A slum is a resilient urban animal, you cannot pry it away. It's like a good parasite—there are some parasites that attack the body and you have to get rid of them. But within the city, the informal settlement is a parasite that acts in harmony with the city; keeps it in check.

Sinclair, whose organization has upgraded slums in Brazil, Kenya and South Africa, believes modern city design should not only tolerate slums but learn from them—and even emulate them. He's building instant shanty towns in disaster zones from Sri Lanka to Japan. 'To be honest,' he says, 'what we lack in a place like London is that the lower classes can't live in central London and have to commute for two and a half hours to do the jobs that keep people going.'

But what's driven this new thinking is not so much vision as a set of ugly economic facts. After the 1970s there was a sharp slowdown in the provision of social housing across the globe. In cities, the move away from state provision of services fuelled the rise of the informal economy and a growing inequality between rich and poor. As a result, we're having to ask ourselves a question that would have made the nineteenth-century fathers of city planning shudder: do we have to learn to live with slums forever?

It's a question to which the Filipino political elite has defiantly answered 'No.'

## *A vision in vanilla*

*Estero de Paco, Manila.* 'Should I buy them ice cream?' Gina Lopez asks me, tilting back her white Stetson and peering over her sunglasses. We're in a slum called Estero de Paco, or what's left of it. The teenage boys are crowding shirtless around Gina, and it's one of their birthdays, so should she buy them ice cream? After all, she is Gina Lopez.

Gina herself is wearing a cool vanilla sleeveless number that reveals her to be lithe and youthful for her sixty-one years. She enters the slum accompanied by about thirty people, including two police officers, a media team of six, some local community guys, her bodyguards, several factotums and a man in dark glasses who is carrying her handbag.

Gina is a TV star, a philanthropist, the boss of Manila's River Renovation Authority and, most importantly, a member of the Lopez family. Lopez Inc. owns half of downtown Manila, an energy company, an entire TV network, a phone company, and has interests in many other kinds of infrastructure, including water. So who better than Gina—in a country apparently untroubled by issues of conflict of interest—to run a charity dedicated to the forcible removal of slum dwellers from Manila's waterways?

The word 'estero' means tributary, but it's also morphed into the word for a riverine slum. The Estero de Paco used to have slums right down to the water's edge, just like San Miguel. One hundred and fifty families lived in the five-foot-high space between the water and a concrete bridge, and several hundred more lived, strung out as in San Miguel, along the banks of the canal. But Gina has sorted this out.

Now, instead of shacks, a neat border of agapanthus and rubber plants fringes the water's edge. State-of-the art oxidation units are trying to turn the brown sludge into something chemically close to H2O. Into the cleared space, work gangs are laying a wide-bore sewage pipe.

As Gina approaches, a group of middle-aged local women forms up into a line. They stand to attention in their shabby garb while Gina goes into a Prada-clad drill routine: 'River Warriors, atten ... shun!' We are treated to some Filipino slogans about honour and playing for the team. Then comes some more drill, before they all fall about laughing: 'I ordered them to dive into the water,' Gina giggles.

But the idea behind the River Warriors is deadly serious. The Estero de Paco clearance was, says Gina, 'non-negotiable'. She set up the charity to train selected slum dwellers to form unofficial security groups, both of men and women. The River Warriors' job is to make sure those who've been cleared don't come back. Gina says: 'They will poo here! They will throw garbage. They would come back if we didn't guard the place. So we work with the ones who are compliant. To make a change like this you have to work with a chosen few, with vanguards.'

The clearance programme works like a giant scalpel. All the engineers need is four metres' width of riverbank to create the easement for the waste pipe, so a second, deeper layer of slums remains: you can see where the demolition crews have sheared through walls, windows, dirt, alleyways. This is social engineering on a vast scale—but it's what the government has decided must happen to half a million people in Manila.

Gina says that she had the idea for the River Warriors

> while I was at a meditation retreat in California. You know how things come to you? You will love this! I thought: I will create something like King Arthur and the Knights of the Round Table. They can kneel down and I will knight them, but with an *arnis*, which is a Filipino weapon.

She is telling me all this without a trace of embarrassment or irony.

The Lopez family is one of ten mega-powerful business families that run the country. If your vision of capitalism is one in which a genetically predestined elite runs everything, where democracy is a vibrant sham, where the minds of the poor are controlled by religion, TV and lotteries, and where patronage and graft is rife, then the Philippines is the ideal embodiment of it.

But the longer I spend with Gina, the more I realize she does have a point. Manila can't be a modern city if its waterways are clogged with excrement. Like the slum-clearers of nineteenth-century London and New York, she has a missionary zeal:

> You can't live well if you are faced with the constant smell of faeces, right? You can't live a decent life on top of a sewer. And even if those people want to stay there, it has a wider impact on the city, the environment: we can't clean the water and bring the river back to life if they are there; and the crime and sickness has a big impact on the overall environment.

But twenty-first-century capitalism has made the ideals of the nineteenth century almost impossible to deliver on. With Gina out of earshot, two River Warrior women tell me that they themselves are returnees from a place called Calauan, where they were moved to when Estero de Paco was cleared. I want to see Calauan, but it's too far to get there and back by road in a single day.

'Oh, but you have to see Calauan,' Gina says. And she flips open her BlackBerry: 'Get me aviation.'

### At the treeline

*Calauan, Laguna Province.* The chopper skims low across Manila Bay; it's fringed with slums and out in the bay itself there are homes on stilts. 'Even the sea is squatted,' Monchet Olives, Gina's chief of staff, tells me.

Soon the skyscrapers of downtown Manila disappear completely and the slums give way to rice paddies; in the distance are mountains. Now Calauan comes into view: neat rows of single-storey housing, the tin roofs glinting. The whole complex houses maybe 6,000 families, and there is room for many more. On the streets of Calauan, density is not a problem. The public space is deserted. There's a playground and a school with the name Oscar Lopez painted on the roof. The problem is—as Monchet admits—there is no electricity or running water, and no prospect of ever getting any:

> When it comes to electricity we're between a rock and a hard place. Many of the new residents have never been used to paying bills—and the electricity company, to make the investment, needs an income stream they just can't provide.

And there are no jobs.

As we walk we're being shadowed by two soldiers in full camouflage and with assault rifles, on a motorbike. Monchet explains that the soldiers' presence is due to the New People's Army, a Maoist guerrilla group going back to the 1950s with currently about 6,000 members nationwide: 'Guerrilla activity is what made the authorities abandon this place for ten years.'

Deep in the jungle? 'No, just up there on the hill.' Monchet waves his finger in the general direction of the landscape, which suddenly looks a lot like that treeline in the opening credits of 'Apocalypse Now'.

Ruben Petrache was one of those relocated to Calauan from the Estero de Paco. He's in his fifties and has been seriously ill. His home now is a spacious terraced hut. It has a tin roof, with tinfoil insulation to keep the heat down, a pretty garden, and a 'mezzanine' arrangement to create two bedrooms, such as you would see in a loft. Ruben's English is not so good, so Monchet translates:

> What he's saying is that although the community [in Estero de Paco] is disrupted, he thinks it's better here. At least for him. Once you get here, after a while, you realize you've become accustomed to conditions that are insanitary; you learn to move on, live in a new way.

Ruben points to the solar panel that provides his electricity; to the barrel for collecting rainwater by the porch that supplements the water they pump from wells. Are there any downsides?

'It would be better if there was a factory here, because we need more jobs,' Monchet summarizes. Later, with a professional translator, I replay the tape and work out what Ruben—handpicked by the camp's authorities—actually said:

> What the people need here is a job. We need a company nearby so that we don't have to go to Manila. Also we need electricity. Many residents here know how to fix electric fans, radios. But the problem is that even if they have the skills, they can't do it because there is no electricity here, so they are forced to go to Manila to find work and earn money to buy food. We are hard workers: and if we don't do anything, we might die of hunger here. That's why many go back to Manila: to look for work and earn money.

In Calauan's covered market the stalls are plentifully stocked with meat, rice and vegetables, but there are more stallholders than shoppers. Gloria Cruz, thirty-eight years old, is performing on the karaoke machine to three toddlers, two other mums, the Armalite-toting soldiers and me. After a couple of verses she hits the pause button and says:

'My husband commutes to Manila to work. He comes back at weekends. It's the same for everybody. There's nothing here.'

### The tolerated slum

*Makati, Manila*. I have an appointment to interview Jejomar Binay, the country's vice president, who is responsible for slum clearance. But when I arrive in the vestibule of his office, he turns out to have a throat infection, which prevents his attendance.

Felino Palafox is more accessible. Palafox is an architect who specializes in vast, space-age projects in the Middle East and Asia: mosques, Buddhist temples, futuristic towers on the Persian Gulf, always for people with money to burn. But now he's come up with a private scheme to save the Estero de San Miguel: to rebuild it, *in situ,* with new materials.

The plan is to clear it bit by bit and put in modular housing. Each plot will measure 10 m$^2$, the ground floor reserved for retail, the floors above extending out over the walkway, just as slum dwellers build their homes—'stealing the air from the planning authorities,' Palafox calls it. 'The slum-dwellers are experts at live-work space design, they spontaneously do mixed use. We just have to learn from them.'

From the roof of the office block in Makati, Manila's central business district, where his practice is headquartered, Palafox gives me a primer in what's gone wrong. He indicates the nearby skyscrapers: 'monuments to graft'. He points out the gated compounds where the rich live, downtown. To the government, which complains that his design is too expensive, he says:

'Okay, if the total cost of rehousing slum dwellers in situ is 30 per cent of GDP, well, I calculate we lose about 30 per cent of the country's wealth through corruption: if we didn't have corruption, we wouldn't need to tolerate slums.'

He sees the Estero de San Miguel as a test case. If he can make his plans work there, the approach could be applied to every one of the city's riverine slums. So the stakes are huge.

Father Norberto Carcellar, who has worked his whole life with Manila's poor, thinks the elites are engaged in a monumental exercise of self-deception over slum clearance:

> We have to recognize the value slum dwellers deliver to the city. These are the ones who drive your car, clean your house, run your store. If these people are cleared from the city, the city will die. The slum dwellers add social, political and economic value to the city.

That sentiment would have seemed alien to our grandparents' generation. I can still hear mine, brought up Edwardian poverty in a coal and cotton town in northern England, spitting out the word 'slum' with disgust. For them, slums meant dog-eat-dog: the dirty world where solidarity could not flourish, where people lived like animals and brutalized their kids.

But thirty years of globalization have produced something in the slums of the global south that defies that stereotype. And with Mena Cinco at my side I'm about to witness it.

### Facebook in the passageways

*Estero de San Miguel, dusk.* As it is Saturday night, there is a full complement of beefy guys with sticks, rice-flails and flashlights: the volunteer police force of the Estero de San Miguel. With Mena—her t-shirt I now realize identifies her as the 'captain' of the slum—I re-enter the Estero down an alleyway opposite a McDonald's. From this entry point you would hardly know the slum was there. As the alley narrows and jinks around, suddenly I am in a novel by Charles Dickens.

On a narrow bridge, a man squats over a barbecue. Because of the smoke I don't see it is a bridge until I'm on it, or that below is a canal, about two metres wide. The dwellings are built so close that the mothers peering out of upstairs bedrooms, made of wooden boxes, could shake their neighbours' hands. If you decided to remake *Oliver Twist* as an expressionist movie, and this was the set design, you would sack the designer for making it too grotesque.

We head down into the tunnel, stooping now: it's less than five feet high here. After passing a few guys playing poker, and a stray chicken, I come to a store run by Agnes Cabagauan. It sells the same things as every slum store in the world: sachets of Silvikrin and Head & Shoulders, the Filipino version of Marlboros, lighters; tiny plastic bags of oil, fish and salt—enough for one meal only.

'My parents helped me set up the store to pay for my education,' Agnes tells me. What is she studying? 'Business Admin. I have a degree. Actually I also have a day job in a large corporation, coding in a sales department.'

But you live here? 'Yes. I was born here.' She is twenty-two years old.

Then we run into Mena's son: he's an engineering student. And as we cross over another bridge, the unmistakable whizz and pop of something digital comes blasting across the stagnant water: it's an Internet café.

Nine computers are crammed into a harshly lit plywood room. A dog yaps around, some kids are on Facebook, others are playing online poker. One young woman is doing her CV; another is engrossed in a multiplayer dancing game called 'Audition'. She too is at college, she tells me, flipping nonchalantly between her BlackBerry and the game. 'Business Admin?' Yup.

In the space of a hundred yards I've met three graduates, a DIY police force and the social media revolution. And as I become used to the smoke, the wailing and chatter of children, the chickens, the confined space, I've learned what one billion people around the world have had to learn: it is not so bad.

'Other places have prostitution: we don't,' says Mena. 'We get drunks and a bit of drug-taking, but it's under control. We look out for each other; we can see everything that happens; it's one big family. The main job for the volunteer police is to look out for arsonists.'

Settlements under threat of clearance have a habit of getting burned down, on the orders—the slum dwellers believe—of the authorities or the landlords.

In the five-foot high niche that is her living room and kitchen, Mena discourses on the finer details of social policy until at last I ask the question I should have asked when I first met her: how did she become so politically literate? 'I majored in political science at the University of Manila.'

What slum dwellers have produced—not just here but in Cairo, Nairobi, Rio and La Paz—is something the slum-clearance Tsars of yesteryear would not recognize: the orderly, solidaristic slum. And the debate, at the global level, is no longer about how fast to tear these places down, but how to meet the rapidly developing aspirations of highly educated people living in shacks.

To those who dream that as capitalism develops it will eradicate slums, Cameron Sinclair says dream on:

> You can't fight something that has a stronger model than yourself. It's never going to happen again. The fact of it is that if you tried to do it in some of these informal settlements they could take out the city. They could march on the central business district and it's game over.

Nevertheless it seems, amid the gloom and trash of the San Miguel slum, that to leave these places as they are is a gigantic cop-out. What the global authorities are really saying is not that they're impossible to clear but that they've become essential to a certain form of capitalism.

The cheap labour of the slum dweller undercuts the organized labour of the core workforce and—given two or three decades—shrinks it to a barely organizable minority. In the process the slum dwellers become the core workforce. Meanwhile, the functions of the state change: in the Keynesian era the state was supposed to care for all, but now, across much of the developing world, it leaves large parts of the urban community to their own devices.

Consequently, the city evolves into a nightmare organism of economic apartheid zones that can coexist quite easily, being economically co-dependent, but which you cannot move between. All you can do is educate yourself and wait for one life-changing bit of good luck. But the global system you are part of is out of your control.

In *The Road to Wigan Pier*, George Orwell describes a coal miner as 'a sort of grimy caryatid upon whose shoulders nearly everything that is not grimy is supported'. Neoliberal capitalism has turned the slum dwellers into something similar. It is on their shoulders that the rich-world economy of 'mass luxury' consumption is balanced; it is from the bottle shredders of Cairo that the Chinese sportswear sweatshops get their recycled raw materials; in Nairobi, it's the slum dwellers who troop in at 5 a.m. to pack green beans in factories right next to the airport, so that you'll be able to serve them up for dinner the next day.

And Mena Cinco is not kidding when she insists there is solidarity in the slum. Unlike the 'dangerous classes' romanticized by the anarchists of the nineteenth century, slum dwellers are part of the modern work-force—albeit semi-submerged, hidden, operating off the books. They are a kind of shadow banking system for the mainstream working class, which nobody cares about until it blows up.

## The crystal spirit

It was Friedrich Hayek who said social justice was unachievable and that the inequality and misery produced by capitalism were both moral and logical. What humanity should do, he said, is to 'suppress the feeling that certain differences of reward are unjust. And we have to recognize that only a system where we tolerate grossly unjust differ-ences of reward is capable of keeping the present population of the world in existence.'[3]

What transpired in 2011 was, in this sense, a revolt against Hayek and the principles of selfishness and greed he espoused.

The present system cannot guarantee the existence of 7 billion people on this planet. It cannot even recognize their basic humanity. It can offer the poorest a brutal route out of poverty, but it is paid for by impoverishing the workforce of the west. And it is always conditional, always contingent on growth, which has faltered after 2008 and may not return for years.

Of all the people I met while writing this book, it was Len-len, the woman in the rural shanty town, whose situation seemed most hope-less. The disjunction between her temperament and her circumstance was so extreme that for me she personifies the overwhelming question facing the human race.

It's the same question Orwell asked in 1943, pondering his time in Spain during the Civil War. In the barracks of an anti-fascist militia in Barcelona, he had met a confused Italian volunteer, fascinated by the ability of his superior officers to read a map, and doggedly devoted to libertarian communism. The man's face, Orwell wrote, though shaped by poverty, radiated hope and solidarity: it embodied what he later called the 'crystal spirit'.

The problem of social justice, Orwell insisted, revolves around a simple question:

> Shall people like that Italian soldier be allowed to live the decent, fully human life which is now technically achievable, or shan't they? … I myself believe, perhaps on insufficient grounds, that the common man will win his fight sooner or later, but I want it to be sooner and not later—some time within the next hundred years, say, and not some time within the next ten thousand years. That was the real issue of the Spanish war, and of the last war, and perhaps of other wars yet to come.[4]

That is the question that swims around my head in the heat of Gapan City. Will Len-len move off the land and find a job? Will she earn enough to feed her kids without having to leave them behind to go work as a housekeeper to some Gulf millionaire? Will the eradication of slum poverty be possible in her lifetime or do we have to wait a hundred years?

Using the methods favoured today, it will take at least a century to drag the rural poor out of their present situation. The process will be brutal, too: from the farm to the slum for one, two or maybe three billion people, and from the slum to where? As with the crimes of Stalinism, it will be rationalized: painful, but necessary, like childbirth.

The imperatives to find an alternative route are not just moral. The economic crisis has begun to collide with the long-term strategic problems we knew were going to come in the twenty-first century, but were not expecting to impact so soon: climate change, energy depletion, population stress.

The events of 2011 showed that ordinary people—the 99 per cent celebrated in the Occupy Wall Street protest—have the ability to reshape their circumstances—to achieve in a day what normal progress achieves in years. The plebeian groups that kicked things off—from Iran in 2009 to Egypt, Libya and Chile in 2011, possess, in fact, a surplus of the most valuable properties on earth: skill, ingenuity and intelligence. Info-capitalism has educated them; social media is allowing them to swap experiences beyond borders. But there is a dangerous disconnect between the mass of people, especially the young, and the political structures and systems in place.

If we go on as we are, the route out of poverty for billions of people will take generations. Meanwhile, a small elite will go on getting richer. That is the picture that persists, despite the scenes of elation that gripped Cairo, Tunis and Tripoli, despite the occupations of public space from Santiago to Wall Street.

But the events of 2011 show simply this: that no situation is hopeless, and everything is susceptible to change. Against the life-destroying impacts of poverty, inequality and monopolized power, millions of people now realize the truth of what was chanted in Tahrir Square:

> When the people decide to live,
> Destiny will obey,
> Darkness will disappear
> And chains will be broken.

# 11

## Spain Redux: Dispatches from Utopia[*]

*City of Valencia, September 2012.* Paula, the pharmacist, has a sharp diagonal fringe and a grin that suggests she not only understands English but could crack jokes in it if she chose to. But she chooses to speak in Spanish. Because what is happening in Valencia is no fun. The sign on the wall tells the story:

> Important information. The government of Valencia owes this pharmacy for all the medicine we have dispensed to you in January, February, March, April and May.

And not just this pharmacy. The government of Valencia—which runs the health system—owes a grand total of half a billion euros to the region's pharmacies. Paula guides me into that back room that exists in all pharmacies, where the prescription drugs are kept. The problem is, now, that there are not many drugs left. 'Look, this drawer is usually full,' she says, pointing to where the suppositories are kept. 'Now there

---

[*] Since the original version of this book was published the Occupy movement took centre stage in the USA, the Russian protests went through the entire cycle of flowering and repression, and important movements such as those in Chile and Canada took place. I've spent the past twelve months trying to cover these events firsthand, mainly as part of my day job as a TV reporter. In the next four chapters I revisit Greece and Spain, survey the impact of the Russian movement up to the jailing of Pussy Riot, and offer a critical re-reading of my original blogpost 'Twenty Reasons Why It's Kicking Off Everywhere'.

are only two packets.' She opens the fridge. 'Look,' she says, 'we're down to our last packs of insulin. We just have no money to buy the stock.'

I ask: 'What happens if several people come in on the same day for insulin?' She makes two fingers walk along the back of her wrist. 'They have to go around the neighbourhood to see if anybody else has it. It's the same with drugs for heart disease, stroke, anti-retrovirals.'

It is an ordinary pharmacy, clean and white, with the regulation green neon cross outside. Now quite a lot of the patients are having to do something that is, for them, extraordinary: they are having to pay for their medicines. There is a sign on the door explaining the new charges. It's all part of the great story of bankruptcy and disillusion that has swept Spain in the summer of 2012. The government, the regions and the banks are effectively bust.

For the regions the problem is particularly acute. They spend money, but have limited powers to raise it. During the property boom, which has now left Spain insolvent, regions like Valencia were collecting some taxes—but they came mainly from property, and have dried up. Now that source of revenue is gone, they are expecting the central government to provide them with the cash they need. But the central government is in trouble too: it cannot borrow—except at punitive rates. The regions cannot borrow, either. Valencia is in debt to the tune of €25 billion—21 billion to the financial markets, 4 billion in unpaid bills to traders like Paula. Who does she blame? She smiles bitterly from beneath the diagonal fringe: 'That is a very hard question to answer.'

In the orange-blossom heat outside Valencia's cathedral, there are people who do not find that question hard at all. They are holding up a banner: 'The Route of Waste'. Activists have organized a coach trip around all the various projects Valencia built in the good times. There is the Formula One racetrack, which was built right through the city so that the roads had to be redesigned. But the city has lost its Formula One race. There is the America's Cup dock, with huge sheds for ocean-going yachts and a massive white control tower. But there is no more America's Cup racing in Valencia. There is the Opera House, a cross between the one in Sydney and something by Gaudí on acid: €400 million to build, 40 million a year to run—fifteen performances a year. 'Yes, I am proud of it,' says Xabi, one of the activists on the tour. 'Yes, the architecture is spectacular. But I would rather have schools.'

Whether by corruption—and there has been a great deal of that—maladministration, or pure bad luck, Valencia is littered with vanity projects that tell their own story. The brand-new airport that has never seen a single plane land. The theme park built in a place where the summer heat rises above 40°C (104°F). The land bought at premium prices, which is now worthless.

The local press were also on the coach trip. And the next day I find out what they were working on. Headlines about me. According to these, the BBC's 'star economics expert' has come to Valencia to pour scorn on their wonderful infrastructure projects. The story makes the national conservative daily *ABC*, and it doesn't stop there. Angry voices at the government's official weekly press conference demand: Why are the BBC here? Have you given them an interview? Will you give us an interview about what you told them in their interview?

'It is Spain,' sighs Máximo Buch, the new financial controller of Valencia, when I finally get to meet him. Yes, Spain—where the arrival of the foreign media makes a nice story for the right-wing papers, but where massive white-elephant projects went unquestioned for a decade, and where the local banks that funded them, known as *cajas de ahorro*, their boards stuffed with appointed politicians, have now gone bust. And where if you need some insulin from the health service, you had better hope you are the first in the queue.

*Seville, Andalusia*. The Spanish version of the soprano cornet is tiny: it curls like a golden snail in the player's hand. There is only one valve, and it is tweaked, like a tap, so that the melody it produces swoops and squeals. In an English brass band there is only one soprano, whose job is to add a sweet echo, one octave higher, to the main melody. In the La Pasión Sevilla band, all the cornets are sopranos. In fact, between the massed ranks of burly working-class men playing their cornetas and the heavy drum detachment at the back, only a few trumpets and horns are present to add harmony and depth. The result, if you stand close as the band shuffles behind a statue of the Madonna through the humid alleyways of the old Triana district, is an aural mixture that is at the same time saccharine-sweet and physically painful.

By the summer of 2012, policymakers across Europe had reason to be thankful for Pasión Sevilla and its cornets, Triana with its statues and incense, the tight knots of local people gathered at the corners of tiny cobbled streets. Because family and tradition, religion, brass bands and social solidarity were all that was holding many communities in Spain together.

One in four adults was unemployed. Half of all young people were jobless. Consumer spending was in free fall, and the country had just learned that to save a single bank would add a third to its already sky-high national debt. Meanwhile its top-thirty listed companies had lost 40 per cent of their market value in a year. Spain was in trouble, on the face of it, because its small savings and loans banks, the *cajas*, fuelled an insane property boom that went bust. They didn't go in for complex structured finance deals, like Lehman Brothers; indeed they were the opposite of 'Anglo-Saxon' capitalism, being small and locally owned.

But behind the purely economic story lies a more complex, political–economic crisis that threatens to send Spain the same way as Greece, shattering the eurozone in the process and placing the whole European project in grave doubt.

You can see how badly the crisis has hit people at the 'Coralla Utopia' apartment block. It's a new, modern, five-storey complex next to a busy road. The flats are small: perfect for young professionals and their minimalist furniture. But the company that built the flats went broke, and now the whole place has been squatted by families turfed out of their own homes, due to repossession. Toni Rodríguez leads me around the darkened corridors (the electricity company has cut the power supply):

'We had weekly meetings for four months and we realized we were all in the same situation, and finally we decided to do something about it. When we took over the building I was frightened, because I've seen things on TV where they drag people out. The banks need to adapt the mortgage system to avoid kicking people out of their homes.'

Toni is forty-four years old, her tanned and weathered skin marked by the kind of tattoos you do with some blue ink and your own needle. She's one of a tight group of women—mainly cleaning workers—who've organized the occupation. They all have children of working age who are unemployed. They resent the banks for evicting them and the politicians for bailing out the banks. Around the edges of the project move people from a completely different demographic: the so-called *indignados* of the 15M movement—anti-globalist youth with trade-mark tattoos and piercings. The *indignados* made world headlines after massive occupation protests in public squares in May 2011, in turn sparking the global Occupy movement.

When you see the Utopia flats, draped with banners announcing 'no homes without people, no people without homes', you see what happens when official politics abandons people. Very ordinary, indeed anti-political people have begun to turn to Spain's radical youth for help. They in turn have found a purpose, here and elsewhere, outside mainstream politics, which they despise. For at the heart of Spain's economic problem is its political system. In the first place, there is the system of autonomous regions: Andalusia, like Valencia, is bankrupt and in need of a bailout. And on top of the regions, there is the highly politicized banks.

Bankia, the bank at the centre of the crisis, was created only in 2011, through a merger of seven troubled *cajas*. They pooled their debts, took bailout money from the government, sunk some of their bad debts into a government fund and sold shares in the merged company, appointing former IMF boss Rodrigo Rato as the CEO. What could go wrong?

As it turned out, Bankia was hiding bad debts that would need €24 billion to sort out. The two largest *cajas* that formed Bankia were both effectively controlled by politicians from the ruling Partido Popular. One has recently walked away with a €14 million payoff, despite presiding over the biggest bank collapse in Spanish history. Rato, the CEO, was officially charged with fraud after the *indignados* brought a class action to the same effect. When opposition politicians called for a parliamentary inquiry into the bank's collapse, the PP used its parliamentary majority to quash the proposal. Ditto any attempt to force Mr Rato to testify before a parliamentary committee.

Raúl Limón, the Seville-based political correspondent for the newspaper *El País*, told me:

'The *cajas* were banks who used regular economic rules but with a political background—so it's like getting a politician to hold your money. That's a *caja*. So maybe the politicians should be answering questions in parliament—and maybe they should be on trial. They paid three or four times the true value of land. They demonstrated economic growth and people believed they used the *cajas* to enhance social well-being—we now know they were buying land and selling illusions.'

If Spain's banking crisis had happened in a sound economy, it might have been containable. But by mid-2012, Spain's debt was growing uncontrollably. It would need a bailout. And EU/IMF bailouts come with one condition: increased austerity.

In a place like Andalusia, austerity will fall hard on people. It's an underdeveloped region where, as in so much of euro-bolstered southern Europe, the biggest economic player is the state. The landscape is spectacular: the Sierra Nevada with its cowlicks of snow, even in summer, floats above rolling hillsides planted with olives, oranges and wheat. But there's a global olive-oil crisis: the regional government had to inject €62 million into olive-oil cooperatives to tide them over the collapse in prices. The regional unemployment rate is 30 per cent, and many farm labourers feel trapped by the current crisis, which, says Lola Alvarez, is just the intensification of a land crisis which is 'always there'.

Lola is a union organizer at Somonte, a farm abandoned as unworkable three years ago, which has now been squatted by some fifty people who are trying to revive it as an eco-farm. The directions to Somonte are 'Drive to a certain kilometre marker and look out for the flags.' The flags, of course, display the face of Che Guevara. It's early, so the occupiers—who sleep nose to toe on the floor of two tiny farm buildings—are still stumbling into the ritual breakfast of black coffee and roll-ups that is the *indignado*'s staple diet. Some are farm labourers, some itinerant anarchists, some both. Lola tells me:

'Before the crisis, because of low pay on the land, the majority of farm workers switched to the construction sector. Their jobs were taken by migrants, and also by mechanization. Now that construction has collapsed, there's very little work on the land.'

But this is not yet a crisis of despair. Whereas in Greece, two years of rioting and political incompetence fuelled the rise of 'anomic breakdown'—social rootlessness and hopelessness—Spain has gone the other way. People have clung to their families, their village roots, their religion (and their secondary religion, which is football). Many young people have formed protest camps. Their bible is Stéphane Hessel's *Indignez-vous!*, a plea for resistance against bank-controlled austerity, and for non-violence.

At the political level, for all the perennial fractiousness of Catalan and Basque politics, for all the allegations of corruption, the system is holding in a way that the Greek system did not. There is no rapid formation and fragmentation of parties; no collapse of elites into warring factions. But it could still happen. And Spanish people know better than anybody in Europe how nasty it can get if politics fails. On the Somonte farm, out of the blue, the occupiers are buzzed by men flying powered microlites. It's a joke at first, until they spot that two of the flyers are displaying Francoist flags, and realize that it's an airborne counter-protest.

Lola points to an old man sitting quietly at the edge of the group of farm workers. 'That's my father,' she says. 'In the Civil War the local landowners, Francoists, made him drink olive oil and eat grasshoppers to force him to vomit up the "red" that was inside him. But don't ask him about it ...' She draws two lines down her cheeks with stiff fingers. 'He cannot tell the story without crying.'

*Colmenar, Andalusia.* 'Drive up this road until we meet Gordillo,' I tell the taxi driver outside Malaga airport, in broken Spanish. The only word he understands is Gordillo. We climb a narrow highway into the Sierra Nevada, the meter ticking satisfyingly towards a hundred bucks. Just where my phone's GPS tells me the demonstration should be, we spot flags in the distance, a procession and the flashing lights of police cars. 'Gordillo!' says the taxi driver, beaming.

It's September now, and the landscape is turning crisp and brown. But the small streets of Colmenar—a farming town—are hot. With my luggage and my jacket and my absence of blood-curdling anarcho-syndicalist rhetoric, I cause a minor commotion as I work my way up the march to find Gordillo.

'What the fuck is this asshole doing?' one old farm worker shouts. 'Journalist,' I say, showing my DSLR camera.

'Fuck journalists!' he shouts at me, and to his mates around him: 'Fuck the journalists.'

'Sindicato!' I call back, waving my NUJ card at them. They laugh, with their weather-cracked faces, and break into some kind of song that either means I am okay or that even unionized journalists are still the running dogs of capital.

In the tiny square of Colmenar, the marchers are receiving their rations: tortilla wraps and bottled water. They're a mixture of activists from the land workers union, some 15M-style youth—but not many— and unemployed people, including numerous women. At the corner of the square, looking dazed, stands Mayor Juan Manuel Sánchez Gordillo. He's wearing a neat Palestinian scarf and his face is sunburnt;

with his gap tooth and wonky eye, the dehydration and exhaustion of the morning's march have left him looking slightly crazy.

Gordillo is mayor of the Andalusian town of Marinaleda, long a legendary place to the social movements for its decades-old communal way of managing the land and its crops. Now it's become legendary for something else: with Gordillo in attendance, the land workers union has begun expropriating food from supermarkets—using force on the odd occasion when the checkout people tried to stop them—and then distributing it to the unemployed.

Now Gordillo has launched this march from town to town, to lay down a marker of more civil disobedience against the austerity to come. Lola Alvarez, who I met on the Somonte farm, is here. Can it achieve anything, I ask? She points at the armada of police cars with their spinning lights. 'We achieved this. They are terrified of us.' Another man chips in, one of the union leaders:

'People don't want to hear about bonds, Merkel, European banks. They want to talk about the cost of a bottle of cooking gas, the cost of medicine, mortgages, work, expectations—and that's what this march is letting them do.'

When I finally get Gordillo to talk to me, it's the wordstream of a man who's making three speeches a day in 40 degree heat.

'Another Europe is necessary,' Gordillo tells me. 'A Europe of the people; a Europe of the ones who have nothing. The unemployed, the poor, the people who demand a new reality.'

But Gordillo has become articulate with actions, not words. The expropriations have started to be repeated, like a meme. There's already been heavy fighting in the northern mining region of Asturias, where the miners made their own RPGs out of dynamite and skyrockets and lead piping, and showed no hesitation in firing them at the cops.

It is the physical demographic of the Gordillo movement that has brought so many Guardia Civil onto these ribbons of melting tarmac in the high hills. These protesters are working-class; they have roots in society; they have more to lose than the young *indignados*. There are not many red flags on display; Che, as always, is the patron saint of the t-shirt. The flags are mainly Andalusian regional flags and union banners.

'They say I'm the Spanish Robin Hood,' Gordillo tells me. 'I prefer William Wallace, like in *Braveheart*. He was a true revolutionary—he came from the lower classes and fought and demanded real change for his people.'

'But he was defeated,' I interject.

'Well, in the struggle you always have winners and losers; but the one battle you never lose is the battle for Utopia.'

*Barcelona, Catalonia.* 'When you go on a Catalan national day demo,' says journalistic folklore, 'your risk assessment has to include the danger of getting blinded. By the diamonds.'

The mass demo on the Catalan national day in September 2012 attracted the usual mixture of the bourgeois and the proletariat. Right-wing nationalists from the Convergence and Union Party, left-wing and communist workers; ladies with Gucci handbags; *indignados* with the word 'fuck' liberally scrawled on their placards. But when 1.5 million people from all walks of life go onto the streets, you can't ignore it.

It certainly riled Francisco Alamán: 'Independence for Catalonia? Over my dead body … and those of many soldiers,' he told a right-wing website. It's a view quite strongly held in Spain. But Alamán is a serving soldier, a colonel in the Spanish army. And it wasn't the only incendiary thing he said. In the week tens of thousands of protesters surrounded parliament, he also observed that: 'The current situation is very similar to 1936, but without blood. Unfortunately, the data indicate that the situation will only get worse in the coming months and years.'

As a journalist covering the aftermath of a financial crisis, you learn to ask yourself a very brutal question as you parachute into the latest theatre of conflict: you look for the social silence. You ask: what is staring me in the face, that nobody wants to talk about?

Colonel Alamán had answered the question. 1936 was the year the Spanish Popular Front government was attacked by rebel forces under General Franco, beginning a three-year civil war in which 300,000 died on the battlefield, and the same number again were murdered off it.

During the early years of Spanish democracy, forgetting about the Civil War was not just a psychological necessity—it was a political choice. The 'pact of silence' instituted after the death of Franco was seen as a price worth paying for rapid, peaceful transition to a functioning democracy—a democracy that, moreover, found space to accommodate a strong, previously clandestine Communist Party alongside the rapidly moderating socialists of the PSOE (Spanish Socialist Workers' Party). The approach was codified into law, with the 1977 Amnesty Law guaranteeing blanket immunity from prosecution for those suspected of crimes against humanity during the Franco era and the Civil War.

But with Spain now reeling from austerity, its riot police dispensing truncheon blows and rubber bullets against demonstrators and passers-by, the 'pact of silence' was falling apart. The images of violence—not all of them made it onto mainstream television, but the Internet did the job—were forcing Spanish people to confront historical memory in a way the various campaigns and lawsuits about the Franco era had not. For the austerity, and the protests, had summoned the spectre of a clash that defined Spain in the modern period: the clash between liberal modernity and religious, monarchic hierarchy: 'A dead, hollow, worm-eaten Spain and a new, eager, ambitious Spain that tends toward life,' as the historian Santos Juliá put it.

It's clear now that these two cultures within Spain—as visceral and rooted as the 'southern' and 'liberal' cultures in the US, or the 'intellectual versus peasant' problem in Russia—never went away. But the culture war had seemed suppressed by wealth: the booming economy, the rapid liberalization of society, and the massive investment in modern infrastructure allowed the two Spains to coexist.

By the eve of the Lehman crisis it was a different Spain—a modernized economy linked to the European core by its single currency and the Schengen agreement, and benefiting on top of that from its links to the rapidly expanding economies of Latin America. When the economy took a nosedive, and the first austerity plans were launched, it was striking that the political and social settlement seemed actually to be helping mitigate the effects. People moved in with their parents, borrowed their grandmother's car; in small towns and villages, barter systems sprang up. Spain's regional government system would also act as a safety net for the needy.

But as the situation worsened, in rapid succession, numerous signifiers of political crisis appeared: acute class divisions, regional politics, street violence, outright civil disobedience in the Gordillo mould, and unaddressed corruption. The removal of migrants' rights to free health care; the sight of uniformed firefighters clashing with riot cops, helmet to helmet, on the streets of Madrid. Such images of fracture feed the resurgence of references to the bloody conflict in which the 'two Spains' tried to destroy each other.

To the right, we find people like Col Alamán. To the left, the *camiseta republicana*. It's a version of the Spanish soccer team's red and yellow strip, with the addition of a big swathe of republican purple: the colours of the flag Franco tore down in 1936. I'd first spotted these shirts on Gordillo's march in Colmenar. They started being produced in 2011 as a limited edition for enthusiasts; now, they are close to becoming the dress code on some protests.

Beneath this battle of signifiers, there is a serious potential for fragmentation in Spain. Once it had been refused a favourable fiscal deal, the Catalan government called snap elections. The ruling party—the Convergence and Union Party—contains a strong minority that advocates outright independence. The far left in Catalonia also supports independence. As the second richest region, with a GDP of €220 billion a year, it's always been seen as an empty threat for Catalonia to go for full independence. Cynics say its flirtation with secession is mere posturing to gain a better settlement with Madrid. In view of the 2012 Independence Day march, however, others on the ground are saying: 'This time they mean it.'

Before the austerity hit, there were a whole series of unthinkables in Spain: that the Civil War wounds, of right and left, could ever be reopened; that the military could ever again intervene into politics (the last time this happened, the attempted Civil Guard coup of 1981, descended into farce); that the modernization and growth that Spain enjoyed could ever be reversed; that the federal state could ever shatter. But numerous unthinkables have already begun to happen.

*Madrid.* To get into Felipe González's HQ you have to be ID'd and searched by a plainclothes cop. Then you step into a rickety elevator, and ascend a few floors of the old mansion block. The air conditioning is basic, so when the man himself greets me, in a denim shirt, we are both perspiring.

González is one of the architects of the Europe that is falling apart. Emerging from the socialist underground after the death of Franco, he put together the PSOE, and after 1982 led the fourteen-year-long socialist administration that made Spain what it is today. He was, towards the end, mired in allegations of corruption and of unleashing a dirty war by police death squads against the Basque separatists. But to some, Felipe is still the Mandela of Spanish democracy.

He rails at Angela Merkel. Germany, he tells me, has become a German Germany, not a European Germany. He still believes Europe can become competitive without trashing the welfare system and dirigiste investment model that Spain relies on.

'But it's in danger, the welfare state. If this economic model disappears, social cohesion is going to suffer, without a doubt. That's what's in danger. People feel the loss of something that they didn't cause—and they're right. But they're not being offered an economic model that permits social cohesion.'

Social democrats like González are seeing their preconceptions hollowed out. The capitalism that could offer a 'social Europe' is disappearing, putting the political consensus in jeopardy: 'The scale of disaffection for the national government, it's enormous. For the autonomous governments it's enormous. There's disaffection with politics —it's quite universal. Representative democracy as we know it is in crisis.'

González led the Spanish left through a peaceful transition away from fascism. The deal was that the old elite would populate both sides of the political spectrum—but without any formal accounting of the events during fascism. Today it is hard not to see that compromise as one of the roots of the corruption that, as an *ABC* editorial claimed two years ago, 'is drowning Spain'. There is heavy and open nepotism in the appointment of business executives; there is—say foreign business people—an unstated regulatory bias in favour of Spanish-owned large companies. And there has been mismanagement of resources, leading to the wasteful spending and lax planning that I found in Valencia.

The problem is not that Spain is a 'young democracy': young democracies can be vigorous, culturally revolutionary, fun places to be. No, the problem is that, as Spaniards gaze at TV images of metre-long truncheons being wielded against passers-by in a Metro station, the discourse tends to head straight to where, for thirty years, they have managed to keep it from heading.

I put it to González that Spain is now paying the price for the compromises made during the transition. He winces. 'That's wrong. We're paying the price for failing to modernize. It's the people who didn't live through Franco who have a lot of difficulty evaluating what we achieved.'

Spain has the potential to explode in a way that Greece does not. It is a major global economy. Its post-fascist political settlement is weakening. Catalan and Basque independence calls mean its survival as a

226

federal state is under threat. Once Mario Draghi decided to save the euro by buying unlimited amounts of Spanish and Italian bonds, in September 2012—Spain knew that even if it avoided bankruptcy it would have to face years of austerity and stagnation.

Faced with all this, what the *indignado* movement represents may correctly be called a 'counter-power' to the old elites, whose money has dried up but whose hands remain firmly on the levers of state. But it is only a counter-power.

It is, of all the mass movements thrown up during 2011–12, probably the one with greatest persistent social weight in its own country. It is one where, until now, non-violence has been rigorously adhered to—and it has forged the strongest links with 'real life': with local cultures, endemic labour movements, popular milieus. Juanjo García, the young activist who took me into the Coralla Utopia occupation in Seville, explains the challenge like this:

'Right now we are so close to disaster that we have to stick to two objectives. One is doing stuff like this, taking over the apartment block—to focus attention on the problems of real people. To show it can be done. But then we have to offer an alternative. We have to force the government to pass new laws that help the people, not the banks.'

With his wispy beard and flip-flops and t-shirt reading 'La Huelga' (The Strike), this twenty-odd-year-old is the kind of person the future outcome of this crisis is going to revolve around.

'Sometimes,' says Juanjo, 'it seems like we've created a collective intelligence that can move very quickly—we can solve big problems in minutes because the situation we found ourselves in demanded it. But we need victories, we need hope, we need to do things that make people think there is a solution. That's what made people from different ideologies, movements, strategies work together in a project like this. Before this we never had such objectives—it's new—but it's because the situation is really critical.'

# 12

# Developments in Greece: Love or Nothing

Of all the operas written during Germany's Weimar Republic (1919–33), probably the most haunting is the last. Kurt Weill's *The Silver Lake*, written with playwright Georg Kaiser, tells the story of two losers—a good-hearted provincial cop and the thief he has shot and wounded—as they make their way through a society ruined by unemployment, corruption and vice.

In 2012, after spending a week in Greece amid riots, hunger and far-right violence, I finally understood it. The opera was meant to be Weill's ticket back into the mainstream. It was his first break from collaborating with Bertolt Brecht, and was scheduled to open simultaneously in three German cities on 18 February 1933.

But on 30 January, Adolf Hitler was appointed Germany's chancellor. The first performances of *The Silver Lake* were disrupted by Nazi activists in the audience, and on 4 March 1933 it was banned. The score was torched, together with the set designs, in an infamous book-burning ceremony outside the opera house in Berlin.

It is easy to see why the Nazis didn't like *The Silver Lake*. Weill being Jewish, their theatre critics found the music 'ugly and sick'. Moreover the plot contains an allegory of the political situation on the eve of the Nazis' rise to power. But there is something else about *The Silver Lake* that goes beyond politics. Something hard to fathom. Spending time in Greece, as the far-right Golden Dawn Party was breaking up theatre performances with impunity, and street violence was rife, I finally understood what that something is.

*The Silver Lake* is ultimately about how people feel when they switch from resistance to hopelessness, and about how strangely liberating hopelessness can be.

Greece right now is a place with a lot of hopelessness. Its own prime minister, Antonis Samaras, has compared the current climate to that of the late Weimar Republic. 'Greek democracy stands before what is perhaps its greatest challenge,' Samaras told the German newspaper *Handelsblatt*. He said social cohesion is 'endangered by rising unemployment, just as it was toward the end of the Weimar Republic in Germany'.

The comparison seems plausible on several fronts. There are far-right gangs meting out violence on the streets (a report in October 2012 identified more than half of all officially recorded racial attacks as perpetrated by people in paramilitary uniform). Every demonstration ends with tear gas and baton charges. There is mass unemployment. There is the collapse of mainstream parties. The press and broadcast media are struggling to remain independent, indeed solvent.

Yet the comparison with the 'end of Weimar' only holds if you know nothing about the Weimar Republic itself. Sadly, this condition is common. School students are rightly taught a great deal about Nazi Germany, but not very much about how it came into being.

In the elections of 1928, the Nazis, who had—like Golden Dawn in Greece—been reduced to a splinter group in the years of economic recovery, got just 2.7 per cent of the vote. But in March 1930, as the Wall Street Crash cratered the German economy, a cross-party coalition government of the centre-left and -right collapsed. It was replaced by the first of three 'appointed' governments, led by Heinrich Brüning and designed to prevent either the communists or the now-growing Nazis gaining power. Faced with a recession, Brüning followed a policy of austerity while keeping Germany's currency pegged to the Gold Standard (much as Greece as follows a policy of austerity dictated by euro membership). This made the recession worse.

As unemployment rocketed, so did the Nazi vote: in a shock breakthrough they came second in the elections of September 1930, with 18 per cent. But Brüning was determined to maintain order: he cracked down on both the right and left, banning the Nazi paramilitary organization, the *sturmabteilung*, along with the rival communist uniformed groups.

As recession worsened, the Nazis grew massively: they came first in the election in 1932, gaining 14 million votes (37 per cent). Although the socialists and communists combined polled higher, while the parties of the centre collapsed, the presidential system of appointing governments nevertheless allowed the remnants of conservatism to go on ruling Germany—now under a new Chancellor, the aristocrat Franz von Papen. Von Papen unbanned the Nazi stormtroopers in June 1932 and, as street clashes escalated, a low-level civil war took off.

By the end of 1932, with the communists now also growing rapidly, the political establishment made one final attempt to pre-empt the move to outright fascist rule—by appointing a right-wing militarist, Kurt von Schleicher, and further constraining democracy. Schleicher had written:

> I am really glad that there is a counterweight [to the Social Democrats] in the form of the Nazis, who are not very decent chaps either and must be stomached with the greatest caution. If they did not exist, we should virtually have to invent them.[1]

Schleicher was appointed Chancellor, and tried to form a government with the support of everybody from the left wing of the Nazis to the Christian trades unions. But this too failed, opening the door to Hitler. The historian Ian Kershaw has written of this fiasco:

> Only crass errors by the country's rulers could open up a path [for Hitler]. And only a blatant disregard by Germany's power elites for

safeguarding democracy—in fact, the hope that economic crisis could be used as a vehicle to bring about democracy's demise and replace it by a form of authoritarianism—could induce such errors. Precisely this is what happened.[2]

The names of Brüning, von Papen and Schleicher, troublesome though they are to remember, should be as famous as the words Stalingrad, Arnhem and Dunkirk. These were the men who tried and failed to use a mixture of economic austerity, authoritarianism and what we might now call 'technocratic' rule to avoid an outright fascist takeover. They thought the Nazis were malleable tools in the continued rule of the old elite, and they played to the gallery of Nazi populism on race and nation.

And therein lies the parallel with Greece: a country committed to austerity, whose centrist parties are clustered into a coalition which represents all the remaining forces of conservatism and social democracy. The coalition, which sees itself as the last bulwark against a government of the far left, is trying to crack down on 'extremism' using a police force which has itself been criticized for extremist leanings.

But despite these parallels, at time of writing Greece was not on the brink of a Weimar-style collapse. Nor was it 'in civil war' as claimed by Ilias Panagiotaros, the deputy leader of Golden Dawn, when I interviewed him for the BBC. If anything, Greece displayed—by the time of the passing of its third austerity memorandum in November 2012—levels of instability and political radicalization closer to the levels seen in Germany in early 1930, not late 1933. The problem was that Greece was approaching 1933 levels of *economic* collapse.

Unemployment was 30 per cent in Germany when Hitler took power; it was 25.1 per cent and rising in Greece in late 2012. GDP collapsed by about 7 per cent in both 1931 and 1932 in Germany. Its current rate of collapse in Greece is roughly the same: 7 per cent per year. Germany's banks had gone bust in 1931. Greek banks are effectively part nationalized already.

You can see the physical impact of this on Stadiou Street in Athens. There was an arcade where, in the summer of 2011, I remember blogging about how its small specialist businesses in Greece were doomed: the pen shop, the coin collecting shop, the stationery store. They're all gone now. So is much of the street itself. The Art Nouveau cinema was burned out last year; the Marfin Bank, next door, was torched with the death of three workers during a riot in 2010. On the walls somebody has spray-canned 'Love or Nothing'. Right now there is a heck of a lot of nothing: shops closed, stripped, barred, graffitied, even the fascias chipped off as ammunition in riots.

And nowhere is the human impact of this weird situation clearer than when you talk to young people.

I met Yiannis and Maria in a bare flat in Exarcheia, the bohemian district of Athens. Despite their bruises and bandages they took some persuading to go on camera—anonymously and in their hoodies—to put on record their allegations of brutality in police custody. What struck me, beyond those allegations (denied by the police, but partially corroborated by a coroner's report), was their detachment from regular life. They expected the police to be brutal fascists. They were outraged that they'd had to listen, they said, to Golden Dawn propaganda in the police cells. But they were reluctant to bring a complaint within the system.

For tens of thousands of young people, life is already lived in a semi-underground way: squatting instead of renting; cadging food and roll-ups from their friends. Drifting back to their grandparents' villages, sofa surfing. Yiannis is a sporadically employed technician in a cultural industry; Maria a highly qualified professional who waits tables. The British author Laurie Penny captured the situation in a recent memoir of a trip to Athens: 'We came expecting … riots; instead we found ourselves looking at what happens when the riots die away and the horrified inertia sets in.'[3]

Horrified inertia is now seeping from the world of the semi-outlawed young activists into the lives of ordinary people. What people do—

whether black-hooded anarchists in Athens, or young farmers in Thessaly on their third or fourth bottle of beer by lunchtime—is retreat into the personal. It's no longer 'the personal is political', it's the personal instead of the political. True, demonstrators still turn out in large numbers, as in the October 2012 general strike. But they go through the motions—of demonstrating, of rioting even. 'It's just for show on both sides, the cops and the anarchists,' I was told by my Greek fixer as we legged it through stampeding people and tear gas.

In 2011 the buzzword was 'anomie': a listless rejection of the rule of law, with individuals beginning to make their own law, from lifting up the gates at road tolls to invading court hearings to disrupt house repossessions. There is not even much of that 'anomic' activism anymore; the movement that defied road tolls in 2011 is tiny in 2012. If anything captures the buzz of late 2012 in Greece, it is the person who sprayed the slogan 'Love or Nothing'. It's less about anomie, more about depression and fear. What has depressed and frightened much of Greek society—from the liberal centre-right to the liberal left—is the rapid rise of Golden Dawn.

In the two elections of May/June 2012 this party scored between 6–7 per cent. That is nothing like a 1930-style breakthrough. But once its MPs were in parliament, while austerity gnawed away at the fabric of society, its support leapt to 14 per cent. Then, like the Nazis in the critical years, it began a low-level battle for control of the streets. It began to do DIY law enforcement against migrants, with no intervention from the police. At street markets in Messolonghi and Rafina its uniformed activists checked the permits of migrant stallholders, demonstratively kicking over the wares of those who lacked the right document.

With electoral data showing—on one count—45 per cent of police personnel voting for Golden Dawn, there is rising concern that support for the far right has begun to skew the operational priorities of the police at the local level.

I met the party's second in command, Ilias Panagiotaros, in the back yard of the store he runs: a militaria shop, selling police uniforms to serving officers and Combat 18 t-shirts to football hooligans. In his opinion, 'Greek society is ready—even though no-one likes this—to have a fight: a new type of civil war. On the one side there will be nationalists like us, and Greeks who want our country to be as it used to be, and on the other side illegal immigrants, anarchists and all those who have destroyed Athens several times. Golden Dawn is at war with the political system and those who represent it, with the domestic and international bankers, we are at war with these invaders—immigrants.'

Panagiotaros, one of eighteen fascist MPs, was clear as to the sequencing of the Greek denouement. It would not be like Weimar: it would begin with a left-wing government, and end with the rule of his own party: 'If Syriza wins the next election, we will win the one after that. It is not a dream that within one, two or three years we will be the first political party.'

He claimed support within the police at '60 per cent or more'. And he gave a chilling explanation of how Golden Dawn's extra-judicial actions were affecting the rule of law. Referring to the market stall attacks, he said:

'With one incident, which was on camera, the problem was solved— in every open market all over Greece illegal immigrants disappeared. There was some pushing and some fighting—nothing extraordinary, nothing special—only with one phone call saying Golden Dawn is going to pass by the police in going there, meaning the brand name [of Golden Dawn] is very effective …'

Greece has a massive and conspicuous problem with illegal migra- tion. The centres of many cities are—or were, until the summer of 2012—full of young male migrants from Afghanistan, Somalia, Sudan and increasingly Syria. Many Greeks do fear them, and perceive them as a threat to social order and a traditional lifestyle. This is a country that never had any colonies, and therefore did not experience high ethnic diversity until recently.

The new policy, known as 'Hospitable Zeus', is to round migrants up and put them in camps: police in plain clothes or uniforms visibly stopping every person of colour on the street, checking their papers, and if the papers are not in order processing them ultimately to a migrant detention camp. Even as human rights groups raise the alarm, demanding access to the camps, Golden Dawn has protested outside them on the grounds that conditions are too good there, and that deportations are not fast enough (about six thousand have been detained, with maybe three thousand deported). And even as the police round up the migrants, Golden Dawn's policy is to terrorize them off the streets, and mount a legal campaign against companies who employ them.

The Greek media, meanwhile, has taken its cue to reinforce the association of migrants with crime. For those seeking an alternative view there are only the newspapers of the far left, since the main liberal newspaper—*Eleftherotypia*, an equivalent to the *Guardian*—went bust and closed down.

Just after the June election I met a senior politician from New Democracy, the conservative party. When I asked what his party was going to do about Golden Dawn, the answer was: 'Get an immigration policy. There hasn't been one. All this Golden Dawn stuff is the product of that.'

In the ensuing months Greece 'got' an immigration policy—albeit one where to claim asylum you have to queue overnight on a Friday, week after week, avoid being beaten by the gangs paid by the police to disrupt the queue, and then somehow bribe your way to the front. A policy where people of colour are shamelessly picked off the streets by plainclothes police and herded onto buses to be processed. One where previously buzzing immigrant neighbourhoods like Agias Pandelemonos in Athens have become, in a matter of months, quiet, orderly, and mostly white.

But it has not stopped Golden Dawn. Theodora Oikonomides, a citizen journalist at the alternative radio network Radio Bubble, who has covered the rise of Golden Dawn, voices a fear common to many:

'Golden Dawn's favourite themes, such as xenophobia, homophobia and anti-Semitism have now become part of Greek public discourse, whether at the political or at the social level,' she says. 'By failing to take action against Golden Dawn while nodding and winking to its elector-ate at every opportunity, the Greek politicians—who are now in power with the support of European partners—have opened a Pandora's box that will not close any time soon.'

On 7 November the Greek coalition imposed its latest and, it prom-ised, 'last' round of austerity: €13.5 billion a year in cuts and tax rises, in order to release €31 billion worth of bailout money. It went through by just three votes—more or less reducing the PASOK party in parlia-ment to a handful of veteran leaders.

Now the Coalition will just hold on, hoping that its own electoral support does not send it the way the German centrist parties went after 1932. But electoral support is slipping. While New Democracy has maintained its poll rating at 27 per cent (compared to 29 per cent in the election), PASOK—the former governing socialist party—was by November 2012 down to 5.5 per cent, neck and neck with coalition partner Democratic Left. The combined poll rating of the pro-austerity parties is now 38 per cent.

In the meantime, for the majority of people who want the austerity to stop and who do not want to be gassed, truncheoned, menaced or even to go on strike, there is only the 'love or nothing' strategy. Anecdotally the use of anti-depressants is rising; Penny's book tells numerous tales of former political activists simply stunned by drink and drugs.

Which brings us back to *The Silver Lake*.

The 'love interest' in Kurt Weill's opera doesn't start until the second half, with the arrival of Fennimore, a young woman trapped in a castle with the two losers and a scheming, reactionary aristocrat who has duped them out of their money. Once Fennimore appears, the music becomes mesmerized and lyrical; it focuses on the combined hopelessness of the two men and the girl. And the final sequence—a dream-like fifteen minutes during which the men set out to cross the castle's lake, certain they will drown—is shot through with ecstasy and despair.

'You escape from the horror,' Fennimore sings, 'that may destroy all we know. Yet the germ of creation will struggle to grow.'

> All this can be a beginning,
> And though time turns our day back to night
> Yet the hours of dark will lead onwards
> To the dawning of glorious light.

I had always struggled to understand this ending. Why, in the last days of Weimar, did Kurt Weill not pen a sustained anthem of defiance against Nazism rather than a work that, ultimately, expresses resignation?

On the streets of Athens there was, by the winter of 2012, an answer. You could feel what it is like when the political system—and even the rule of law—become paralyzed and atrophied. The 'horrified inertia' begins to grip even the middle classes, as the evidence of organized racist violence encroaches into their lives. Faced with an economic situation dictated by the European Central Bank and the International Monetary Fund, and a street atmosphere resembling Isherwood's Berlin, the natural human urge is not fight but flight. Flight from danger into the cocoon of drugs, relationships, alternative lifestyles, one's iPod. After the first-night disruption of *The Silver Lake* in Leipzig this is how its director, Douglas Sirk, described the scene at the theatre:

> The *sturmabteilung* filled a fairly large part of the theatre and there was a vast crowd of Nazi Party people outside with banners and God knows what, yelling and all the rest of it. But the majority of the public loved the play... And so I thought at first, well, things are going to be tough but perhaps it isn't impossible to overcome ... [But] no play, no song, could stop this gruesome trend towards inhumanity.[4]

And this is how a Greek theatre director in 2012 describes the situation after his own theatre was disrupted by fascists. Laertis Vasiliou's production of *Corpus Christi*—a play with a gay theme—was shut down by demonstrators from Golden Dawn after several nights of rock throwing, tear gas and the beating of audience members:

'We went ahead with the performance, which started with two hours of delay because of the fight outside the theatre between the police against the Christian fundamentalists and the Nazis. It was like hell. The noise from outside was clear inside the theatre during the performance. People were beaten up by Nazis and Christian fanatics. This was the Greek Kristallnacht. Every day they phone me now, they phone the theatre, saying: your days are numbered.'

His eyes redden and his face begins to tremble as he tells me: 'They phoned my mother, Golden Dawn. They said we will deliver your son's body to you in a box of little pieces. I want to be told if we are in a democracy or a dictatorship?'

The differences between today's Greece and the last days of Weimar, then, are clear. Under international pressure, the Greek state is still capable of upholding the rule of law; centrist parties, though atrophied, still hold the allegiance of more than one third of voters; there has been no decisive electoral breakthrough by the far right. Crucially, no major business or media groups, and no significant portion of the elite, have swung behind the far right as happened in Germany. But these conditions are eroding.

And the flight to inertia, depression, to personal life may also be more pronounced than in Weimar. Weimar Germany was, after all, a society of intense political engagement; of hierarchical politics, lifelong commitment to social movements, trade unions for the left and centre, military veterans' groups and churches for the right. So while the crisis may be on a scale weaker than the one that collapsed democracy in Greece, the forces holding democracy together may also be weaker.

The leaders of the international community know what the stakes are. Greece is the test bed for an austerity programme dictated by international capital. It is being imposed so that globalization can go on existing: so that bankers will still be able to afford yachts, and banks will never have to write down the mountain of toxic debt hidden inside their balance sheets. Instead of debt, Greek people are being asked to write down their lives and see their society destroyed. It might work: we might get to the exhausted end of it with 'only' pogroms, broken glass, cancelled plays and a severely curtailed democracy.

If it fails, a whole generation of Greek young people will be left, like Weill's protagonists in *The Silver Lake*, with a choice between love and nothing.

Or to put it another way, they will be left with a choice between the politics of solidarity and what the director of *The Silver Lake* observed: a gruesome trend towards inhumanity.

# 13

## Russia: 'Putin Got Scared'—
## From the Football Riots to Pussy Riot

To those who remember Russia straight after the collapse of communism, it is a country radically transformed. In Pushkin Square, twenty years ago, I remember the way forlorn Muscovite women would stand in a line, dazed, their cheap shoes disintegrating in the snow, to sell the last of their possessions. Today Pushkin Square is a monument to economic progress—and progress not just for the oligarchs and crooks who've flaunted their designer watches and girlfriends across the top hotels of Europe for the past two decades. Vladimir Putin's Russia has delivered progress for large numbers of ordinary people.

The raw figures tell the story. In ten years GDP per head grew from $7,000 to $20,000. Though economic growth went into reverse during the global crisis, it resumed afterwards: the Russian economy, which produced $250 billion ten years ago, is now closing in on $2 trillion GDP. In the same period, the value of the country's exports increased fivefold. Unemployment in the Moscow district was down to 2.8 per cent at the start of 2011, and though it remained high in the south and east of Russia, in the politically crucial cities of the west it was below 8 per cent and falling. Russia has become an energy-exporting economy, with a conspicuous consumption sector attached. Its Internet market is second only to Germany's in Europe. Its public finances are in massive surplus.

For Vladimir Putin, his return to the role of president in 2012 was set to be the crowning event of this growth, this new self-confidence, and the oil windfall on which it was all based. With the constitution changed, Putin would be set for two six-year terms, which, if you count his time as prime minister under Dmitry Medvedev, would give him one more year in power than Tsar Nicholas II.

Only one statistic remained troublesome. Despite a rising currency and strong public finances, capital was still pouring out of Russia: out of the banks, out of the business sector. Russia's new wealthy did not want to invest in Russia. The middle class did not want to keep their money there. And the World Bank quietly suggested why: it cited 'structural factors such as the quality of the investment climate', and 'rising domestic risks at least partly attributable to political uncertainty associated with the upcoming elections' as reasons for the relentless capital flight.[1]

Corruption, arbitrary rule, the stifling power of the FSB (a successor to the KGB), and the arrogance of the '*siloviki*'—the security elite Putin had brought to power after he broke with the so-called oligarchs: these were the factors driving money offshore on a scale not warranted by economics. And not just money: in their minds, many of the sharp-suited, iPad-toting professionals on the Moscow Metro were already somewhere else, living a 'virtual' Western lifestyle amid the political barbarity.

Katya, a democracy activist whose identity I am masking for legal reasons here, describes how it feels to live like this:

'There is no freedom to own property, to do business. There is so much corruption, people don't work with any real professionalism or sincerity. There is a culture of learned helplessness. There is very little trust in society; people are naturally suspicious of each other's motives.'

So there was discomfort among the middle class, even disgust. But was there really 'political risk', as the World Bank's economists suggested? Putin believed not. There would be no 'Occupy Moscow', he told an audience of global CEOs two months before the 2011 parliamentary elections, when all across the West 'hundreds of thousands of people—not just a bunch of outcasts but hundreds of thousands—are coming out onto the streets to demand what their governments are unable to fulfill.'

Russia, by contrast, would fulfill its social obligations, he promised, scheduling a 20 per cent increase in welfare spending for the coming budget.[2]

If Putin was worried about anything as he prepared to swap roles again with Medvedev, it was the racist and nationalist mobs he had encouraged. The football riot in Manezhnaya Square, on 11 December 2010, two days after London's 'dubstep rebellion' (see Chapter 4), displayed a neat, dark symmetry with the student rebellions in the West.

Fans of Spartak Moscow protested beneath the walls of the Kremlin over alleged police bribe-taking during the investigation of a fan murdered by a Chechen hoodlum. They pelted the cops with missiles, before being dispersed amid freezing fog and the smoke from orange distress flares. Nazi salutes were given, racist slogans were sprayed and shouted, numerous people who looked foreign were attacked, and 1,300 people were detained. The presence of members of the pro-Putin Nashi movement, and the more extreme Movement Against Illegal Immigration, completes the picture of a classic Russian pogrom.

But even on Manezhnaya there was a foretaste of the trouble to come. Nashi and similar right-wing youth movements had been created as extra-parliamentary activist groups to support the Putin regime. But there was also a strong anti-government sentiment among the rioters.

Oleg, a thirty-three-year-old Spartak fan who spoke on condition I changed his name, said: 'I came to Manezhnaya Square out of solidarity with the announced purpose of the gathering, which was to protest against what is seen as a corruption-based symbiosis between the country's authorities, in particular police, and ethnic collective entities— mostly from Russia's North Caucasus region.'

He reeled off a litany of complaints about the Caucasus: the way football fans are treated when they travel there, the way Putin has granted it virtual autonomy so that 'many of yesterday's gangsters have now turned into police or security officers who enjoy all sorts of rights and authority, and can wander around Russia with guns and de facto immunity against criminal liability'.

Alongside racism there had been heard, at Manezhnaya, much rhetoric along the same lines condemning corruption, unaccountable government and the blatant contempt of the political elite for the masses. By 2010, says Oleg, 'in the subculture of football fans, Putin was widely seen as a crook and a traitor.'

For despite the emergence of a broad middle class, many of the Spartak fans were not part of it. They were from that segment of the population we find in all the places where it has kicked off: low-skilled, poorly educated, resentful of the economic challenge posed by migrants, and now unwilling to act simply as operatic spear-carriers for Putin and Medvedev. Ivan Katanaev, former leader of a Spartak supporters group, told reporters: 'The crowd who came to the rally has no leaders—only the consciousness that we cannot go on living like this and the desire to change everything.'[3]

Putin sent flowers to the grave of the murdered fan, and then called the football fan leaders into the Kremlin, where he delivered himself of a long lecture whose theme can be summed up in a single excerpt:

'I believe that you are a strong force. But unless we learn to control your strength, if we handle it like a lunatic handles a razor, we can destroy our country.'[4]

The Manezhnaya riot was a minor earth tremor, it seemed, nothing more. Any serious challenge to Putin would need the middle class—so long bought off by Putin's statecraft, by the oil money and the paraphernalia of affluence—to take to the streets. Surely they would never do that?

Russian liberalism and the Western-oriented middle class were sickened by the nationalist right. As discussed in Chapter 7, the working class of a modern economy tends to be culturally divided between those exposed to global labour markets and technocratic conditions, and this beleaguered group oriented to traditional values and national economic solutions.

Absent any solidarity between the plebeian right and the left intelligentsia, the protests against Putin would continue to be small, repressed and ghettoized. Sergei Udaltsov, the leader of the Left Front, would, in the twelve months before the 2011 election, spend a total of eighty-six days in detention. And for some the price of dissent could be higher still. Ask Alexander Litvinenko. Ask Sergei Magnitsky, the anti-corruption lawyer imprisoned without trial, who died in custody after being denied medical assistance. Ask Anna Politkovskaya.

Putin, it seemed, would coast to victory in the 2012 presidential election and the oil and gas money would keep on flowing. Economics, ignorance and brute force would shield Russia from the great wave of unrest that was, by now, sweeping the world. Wouldn't it?

It's November 2011. Two large men—white, fat and shaven-headed—are punching seven bells out of each other in a Moscow sports stadium. They look like giant babies: Fedor Emelianenko, belly wobbling above his swim trunks, and Jeff Monson—stockier, with bigger biceps and a rash of tattoos. This is 'mixed martial arts'—MMA for short—and the crowd is full of exactly the kind of men and women that have made Russian liberals despair. Men brought up in the 'cult of the real man'; women who seem happy to be blonde and ornamental.

By round three, as MMA is more or less bare-knuckle, Monson's face is spurting blood and Fedor is landing punches onto his bare skull. This is political theatre, too. Fedor is a deputy for Putin's United Russia party; Monson is a veteran of the Seattle protests in 1999, his skin covered with anti-capitalist body art. As Monson goes to the floor it is the ultimate postmodern spectacle: real violence, real blood, but steeped in irony and histrionics.

And then, as Fedor is given the prize, into the ring steps a third adult baby, also stocky and bald-headed, but in a suit. He takes the microphone and begins to speak. 'Fedor,' he says, 'does not only have great muscles: he is a real Russian hero.' It is Vladimir Putin.

And the crowd begins to boo. They might be booing because they don't want to hear corny words; or—as some will later claim—because there are not enough toilets in the venue. But it doesn't matter: the booing, cat-calling and whistling continue until he stops.

Russian TV cut this scene, of course. Putin's media is conditioned only to collude with publicity stunts when they go right, as with his shirtless Siberian photo-shoot, or his miraculous discovery of two sixth-century Greek vases, bang in front of the TV cameras, while diving in the Black Sea. Only when the MMA video was circulated on YouTube, and the blogosphere erupted with sarcasm, did the booing become public in Russia itself.

Putin looked shaken—and he had reason to be. It was the second tremor of the quake to come.


A young man sprints down a long, dim-lit corridor, yelling 'Stop her!' He's breathless and trying to film with his cellphone as he runs. The scene is polling station number 2945, in Moscow, on 4 December 2011.

Eventually the pursuer—Konstantin Yankauskas, from the youth movement Solidarnosc—gets the cops to listen to his story. He has infiltrated a group trying to submit false ballot papers in the election: they've been equipped to submit eight ballot papers each, for 1,000 roubles, and this is the seventh place they've done it. The woman, and the man with her, place their hands in front of the pursuer's camera. She is the alleged leader of the vote-rigging group and has handed out 'special passes' to show the election officials, who are also involved.

Yankauskas recovers the fake ballot papers, stuffed into a nearby toilet, and counts them on the floor. They're all stamped and legitimate: in the ballot box they would have counted as votes. 'The vote riggers are from out of town, poor, and beyond caring about themselves or what happens in their country,' says one of the journalists who've staged the exposé.

It would have made great TV—it would not get on Russian TV, of course. But by the time the polls closed it was already on YouTube.[5] Within minutes it had been shared by 50,000 people, then somebody tweeted it. Within forty-eight hours it had been seen by 1.2 million people. And it was not the only evidence: there were scores of videos showing systematic ballot rigging and manipulation of the count. As they circulated through the Russian blogosphere, it dawned on democracy activists that this was the start of something big.

The party supported by Vladimir Putin had won the parliamentary election. But its support had collapsed, despite the systematic abuse shown in the videos.

The Duma elections of December 2011 faced voters with unedifying choices. Electoral law effectively impedes the creation of new, minor parties, and prevents those who poll below 7 per cent from winning seats in parliament. So the choice was, effectively, between the four political blocs that have existed in Russia since the fall of communism.

There was Putin's United Russia party, the party of power, representing the interest of the state, the secret service, the pro-Kremlin rich and the hydrocarbon industry. Then the old Communist Party (no longer just a pensioners' club, it is also supported by some middle-class liberals and social democrats). Then the Liberal Democratic Party—more precisely a far-right nationalist party, led by eccentric anti-Semite Vladimir Zhirinovsky. Finally, the 'Fair Russia' party, an alliance of social democrats and ex-communists who—though opposing Putin—had aligned themselves with outgoing president Dmitry Medvedev. These were the parties with deputies in the Duma.

Also on the ballot paper were Yabloko, a Western-oriented liberal party; 'Right Cause', a free-market conservative party, and a communist splinter faction called Patriots of Russia: none of them had seats in the Duma and there was little chance of winning any this time. Sergei

Udaltsov's Left Front—the closest Russia has to the Greek Syriza party—had been repeatedly denied registration.

The campaign had been sporadic: the media, owned and dominated by Putin's allies, had provided one long desultory valediction for United Russia. The party's network of officials had, as always, used their public office to promote their own camp. The opinion polls had showed a steady slippage for Putin's party, but still placed it well above 50 per cent on the eve of the vote. The same polls showed that 36 per cent of Russians believed their vote would have no effect.[6] So, as the citizens trooped into the polling booths, they might well have expected business as usual.

But by nightfall Russia was seething with discontent. There had been, right in front of the international observers and video monitoring systems, blatant vote rigging. And the count was a farce. 'The vote count was assessed as bad or very bad in every third polling station observed,' was the verdict of monitors from the OSCE. GOLOS, a Russian NGO set up to promote civil rights, reported widespread ballot-stuffing, miscounting, and a systematic discrepancy between votes tallied at the polling station and the eventual numbers counted.

The election had been conducted on the same principles as an MMA fight: without rules, and to provide a predictable result. But in moral terms Putin had lost. His support had collapsed, from 64 to 49.8 per cent. Worse still, in the big cities—not just in European Russia but in the Urals, Siberia and the far east—United Russia's percentage of the vote had fallen to the low 30s.

'This party of crooks and thieves like to tell us they represent teachers, doctors and engineers,' wrote the thirty-four-year-old lawyer Alexei Navalny on his influential blog that night. 'In fact they represent only Chechnya, the corrupt elites in the national republics, oppressed rural areas and the Moscow municipal mafia. That's all that saved United Russia from total failure.'[7] And that's what the map showed: only in Chechnya, Dagestan and Ingushetia did Putin's party score the kind of 70–90 per cent that is the mark of the successful autocrat.

At 9 pm on election night a few hundred protesters assembled at Ploshchad Revolutsii, calling for the results to be annulled. They were quickly dispersed, the police making more than 200 arrests, including of leading figures from the far right.

The next day, 5 December, 8,000 people gathered in central Moscow and tried to march on the Lubyanka, the secret service headquarters. By now the left, the radicals and the democrats were out in force, with Navalny prominent among them. Navalny's blog had become a focal point for the democracy movement in the run-up to the election and— via LiveJournal—he now distributed YouTube videos and documentary proof of the rigged election. The elite's monopoly of TV news did not matter anymore. Using the same leverage mechanism as the Arab Spring—the social media amplified by Internet TV stations, and then further amplified by the international media—the story was out.

'For the first time in many years,' wrote Navalny, 'millions of absolutely different people have chosen a common political strategy and implemented it without serious coordination and succeeded. The main enemy—Mister Nothing Can Ever Change—is not dead, but he has suffered a stroke.'

Andrei Piontkovsky, a seventy-two-year-old maths professor and veteran of the democratic movement, puts it like this:

'Social media played a crucial role, actually the main role. First, from the point of view of organizing the meetings and uniting people. It was the only channel, the only means of communication. That was its primary function. But it had a broader significance, too. With social media, there are two Russias: the Russia of Channel One and RTR, and the Russia of the internet.'

The Russia of Channel One now responded with systematic and pre-emptive repression. Navalny was arrested on the 6 December demo, together with Boris Nemtsov, the one-time deputy prime minister who had joined the protests. The left's Udaltsov had been pre-emptively arrested on election day itself, 'for refusing to cross the road as indicated by police officers'. Nashi mobilized thousands of pro-Putin youth in counter-demonstrations and, with the police swamping and arresting any public gathering, the first phase was over.

Now, via Facebook, and in the face of truly herculean efforts to disrupt the mobilization—including a warning from the health minister that demonstrators would catch SARS—60,000 people marched to Moscow's Bolotnaya Square.[8] This was the day the opposition politicians moved in, en masse, to shape the movement. The speakers' list read like a roll-call of liberals and social democrats going back to the Yeltsin era. Piontkovsky was aware of the contradiction from the start:

'Just like after the French Revolution—with the Jacobins—you have the radical wing: Udaltsov, Navalny, Gary Kasparov and me. Our strategy was to cause a rift in the ruling elite: to eliminate the current powers-that-be, and force Putin to resign. And then there was the moderate wing—the "managed" wing, and its messengers; the liberals within the system. Their aim was to force Putin to compromise, with an eye on the 2018 election. They hate the *siloviki*, but in reality they are its counterbalance within the system.'

The political fragmentation in the movement was revealed the next weekend, when the Yabloko party and the communists both staged their own, party-branded demonstrations (Zhirinovsky's LDP had denounced the demonstrators as foreign puppets early on).

The high point of the post-election wave came on 24 December, when between 60,000 and 120,000 people assembled at Sakharov Avenue. Here the platform reflected the younger, more diverse, more radical coalition that was growing up outside and between the party machineries. As protest followed protest, something else was noticed: a community of opposition had coalesced. 'We made friends in the protests, we made friends in detention cells. It was like we found our voice,' says Katya; 'we found each other.'

People who had never been on a demonstration, who enjoyed good jobs and decent salaries, now took to the streets alongside pensioners and radical youths. Many spent their first night ever in a cell in those weeks. They shared their experiences openly on Facebook,

VKontakte, LiveJournal. Some were sacked for taking part—and soon the letters of dismissal were being circulated online. And while Moscow remained the centre of the protest, there were now—on every day of action—protests in the key provincial cities as well.

Though outrage at the election result was what sustained the movement between its big street demonstrations, it survived from day to day as a cultural movement. It survived because a few prominent media figures—including TV host Ksenia Sobchak, with half a million Twitter followers—came over to the opposition. But it also survived through the small actions of hundreds of thousands of more anonymous people. In the white ribbons protesters pinned to their clothes, and in the condoms they displayed after Putin compared the ribbons to condoms. In the Internet clips and live performances of Citizen Poet, a duo of comedians dedicated to ripping Putin's reputation to shreds with satire, speech by speech; in the fake tickets for the police arrest bus handed out on every demo. And sometimes just through bitterly earnest songs, in journalism, in 140-character tweets going viral to an online community of millions—actions Putin could never understand, and the FSB could never totally repress.

Two months before his election, Vladimir Putin had crowed to the West about its problem with the Occupy movement, who were 'not just a bunch of outcasts but hundreds of thousands'. Now he had that problem too.

Russia is a lucky country. Since the fall of communism it has been blessed with not just one kleptocratic elite, but two.

Under Boris Yeltsin, the so-called oligarchy was created when a small group of businessmen, initially emerging from the Gorbachev-era elite, seized the country's privatized resources with all the subtlety of a lion enclosure at feeding time. Their guiding principle was the free market without the rule of law. Their seizure and re-division of the massive spoils was attended by murders, extortion and the trampling of investors' rights. By 1996, claimed the media magnate Boris

Berezovsky, he and six others owned half the country's assets. On top of that they owned the Yeltsin government, and presumed, on his rise to power, that they would own Putin also.

But the history of Putin is the history of the fall of the oligarchs and the creation of a statist capitalism, in which oil, gas and mineral companies would be used to enrich the *siloviki* and their allies.

Berezovsky was forced into exile in 2000. A younger generation, including Oleg Deripaska, Mikhail Prokhorov and Roman Abramovich, moved some of their assets abroad and 'largely abandoned politics in favour of business, skiing and football clubs'.[9] Today Russia has 110 billionaires, the top 100 of whom own combined assets worth half a trillion dollars. But it's impossible to speak of them as an 'oligarchy' in the sense of the group that thrived under Yeltsin, whose project Berezovsky has described as direct interference in politics to prevent the emergence of an authoritarian nationalist state.

Under Putin, it is just this authoritarian nationalist state that has ruled the roost, forming a new elite whose implicit bargain with the private-sector billionaires—'Get rich and stay out of politics'— was demonstrated by the fate of the man who broke it. Mikhail Khodorkovsky, the former owner of oil giant Yukos, was jailed for tax evasion in 2003 and remains behind bars. However, he also remains at the centre of a network of influence that extends via his well-funded public affairs machine into Western liberal and social-democratic circles, and now to the protest movement on the Russian streets.

Since 2005, Khodorkovsky—who has been declared a prisoner of conscience by Amnesty International—has embraced a social-liberal agenda, arguing for a 'left turn' in Russian liberalism, away from the chaotic free-market politics of the Yeltsin years. During the White Ribbon protests, Khodorkovsky publicly threw his weight behind the younger, more radical faction, less tainted by its association with the Yeltsin years, and distanced himself from his former allies.

'What is going to be taking place is called a revolution, whether we like it or not,' Khodorkovsky wrote from prison in July 2012. 'The time for soft, slow reforms has slipped away. Our main task is for a non-violent process to "get going". The former leaders don't have enough drive for a revolution.'[10]

The presence of Khodorkovsky 'within' the radical wing of the protest movement—albeit virtually—further complicates the political challenge it faces. For Khodorkovsky's prolonged imprisonment is the direct result of the scale of Putin's fear of him. This is a man who wields power even from a cellblock in a Karelian prison, power of a type most of the other protest movements described in this book could only dream of.

As the Russian protest movement grew in strength, staging another massive demonstration in February 2012, and a huge protest in Pushkin Square in May, it faced four linked problems that have made its evolution unique among the global protest movements.

First, the problem of powerful allies such as liberal capitalists, the US state department and the remains of the Yeltsin-era free-market elite, plus the leaders of the Duma opposition parties. This gave the movement, at times, the character of a traditional, hierarchical and party-led opposition. Furthermore, the support of the Communists, Yabloko and Fair Russia have, at times, come with conditions, and an agenda.

Second, and in response to that, there is the tendency of the radical wing themselves to operate in a non-horizontal, non-networked way. True, they have understood the need for street power to remain 'soft', to avoid violent confrontation, etc. But at the May 2012 demonstration they co-signed a manifesto calling for the creation of a Coordinating Committee, elected from across the political spectrum, and authorized to call demonstrations. They set out a basic series of democratic demands, focused on free elections and a new constitution.[11]

While this kind of shift towards 'structure' has sustained the movement's momentum, it has arguably stifled the emergence of the low-level, multi-directional direct action and occupation movements that characterized the protests in the West (although, to be fair, when Udaltsov threatened to erect a tent in Pushkin Square he was, once again, immediately arrested).

A study by web analytics group Nodus Labs outlined the relationship between organized politics and activism in a series of graphics. It found that membership of the huge Facebook group 'Putin Must Leave' was in fact dominated by four (fairly separate) sub-networks linked to political parties. Journalists, lawyers and politicians were identified as powerful nodes in such networks. By contrast, 'the groups formed around a specific practical goal, such as volunteer action and meeting organization, were led by the people who had little to do with politics: event organizers, scientists, researchers, media and creative industries workers, activists of minority rights organizations'.[12]

The third factor, and with massive implications, is the growing presence of right-wing and nationalist movements within the protest movement. This was most evident on the June 2012 demonstration, where the Nazi salutes and near-replica SS uniforms of the Velikye Rossia movement ranged—surreally—alongside the red flags of the far left and rainbow flags of the Lesbian and Gay movement. And some of the radicals themselves have a closer than comfortable relationship to right-wing nationalism: Navalny attended the 'Russian March' alongside skinheads and fascists in November 2011, and, when challenged, made clear he favours the emergence of a 'modern', liberal nationalism.[13]

Finally, there is the scale of the repression. After the May 2012 demo became violent, the authorities were able to inflict a sustained harassment campaign on most of the recognized leaders of the movement—most importantly Navalny, who was charged with embezzlement, and Udaltsov, who was charged with 'plotting mass disorder'. Katya, the protest activist, says much of her time is now spent supporting the core dozen people being subjected to prosecutions for the various 'crimes' they are supposed to have committed during the December days, when hundreds were arrested:

'This dozen—they are just regular people, like many of the others who went through the same procedures of detention and so on. Why just them? If [the authorities] expand this approach and do it to everyone that was detained, we could be talking about hundreds of people. Now people are worried. They are concerned that there will or might be some kind of payback; some kind of consequences. They don't know how far the state will go.'

Though the Egyptian radicals also faced repression, during the military's year-long fight-back after Mubarak's fall, it was never on a scale to preoccupy or cow them. And though high levels of pre-emptive repression managed to defocus the Occupy movement in America, the radicalism that was driving it did not go away. This leaves the Russian movement as probably the most imperiled of all the democracy movements unleashed in 2011—and intensifies its tendency to adopt hierarchies, lean on foreign support and ignore the dangers posed by the far right.

It was Marx who wrote that 'men make history but not in conditions of their own choosing'—and rarely has this been better illustrated than by the Russian democracy movement. In its youthful makeup, its use of social media, its adoption of humour, cultural activism and non-violence, it is almost a carbon copy of the Occupy and *indignado* camps that Putin believed could not exist in Russia. Yet it is disfigured—possibly fatally—by its emergence from a society in which humanity and public discourse were crushed for nearly seventy years.

The anti-Semitism, the anti-Caucasian prejudice, the dysfunctional nationalism, the infatuation with uniforms and flags, sit in nightmare juxtaposition to Pussy Riot and the condom-headed Putin pastiches. They are as much part of the same reality as when Salafist Muslims protest alongside liberal atheists in Cairo; yet they speak of a nightmare that is ever present, not fading. They are symptoms of the same desperate problem that confronted Russians in those first days after the fall of the USSR, twenty years ago: the atomization of the poor and the extreme power of the rich.

As these tensions have played out, especially during the demonstrations in May and June, 2012, the social character of the movement has changed significantly, says Piontkovsky. 'In December, the protest crowd mostly consisted of bourgeois people, successful people, with full bellies, good clothes and shoes. In May and June there were, first of all, many more people from outside Moscow. Second, more people from the public sector: teachers, engineers, military officers. Third, the protests have become more radical in terms of their demands and in the way they act when facing the police: they are harsher, tougher.'

And they would have to be. On 21 February 2012, members of the feminist punk performance collective Pussy Riot staged a guerrilla performance in the Cathedral of Christ the Saviour. In a performance filled with f-words, they implored the Virgin Mary to 'throw Putin out'—a protest aimed at the patriarch of the Russian Orthodox Church, who they alleged had been campaigning for Putin.

It was the latest in a series of brilliant, impromptu performances: they had raged from the tops of buses, in luxury shopping malls, at fashion shows and from a rooftop in Red Square, and performed outside Navalny's cell when he was detained. The group drew inspiration from the same mixture of postmodernism and performance art as the OccupyArt movements in America and the student protesters in London in 2010. As they told an interviewer:

> Some of us are anarchists, some have leftist liberal positions. We would like horizontal political activity, self-organization and the capability to be aware of oneself as an equal participant in civil politics, to understand one's rights and fight for them to develop. Russian society lacks tolerance and lenience.[14]

The immediate aim of the culture war they'd started was to fight for the right to unauthorized public demonstrations. But this culture war—previously seen by many as the softest and least threatening part of the Western protest movements—proved to be the scariest thing of all in the eyes of the authorities.

After the Cathedral stunt video went viral on their YouTube channel,[15] the three members of Pussy Riot who had been involved—Maria Alyokhina, Nadezhda Tolokonnikova, and Ekaterina Samoutsevitch—were arrested. They were denied sleep and food and staged repeated hunger strikes during their detention. Their trial turned into a vintage Putin-era farce, and turned them into global heroines way beyond the activist movement.

On 17 August 2012, the three women were convicted of 'hooliganism' and sentenced to two years in prison. 'Putin Got Scared', they had sung from the rooftops of Red Square. Their conviction would prove a signal moment for the Putin regime: it revealed what the hero of Chechnya, the great bare-chested leader of the Russian people, is actually scared of. It is the thing that will bring that elites with untrammelled power always fear. It is freedom.

The argument of this book is that the crisis of 2008 shook every part of the global order: not just because of the economic impact, but thanks to its coincidence with an upsurge of self-expression using social media that amounts to a change in the human character; and also because of the expectations that had built up during the neoliberal years, which were now dashed. In the eight months since the English edition was published I have spent hundreds of hours discussing the issues with academics, activists, bloggers, festival-goers and security experts. From such diverse directions the questions are nearly always the same: can non-hierarchical movements ever be more than irritants to those with power? And which is the bigger revolution—the economic discontent, or the human and democratic issues?

Russia's experience since December 2011 helps answer these questions. Those who took to the streets were those to whom Putin's gas-fired state capitalism had delivered a lot. But beyond the iPads, UGG boots and Android phones, what they most wanted was the freedom to live and work in a society that tolerates free speech and diversity, under the rule of law.

This is what the Putin regime cannot offer. It has met every stage of the movement with repression: raiding the homes of its leaders before the May 2012 protest; imposing severe financial sanctions on those participating in unauthorized demos; forcing GOLOS and other NGOs to register as 'foreign-backed' organizations; re-criminalizing libel, taking powers to ban 'extremist' content on the Internet and making 'homosexual propaganda' a crime.

Putin has created an authoritarianism that dare not bend. It rightly fears swift justice from any new regime brought to power by free and democratic elections.

By the time of the Pussy Riot verdict, large parts of the Russian people had, for certain, given up on Putin. They'd experienced the same kind of 'regime change of the mind' I saw in Greece, after which official politics becomes an irrelevance, especially to the youth. But the liberal politicians who flocked to support the movement in December 2011 create the same problem for the workers and youth as Moussavi did in Iran in 2009: for the poorest, there is no escape route to the West once you've attempted a revolution and failed. No working class in history—and no intelligentsia—ever launched an all-or-nothing fight for power merely in order to bring in a different set of men in mink *shapkas*.

Russia, on the basis of the events so far, has seen an insurrection primarily driven not by economic grievance but by the more complex social, demographic and human changes I describe in Chapter 7: the rise of the networked individual, their desire for enhanced personal and social freedom, and their extreme disenchantment with authoritarian state capitalism.

Putin's main advantage is not his ability to deploy the FSB and the riot squad, nor even his ability to spend tens of billions of roubles on social programmes. It is the sheer scale of social atomization that occurred in the last years of the Soviet Union and the first years of the Yeltsin regime. It is arguable that, even now, the generation that lived through the 1980s and 90s—the Afghan wars, perestroika, the Yeltsin shock—remains so fatally mesmerized by authoritarian nationalism that it would, given the chance, simply replace Putin with a straight Communist or far-right replica. Even if this is not true of the Pussy Riot generation—which has known only cellphones and social media, and which breathes the same radicalism as the youth of Cairo and New York—it creates yet another division within the movement.

All these factors make it unlikely that the democracy movement, on its own, could topple Putin. Expanding the space for social activism and democratic debate might be the most it could hope for, under its own steam. But this, at root, was all that Pussy Riot were trying to do, and in the end the regime could not even tolerate that.

However, there is a strong external dynamic—and the regime is right to fear it. Putin is said to read the annals of Russian despotism not as a history book but as an instruction manual. The centrality of the FSB in his statecraft mirrors that of the Okhrana under Tsarism and the KGB under Brezhnev. The turn to aggressive militarism, nationalism and the muscle of semi-fascist street gangs are, likewise, well-thumbed pages from the Tsarist playbook. But these vital traits of Putinism lead in directions that make his rule decreasingly functional within global capitalism, and tend to alienate even sections of the elite.

And now, the Arab Spring has injected a new, unpredictable element which Putin's statecraft is struggling cope with.

For years, Pentagon strategists have dreamed of a scenario in which Lebanon evicts Hezbollah, Syria goes over to the West, Iran's hardline mullahs get overthrown, and the dominoes of Russian influence topple one by one, in a straight line, from Beirut to the borders of Turkmenistan.

By vetoing sanctions against Assad in Syria, and repeatedly supporting Ahmadinejad against his own people in Iran, Putin has put himself on the opposite side to something more powerful than Hilary Clinton. He has set the Kremlin's face not just against a weak domestic revolution, but against a global revolution that will, in the next few years, arrive on Russia's doorstep.

To lose Syria and Iran would be the diplomatic equivalent of the battle of Tsushima (the 1905 naval battle in which Tsar Nicholas sent Russia's fleet halfway around the world, only to see it instantly sunk by Japan). Revolution in Syria and Iran would leave Russia's power in the world severely curtailed. But with every speech, every veto, every attack helicopter shipped to his failing allies, Putin seems determined to prepare this diplomatic Tsushima.

Thus are the global revolutions and the Russian struggle for democracy linked. The White Ribbon revolution is not just a local reflection of uprisings elsewhere: its fate is intertwined with them.

# 14

## The Twenty Reasons, Revisited

It is nearly two years on from Tahrir Square. The president of Egypt is from the Muslim Brotherhood; on the streets of Athens the Golden Dawn party is staging anti-migrant pogroms; the most prominent leaders of Russia's democracy movement face criminal charges. Around 200 people a week are being killed by Assad's regime in Syria.

It's an easy step from such manifest negativity to the conclusion that 2011, the year it all kicked off, was a flash in the pan. But to conclude that would be totally wrong.

The Arab Spring and the Occupy movement—with their echoes as far afield as Santiago and Quebec—have unleashed something real and important, and it has not yet gone away. I am confident enough now to call it a revolution. Some of its processes conform to the templates laid down in 1848, but many do not. Above all the relationship between the physical and the mental, the political and the cultural, seem inverted.

There is a change in consciousness, the intuition that something big is possible; that a great change in the world's priorities is within people's grasp. The essence of it is, as Manuel Castells has written, the collapse of trust in the old regime, combined with the inability to go on living the pre-crisis lifestyle: 'The perceived incapacity of the political elite to solve their problems destroyed trust in the institutions in charge of managing the crisis.'[1]

If anything, the impervious nature of official politics—its inability to swerve even slightly towards the critique of finance capitalism intuitively felt by millions of people—has deepened the sense of alienation and mistrust. But the changes in ideas, behaviour and expectations are running far ahead of changes in the physical world. Here 'progress' is hard to find. There is greater space for democratic movements in the Arab world, but it is constantly menaced. 'The Protester' may have made it on to the cover of *Time* as Person of the Year but, to date, not a single anti-austerity protest has achieved its aim.

If we take 1848–51 as a template, the critical events that would close the period of upheaval lie ahead. Pessimism of the intellect leads you to expect them to be episodes of reaction: a police-led coup in Greece, where democracy is already constrained; a suppression of the secular, liberal and leftist forces in Egypt; an intelligence-led bust up of the Occupy movement in America; and for good measure a war— probably with Iran. But, as I argued in the first edition of this book, there is one powerful factor militating against a return to stability and order: the economy.

Europe's great slide backwards, beginning in October 2011, as the G20 summit at Cannes ended in paralysis, has dragged the world economy backwards. In a balance-sheet recession, where recovery is impaired by overhanging debts, all policy can do is to keep the patient alive. Sustained recovery can only begin when the debt mountains are diminished—either by inflation, currency wars or aggressive defaults. In turn, each of these shatters the basis of the old economic order: inflation wipes out the savings of the salaried workforce and the middle class; currency wars trigger the break-up of globalization; default—by states, banks and individuals—reduces parts of the finance system to rubble. As a result we are maybe only halfway through the depressive effects of the 2008 crisis. In countries such as Greece, Spain, or Portugal, a 1930s-style death spiral is a serious danger.

The title of this book asks 'why' social movements erupted as they did from late 2010. It does not and cannot answer the question why they fail; as a work of analysis it was never intended to answer the question 'what should they do?'

In general, throughout history, social movements failed because they were not resolute enough, because they were self-deluding, bureaucratized or badly led, or because they were disunited. Often they failed because they were launched at a time when conditions made it impossible for them to succeed. Generally, for those that did succeed, these conditions were overcome. It is impossible to tell at this stage whether the movements described here will fail: but if they do, the conditions of their failure may turn out to involve—as in Greece—a retreat from democracy and from the welfare state, and quite possibly a retreat from globalization.

With this in mind I want to revisit the 'Twenty Reasons' post that originally inspired this book, written as a blog on 5 February 2011.[2] Its insights were provisional then, and the conclusions below remain provisional. I will argue that the thrust of the original bullet points—reprinted in italics below—remains valid, but new questions are raised as follows:

## 1. At the heart of it all is a new sociological type: the graduate with no future

When I wrote those words the *indignados* had not yet flooded into Madrid's Puerta del Sol; the Occupy camps had not been thought of; the Quebec student protest was a year away. The 'graduates with no future' have been central to the events of 2011–12, although—as we will see, now that we have more case studies—the limits of what they are prepared to do are more obvious.

Free-market capitalism offered the generations born after 1985 the moon and stars. Now it can offer very little. For the unlucky ones, there is unemployment. In the small Spanish town of San Miguel de Salinas I found jobless youth lounging on the streets, smoking and drinking too early in the day. 'We have no car,' one young woman told me, 'not even a drivers' licence, because what's the point of paying for it if you are never going to get a car?' As one year spills over into the next, there is a quiet migration out of the crisis zone; a chemistry graduate I met in San Miguel is a bartender in Edinburgh. 'I'll save some money and then look for something to do with chemistry,' he said.

But even for those with jobs, there is a dramatic change of story that makes no version of the future seem palatable. In Athens, I interviewed a female anti-fascist, who'd been strip-searched and abused in the police HQ: what was her job? 'I wait tables,' she said, adding with an embarrassed laugh, 'but I am a qualified civil engineer.' On the streets of Madrid and Barcelona, late into the night, with the once vibrant bars now closed, you see young adults squatting in groups on the pavement, drinking warm beer out of cans, sold by itinerant migrants. The lifestyle of the small-town poor is forced on the glamorous youth of the most glamorous cities.

To survive, the young have become a generation of drifters, reliving the plotlines of movies from the 1930s. For those graduating since the crisis began, there is the offer of wages pegged close to the minimum; work contracts stripped of traditional benefits; a collapsed housing market that they cannot enter—even as properties lie crumbling and weed infested, from Las Vegas to Valencia. Rising taxes, massive debts from the day you graduate, a retirement age raised so far you might as well stop thinking about it. And above all stories that no longer make sense: the American dream, the social Europe. And if it's bad now, the avatars of emerging market capitalism have only scorn for the idea that living in the West, and getting educated, should be a guarantee of decent living standards.

'The minimum wage is a machine to destroy jobs,' multimillionaire Tidjane Thiam, the Ivorian-born boss of Prudential, told an audience at Davos in 2012. 'The minimum wage is the enemy of young people entering the labour market.' Unions too were the enemy of the young, defending the conditions of those with work. The logic is that to get into the labour market at all, this generation—probably the best-educated, healthiest, most emotionally literate generation ever—will have to work for starvation wages and forget about unionization.

It is a common refrain. At the United World Colleges summit in London, Ruben Vardanyan, the boss of the $1 billion Troika Dialog hedge fund, told me: 'European people need to work longer, harder and be less paid. Or take a later pension. Otherwise there will be no economy left.'[3]

Without some massive and cathartic turnaround, the generation in their twenties, across much of the Western world, will never accumulate savings at the level their parents did; they will never accumulate pension rights at a level that could realistically support them in retirement. What they are accumulating is resentment.

*2. ... with access to social media, such as Facebook, Twitter and yfrog, they can express themselves in a variety of situations ranging from parliamentary democracy to tyranny*

The state, of course, had other ideas. Facebook pages have been closed down by the US media company, at the request of those in power. And, while states were prepared to ignore social media before they became a venue for opposition, the past two years have seen the imposition of 'normal' media law against blogs, Facebook and Twitter. Incitement and libel are now regularly prosecuted on the social media and summary action is common at corporate level. For example, on the eve of planned protests during the UK's 2011 Royal Wedding, some fifty UK Facebook groups dedicated to organizing protest events were deleted by the company, on the grounds that they were being maintained by people with false names. During the English inner-city riots of 2011, the prime minister floated the idea of banning rioters from using Facebook and Twitter, and two young men who had publicly incited riots in small towns were jailed on the evidence of their Facebook pages (even though in both cases, no riot had ever happened).

Meanwhile, among the young, poor and disenfranchised demographic who formed the core of rioters, research by the *Guardian*/LSE confirmed—as everyone understood at the time—that the secure Blackberry BBM service was the key conduit of riot agitation, not Facebook. RIM, the maker of Blackberry, quickly pledged to do what it could to unsecure the data.

However, in response to increased surveillance and repression, activists have evolved new uses for social media. Tumblr emerged as the platform of choice of the Occupy movement in America after it hosted the viral 'We are the 99%' blog. The blog, and the '99%' meme it created, form a case study in the mass dissemination of ideas possible with social media. The slogan itself originated at a general assembly in New York's Zuccotti Park in August: a blogger posted an appeal for posed photographs with one-line summaries of their subject's economic problems. The first, showing a young woman, read: 'Single mom, grad student, unemployed and I paid more tax last year than GE. I am the 99 per cent.' Soon the site was getting more than 100 submissions a day. And it was picked up—at first by the niche websites associated with Occupy, then by the mainstream media.

When protesters took Brooklyn Bridge on 17 November 2011, a guerrilla art group called The Illuminators shone '99%' in the style of a Batman searchlight signal onto the HQ of Verizon. Mark Read, the instigator of the group, told me:

'The bat signal is really simple. It's big and it reads as a bat signal— it's culturally legible. It's a call to arms and a call for aid, but instead of a super-hero millionaire psychopath, like Bruce Wayne, it's ourselves— it's the 99% coming to save itself. We are our own superhero.'

The cat and mouse game between social movements and the authorities over the use of social media has, if anything, made its use more sophisticated. Most of the protests of 2011–12 have involved inchoate groups, overlapping networks, complex demographics. By shutting down one service—as the Iranians did with Facebook in 2009—you tend to push people in the direction of bleeding-edge platforms that are not yet monitored, or back onto the plain, old, pre-social digital comms like email and bulletin boards, and of course word of mouth.

Underpinning the use of social media, the years of crisis have seen massive combined and synergistic growth in smartphone use, smartphone technologies and social media applications designed for them. The iPhone grew from scratch in 2007 to 35 million units sold per quarter by 2011. Facebook had 400 million active users in 2010, and has one billion in mid 2012.

David Karp, the twenty-six-year-old CEO of Tumblr, told me: 'All of this stuff is gated on the hardware: Apple and Google are pushing the hardware so far, so quickly … and as the creative horsepower moves faster and faster, the software is going to explode.' Karp is one of the few CEOs you'll meet whose eyes light up as he describes the momentum behind Occupy Wall Street: 'The reach you can build out of a network like Tumblr, and the mass communication that's able to go down in a network like Twitter is incredible: it's just something that's never existed before. The other thing is the media itself: it's easier than ever for you and me to make something that's really compelling, tells a story, put that out into the world and really move people.'

It seems, in the near future, highly unlikely—given the overlap of complex and changing networks—that the state, except in outright dictatorships, can do anything more than play catch-up with the social media.


## 3. Therefore truth moves faster than lies, and propaganda becomes flammable

I should have explained this better, because the way this happens involves more than just the social media. It's clear now—from the examples of Cairo's 'Day of Rage', Wisconsin's Capitol occupation, the global explosion of the Occupy movement on 15 October 2011—that protesters' ability to leverage the mainstream media has also been crucial.

In the first place, it is important for real-time information-spreading. On protests you have started to see geeky men wandering around with a GoPro camera on a bike helmet, linked to a computer and a makeshift aerial, effectively livestreaming the action to niche video blogs. But you also now have mainstream news networks livestreaming the protests, albeit sometimes from the safety of a rooftop or helicopter.

Two examples spring to mind: first, the notorious clash of 22 October 2011, in Syntagma Square, between anarchist and communist demonstrators. This unfolded in real time on the website of the mainstream Greek TV station Skai, and allowed all segments of the protest movement to react to its full horror (molotovs were thrown). Significantly, those who wanted to follow the news without the constant moralizing of the TV anchormen split-screened with it were forced towards Skai's unmediated output. The mainstream media was effectively being forced to mimic the output techniques of the guerrilla media.

The second example was the 26 September 2012 demonstration outside the Spanish parliament, where a broadcast media that usually put a heavy pro-government spin on events, ended up showing the entire, stage-by-stage police attack on a largely peaceful demonstration, including the firing of rubber bullets. For several hours the world could click on a livestream and see protesters repeatedly showing their open hands, trying to calm things down even as the police wound things up.

What this means is that, wherever the mainstream media has the guts to do it, they can show the unedited truth about protests: who starts them, who escalates them, who behaves stupidly, who not.

Of course, in the 'built' news bulletins you are always going to get ideology and constructed narratives; but in addition to the livestream record of events, and the storm of visual testimony via Twitpic and Instagram, traditional journalists also now have numerous other outlets to triangulate against.

Russia Today's coverage of the Greek riots, for example, while descending occasionally into histrionics, provided a very different visual and editorial take to that of Greek TV and the American news channels. Al Jazeera English, HuffPo—in both English and Spanish— and the numerous semi-professional blogs are, effectively, holding a

mirror up to the state and corporate media. And what they see sometimes alters the mainstream's vision of the story.

At the base layer, of course, remains the social media, which grew
more complex during 2011 and 2012. With blogs reducing the price of
publishing words, movies and pictures basically to the labour and
hosting costs—and Twitter, Tumblr and Facebook providing a
massive and unpredictable echo chamber—the whole relationship
between mainstream and social media has changed. Slowly, quietly
and, for now, unmeasurably, the mainstream media has become, for
many involved in activism, politics and journalism itself, a *secondary*
source of information, while social networks have become the primary
source. This, in turn, speaks to the emergence of an undeclared dual
power between the world of ideas and the world of official politics.

## 4. They are not prone to traditional and endemic ideologies: Labourism, Islamism, Fianna Fail Catholicism, etc., in fact, hermetic ideologies of all forms are rejected

This sentence does not even begin to capture the scale of detachment
from mainstream politics among those protesting—nor its implications. In the event, this disengagement from ideology and structure was
to play a major role in the defeat or failure of the progressive movements, from the USA to southern Europe, and above all in Egypt.

In Egypt, the first year of the revolution had seen spontaneous and
popular upsurges in which the youth and the more radical forces played
a significant role, demanding—in repeated clashes around Tahrir
Square—the transfer of power from the military to civilians. But the
secular and leftist youth who had led the revolution had failed to form
anything like an effective electoral bloc, or even to design an electoral
strategy. Thus the parliamentary election, and the final round of the
subsequent presidential race, would be fought essentially between the
remnants of militarism and the two forms of political Islam: the Muslim
Brotherhood and the more radical Salafist movement.

On 23 January 2012, parliament convened with a majority for the MB and a stunningly large minority of Salafists. Liberal, secular and leftist parties made up a small minority. However, Egyptians quickly realized that the parliament was effectively neutered, and that real power lay in the hands of the Supreme Council of the Armed Forces (SCAF).

Outside parliament two struggles raged: one conducted by the remnants of the Mubarak regime to retain control of the state; the other by the workers' movement to improve conditions in the factories. But they rarely collided.

Here the fundamental weakness of Egyptian democratic and secular politics—the so called 'civil camp'—was exposed. Some of those who had led the masses to Tahrir fought to push the Islamist-led parliament into a clash with the SCAF, and take full power. But many among the liberal and leftist movements rejected the idea of an alliance with the parliament against the SCAF. The liberal Al-Wafd Party even agreed to join an 'advisory council' that SCAF had set up to give the impression that it was sharing power. There was, even among NGOs and currents that would be described as social democratic, a preference for an 'Ataturk-ist' option: that is benign, secular military rule as a guarantee against Islamism.

The underlying problem throughout was that, even as the popularity of the MB and the Salafists began to wane, liberal and leftist forces proved unable to fill the vacuum. And this was not because they lacked support. In the presidential election of May–June 2012, the veteran Nasserite Hamdeen Sabbahi—a secularist—came third in the first round, just 700,000 votes behind the SCAF's candidate Ahmed Shafiq. And the two candidates who were to fight it out—Shafiq and the eventual winner, the MB's Mohamed Morsi—did not even poll half the votes between them in the first round. The election of course was marred by the arbitrary disqualification of other candidates who would have inhabited the secular ground between the MB and the SCAF.

With the MB in power, and consolidating its power in a series of constitutional moves following the presidential poll, the dynamic of the Egyptian revolution changed. It became, for the left, a question of exposing the differences between the social justice rhetoric of the Brotherhood on the streets and its actions in power; a question of organizing the working class in preparation for the moment when political and economic struggles would merge.

As Hossam El-Hamelawy (see Chapter 1) puts it: 'The leadership is reactionary, reformist, opportunist as with the Labour Party in Britain. But at the same time the base cadres are moving in a different direction. When Morsi speaks about the Islamic Sharia, maybe the Sharia in his head translates into neoliberal norms. But for the Muslim Brotherhood worker it actually means social justice.'[4]

However, after two years of riots, crises, scandals and crackdowns, Egypt has produced no large force on the left that is simultaneously against Islamism and in favour of a rapid completion of the revolution against the old militarists and businessmen who stand behind the SCAF. The left of all colours remains frustrated by the fact that the revolution has failed to break out of its 'political' stage.

Egypt, in short, is the clearest example of the revenge of the hierarchy: the revenge of the twentieth-century ideologies that globalist, secularist netizens had convinced themselves would expire of their own accord. The revolution is not over. Its next phase will seem quite familiar to those who studied 1848, or the classic revolutions of the twentieth century—but with this crucial difference: its fate will depend on whether large numbers of the Islamist poor, the lower middle class and workers can be convinced to break with the MB towards a social justice agenda that is not, at the same time, even more radically Islamist. That, in turn, depends on the ability of those who led the masses to Tahrir in January 2010 to break out of the political ghetto described above. (As I read the proofs of this edition, on 6 December 2012, six protesters have died and hundreds have been injured in clashes between Muslim Brotherhood supporters and the radical, more secular forces resisting President Morsi's grab for extra-constitutional power.)

And while there are many specifics to the Egyptian situation that are not likely to be replicated elsewhere, the year 2012 closed with a foreboding among the social movements of the world that maybe the old forces—religion, fascism, Stalinist communism, militarism—could revive and conquer elsewhere.

*5. Women [Are] very numerous as the backbone of movements. After twenty years of modernized labour markets and higher-education access, the 'archetypal' protest leader, organizer, facilitator, spokesperson now is an educated young woman*

With more examples to draw on, this pattern is confirmed. But beyond women's demographic and political presence, the noticeable thing is how unprepared feminism has been to deal with what's happened during the struggle.

There's been an obvious and predictable backlash, such as the sexual assaults in Tahrir Square, the crazy debate in the Egyptian parliament over a husband's right to have sex with the corpse of a recently deceased wife; the rapes and sexual assaults in various Occupy camps. Within the developed-world occupation movements there's been the consistent problem of men assuming leadership, and dominating the discussion, even in forums where 'consensus' and the various speaker stacking systems were supposed to prevent it.

In general, women have been able to organize to combat such instances of outright sexism. But the wider problem remains: if a movement has no demands, then how does it articulate what women's liberation consists of? How does it fit the issues raised by women's long-term and strategic oppression into the immediate social issues of the day?

Such questions perplexed and even tore apart the left-wing movements that emerged after 1968. Once women had won the battle against blatant sexism inside the left, there was still the issue, day to day, of how you advance the self-organization of women in an industrial labour movement that could be simultaneously militant, anti-capitalist and sexist.

In the horizontalist movements, this problem has hardly begun to be addressed. At root it is because feminism has achieved social mobility for some women, and even a symbolically liberated lifestyle, but at the price of a truce over the economic and social subjugation of all women. The journalist Laurie Penny summed up the limitations of what 'post-left' feminism has achieved:

> I wonder if the shiver of impossible yearning I experience when I watch space-battles on the television is what my nanna and women like her felt when they watched us going to university, having boy-friends … dancing all night … For her, my life was, is, science fiction: strange and frightening, enabled by technology … We handle it all casually because we're unable to conceive of an even better world. We've been told that this shaky picture is the best we're ever going to get.[5]

If you take a long-lens view of this dilemma—personal liberation replacing a struggle for general economic and social liberation—you could say it's simply subset of the overarching problem with the movements of 2011–12. Being a counter-culture—or even a 'counter-power'—is a viable strategy only as long as the dominant cultures and powers are benign and stable. Here the experience of the early labour movement contains a lesson.

The agenda of women's liberation—not just women's rights, but an actual route to sexual and economic equality—had to be imposed onto the early workers' movement by—guess who?—Marxist men with beards. Written in 1879, August Bebel's book *Woman and Socialism* became required reading for working-class men who wanted to be activists in the German socialist party, the SPD. It pledges that the woman of the future will be 'entirely independent, both socially and economically. She will not be subjected to even a trace of domination and exploitation, but will be free and man's equal, and mistress of her own lot … In the choice of love she is as free and unhampered as man.'[6]

But what the male lathe-turners of nineteenth-century Germany took for granted—the goal of economic liberation for the poorest and most downtrodden women—late twentieth-century mainstream feminism could not dare to imagine. It had become embattled by a sexual counter-revolution, detached from the politics of poverty and class, trapped in academic language.

So horizontalism in Europe and America, or the secular activists in the Middle East, often failed to successfully organize working-class and low-income women. Where it did so—as with the Spanish *indignado* movement once it moved out of the tent camps and immersed itself in everyday life—you find women, again and again, at the forefront of the resulting actions. The Coralla Utopia squat in Seville, where evicted working-class families took over a deserted apartment block, was run by a core of poverty-stricken women in their forties and fifties.

In the debates outlined below, about how the social movements of 2011–12 might break out of their isolation, the ability of feminism to see beyond the 'personal' into issues of economic freedom and a redesigned society will probably be decisive.

However, the scale of the sexual counter-revolution in some countries means women are not going to wait for the social movements to get their act together. Mitt Romney's stunning defeat among women voters in the November 2012 US presidential elections can be seen as the direct result of the Republicans' obsession with attacking abortion and contraception rights. The GOP's state-level war on abortion rights in particular during 2011–12 mobilized tens of thousands of women in local campaigns, not to mention the overwhelmingly female and minority workforce of the abortion clinics themselves. Nevertheless, their most effective defensive act in all this was to vote, and to vote in that most hierarchical of competitions: the race for the White House.

*6. Horizontalism has become endemic because technology makes it easy: it kills vertical hierarchies spontaneously, whereas before—and the quintessential experience of the twentieth century—was the killing of dissent within movements, the channelling of movements, and their bureaucratization*

With hindsight, late 2011 was the moment the sheen on horizontalism faded. In Egypt, the atmosphere of networked tolerance that had prevailed during the initial Tahrir Square occupation dulled as real, hierarchical forces emerged. In Spain, the leading voices within the *indignado* movement became frustrated as the obsession with 'process', the tyranny of consensus and the refusal to advocate political demands sucked away its momentum. With Occupy Wall Street, critics point to an emergent self-obsession, which the philosopher Slavoj Žižek warned about when he spoke in Zuccotti in October: 'There is a danger. Don't fall in love with yourselves. We have a nice time here. But remember, carnivals come cheap. What matters is the day after, when we will have to return to normal lives. Will there be any changes then?'[7]

The journalist Thomas Frank excoriated Occupy for its self-obsession, its refusal to express demands, comparing its minimal achievements with those of the Tea Party, which abandoned horizontalism and moved into the hierarchies of the Republican Party—gaining heavy representation in Congress, state legislatures and their own man on the ticket for vice-president.

'It is as clear to me today as it was last year', Frank wrote, 'that the conservative era will be brought to a close only through some kind of mass social movement on the left. But what kind of movement might succeed? Well, for one thing, a movement whose core values arise not from an abstract hostility to the state or from the need for protesters to find their voice, but rather from the everyday lives of working people.'[8]

However, both in the USA and Spain, the occupiers did—once their ability to capture physical space was suppressed—attempt to move towards 'everyday' or 'normal' life. By mid 2012, wherever you went in

Spain you could find movements of the working class and poor that had become infused with a maybe 5 per cent dose of horizontalist activism. The landless labourers I found occupying and working a deserted farm in Andalusia had attracted a small band of itinerant *indignados*: they slept on the concrete floors of the abandoned farm and tended the sheep in their Che Guevara t-shirts. Likewise it was 15M activists who acted as a kind of facilitation service for the mainly working-class occupiers at Coralla Utopia in Seville. Castells writes of the Spanish *indignados*:

> The movement did not disappear; rather it spread out into the social fabric, with neighbourhood assemblies, defensive actions against injustices, such as opposition to evictions of families, and the spreading of alternative economic practices such as consumer cooperatives, ethical banking, exchange networks and many other such forms of living differently so as to live with meaning.[9]

In the USA, though the Occupy movement had been reduced to a smaller bunch of activists by mid 2012, you began to see, around the edges of their attempts to infest Union Square on a nightly basis, small clusters of activists from what Žižek might have called 'normal life': Orthodox Jewish youth complaining of being oppressed by their community's internal security force; African American kids—from projects, not colleges—who'd mobilized in their thousands in the wake of the shooting of Trayvon Martin. When Superstorm Sandy devastated parts of New York and New Jersey in November 2012, overwhelming the federal emergency response services, Occupy activists surged into the breach, organizing food kitchens, rigging emergency power supplies, setting up informal car ferry schemes and emergency shelters. Soon the hashtag #OccupySandy was trending.

So, if you look hard enough, the Occupy protests did leave an imprint on 'normal life'—and of course they made a massive imprint on intellectual and cultural life. But to those who know the history of radical politics, the pattern of 'reaching out' as facilitators towards the struggles of the severely dispossessed bears a fatal resemblance to the actions of the Russian 'Narodniks' of the 1870s.

The student Narodniks, or Populists, left Moscow and St Petersburg in their thousands in what became known as the 'mad summer of 1874'. Dressed as labourers or peasants, they sought jobs alongside the recently emancipated serfs, whose village communes they believed to be the basis of a future economic system that could bypass industrial capitalism. Equally important to the Narodniks was the perfection of the self: revolutionaries ought to be 'fully rounded characters who opposed the crushing of individuals under the wheels of a runaway historical tractor'.[10]

Though their work was later derided by Marxists, and after it failed some became terrorists, it was not a total waste of effort. Over its forty-year arc of development, Russian Populism would produce numerous activists who eventually concluded that it was better to spread radical politics among the workers rather than the peasants, because the route to social justice lay through seizing hold of capitalist industry, and indeed government—not in the attempt to avoiding a capitalist stage of development. Some became reformist social democrats, others, leaders of the Bolshevik Party: the phrase quoted in the paragraph above was flung by Leon Trotsky, then a teenage Narodnik, at his Marxist girl-friend at a clandestine meeting in the 1890s.

But the route away from horizontalism to more traditional structured politics looks blocked today: blocked by consciousness of how entrapped activists become when they enter structures like the trades unions, the US Democrats, social democracy and even the major NGOs. Though many activists do live parallel lives—working for a union by day, for example, mobilizing for occupation protests by night—it is rare to find horizontalist practices imported into unions and official parties. It is far more common to find social movement activists com-plaining that their time is wasted working for the union bureaucracy. Castells argues that this is logical, and that the turn to 'alternative economic practices'—by choice among the activists and by necessity among the poor—is where the movement goes next, along with the spread of anti-establishment consciousness.

But a changed consciousness is not enough. It does not resist austerity, stop fascism, or liberate women from drudgery and sexual violence. Though they have developed in fertile directions via communes, land occupations and hurricane relief work in 2012, the social movements have not yet found a tactic that can dictate the agenda on the scale it did during the occupation of symbolic space in mid-to-late 2011.

*7. Memes: 'A meme acts as a unit for carrying cultural ideas, symbols or practices, which can be transmitted from one mind to another through writing, speech, gestures, rituals or other imitable phenomena. Supporters of the concept regard memes as cultural analogues to genes, in that they self-replicate, mutate and respond to selective pressures' (Wikipedia). So what happens is that ideas arise, are very quickly 'market tested' and either take off, bubble under, insinuate themselves or, if no good, they disappear. Ideas self-replicate like genes. Prior to the internet this theory (see Richard Dawkins, 1976) seemed an overstatement, but you can now clearly trace the evolution of memes.*

When the history of this crisis is written, one of the most fascinating tasks will be to comprehensively document the memes that flowed throughout it. It will not be easy: the digital human consciousness is playful. Thousands of jokes are made each day on Twitter consisting, for example, of fake book titles on some iconoclastic theme. It will not be enough to document what they were, but who made them—the speed at which the irony flowed; were people at work when they retweeted, or added their own contribution? Did the meme stay local, or did it go global?

And not all memes were digital. The 'V for Vendetta' mask associated with the Anonymous hacker collective was physical: it was worn on faces, and spray-canned on the bent shutters of the posh hotels in Syntagma Square, by people with no links whatsoever to Anonymous.

There is the global phenomenon of holding up verbose, personalized hand-drawn placards, whose clear subtext is defiance of the pithy, uniform, printed ones supplied by trade unions and leftist groups. 'We want everyone to wake up to the beauty we can create', read one I spotted on the first day of the Occupy protest at St Paul's in London. 'This is not a violent riot. This is a human awakening,' said another.

Then there is the chant—'*Ash'ab nurid izqat al-nizam*' (the people demand the fall of the regime)—which spread from Tunisia, Bahrain and Egypt to Libya and Syria without textually morphing at all. Journalist Suby Raman has produced a 'deconstruction' of the slogan for non-Arabic speakers that reveals fascinatingly significant choices in the words themselves: the term for 'the people' is the most radical, most secular on offer; the term for 'the fall of' is not radical at all—signifying more 'the cutting down to size'. The term for 'regime' means more than just government: 'Instead, it refers to a sociopolitical order that the people are trying to bring down, an entire mechanism of terror and discipline that they have broken free of.'[11] This, in turn, allowed the slogan's meaning to morph from literal to metaphorical, as noted early on in the process by the Middle East scholar Rashid Khalidi: 'They are not only referring to their corrupt governments; they also mean the old regime that has prevailed for decades in the entire Arab world, from the Atlantic to the Gulf.'[12]

The most important thing about these slogans, images and gestures is not what they said in isolation but what they expressed cumulatively, as they interacted: the woman who walked naked through the riot in Plaza Neptuno, outside the Spanish parliament, holding a sign saying 'peace'; the video of Loukanikos, the Greek riot dog, which went globally viral in the summer of 2011; the very name of the band Pussy Riot, which newsreaders in some Catholic countries were ordered to avoid saying on air, even as their jail sentences were reported.

What did it all mean? These were first of all signifiers of rejection: scorn not just for the elite world of yachts, diamond watches and bodyguards from which the 99% are excluded, but for the world of corporate conformity. Scorn for the charade played out in the workplace: for discipline, hierarchy, targets achieved, the cheap business suit, the insincere smile, the dead language of corporate communications. Through these signs and symbols, large parts of humanity were signalling their solidarity to one another; their belief that a kinder, more human system is possible; and that it would be born out of the chaotic, ironic, playful qualities of human life—not by pitting one cruel hierarchy against another.

*8. They all seem to know each other: not only is the network more powerful than the hierarchy—but the ad-hoc network has become easier to form. So if you 'follow' somebody from the UCL occupation on Twitter, as I have done, you can easily run into a radical blogger from Egypt or a lecturer in peaceful resistance in California who mainly does work on Burma, so then there are the Burmese tweets to follow. During the early twentieth century, people would ride hanging on the undersides of train carriages across borders, just to make links like these.*

In the Soviet war movie *The Commissar* (1967), a Jewish blacksmith admits to a female military commissar, as they both prepare to be killed: 'I'm not spiteful. I am for the International of Kindness. There are so few kind people left in the world.'

She counters: 'Where did you get those fairy tales from? About the International of Kindness? The International is founded on the blood of workers and peasants. People swallow gunpowder for it and become very spiteful: they endure fighting, marching, lice.'

'If you take fairy tales away from people,' he replies, 'how would you explain to them what they should live for?'

This, the central question for all progressive movements, was unequivocally answered in the twentieth century in favour of the commissar and against the fairy tales: a narrative that preferred 'dying for' to 'living for' was what prevailed.

*The Commissar* is one of the masterpieces of Soviet cinema. It goes without saying that it was immediately banned, and the single print was ordered to be destroyed. Director Aleksandr Askoldov was expelled from the Communist Party, accused of 'social parasitism' and never allowed to make another movie. Only in 1988, having been secretly preserved by workers in a film archive, was the work revived, to wide acclaim—by which time Askoldov's career had been destroyed.

Today Askoldov's phrase 'The International of Kindness' seems a strangely apposite label for what the activists have created. Over the past three years a vast, chaotic network of discontented people has has evolved into something close to what the characters in *The Commissar* describe: an 'international' without leaders, formal structures or strategy—and above all without bitterness.

And this is the problem for all those within the radical movements who wish them to take a 'turn to the workers', a turn towards 'everyday life', to structure, demands and engagement with official politics. Such exhortations miss the point: their unwillingness to engage is precisely what allowed radical activists, up to now, to disrupt the timetable of official politics.

Paradoxically, this very un-Marxist generation of rebels has begun to do what Marx urged during the 1848 revolutions. It has stopped trying to clothe its radicalism in the costumes of past revolutions, and embraced the essence of revolution: 'revolutionizing themselves and things, creating something that did not exist before'.[13]

Things 'kicked off' because what Marx called the 'poetry of the future' broke through the prose, and the structures of the present. But they did so for quite prosaic reasons, as I outlined in the ninth of the Twenty Reasons.

*9. The specifics of economic failure: the rise of mass access to university-level education is a given. Maybe soon even 50 per cent in higher education will not be enough. In most of the world this is being funded by personal indebtedess—so people are making a rational choice to go into debt in hopes of being better paid later. However, the prospect of ten years of fiscal retrenchment in some countries means they now know they will be poorer than their parents. And the effect has been like throwing a light switch; the prosperity story is replaced with the doom story, even if for individuals reality will be more complex, and not as bad as they expect.*

As an explanation for radicalization, this needs little further comment. However, the long-term economic implications of hollowing out the middle class like this are worth spelling out.

Even before the financial crisis, policymakers were concerned about the impact of ageing populations. In advanced countries the so-called dependency ratio—between the older generation drawing pensions, and a younger generation whose economic activity pays for those pensions—is set to double between now and 2050. In Spain, Italy and Japan—countries with unsustainable debts and low economic dynamism—the ratio is set to reach 60 per cent: that is, for every six pensioners there will be just four citizens of working age. Worse still, in China—the economy we relied on to drive global growth during the recession of the 2010s—the dependency ratio will rise rapidly to around 60 per cent by 2050, two-thirds of which will be dependent elderly people. Meanwhile, already something like one in five graduates in China are having trouble finding permanent, graduate-level jobs: when I visited there in November 2012, I was struck by the rapid convergence of the Starbucks workforce there with that of other countries. It contains more graduates, many English speakers, and for some their future—indeed their present—looked as uninspiring as it does for the graduate baristas of Europe and the USA.

Globally, even without the financial crisis, the arithmetic of ageing would have made it impossible for the existing financial system—of saving via pensions invested in the equity and debt markets—to go on serving the middle class.

Now however, the realization is dawning that the generation who started work in 2010, and who will retire in 2050, will have been poor through much of their working lives; they will be 'asset poor'—unless the house-price bubble can be pumped up again—and dependent on a generation being born today to join the 'race to the bottom' in terms of wages and lifestyles.

*10. This evaporation of a promise is compounded in the more repressive societies and emerging markets because—even where you get rapid economic growth—it cannot absorb the demographic bulge of young people fast enough to deliver rising living standards for enough of them.*

*11. To amplify: I can't find the quote, but one of the historians of the French Revolution of 1789 wrote that it was not the product of poor people but of poor lawyers. You can have political/economic setups that disappoint the poor for generations—but if lawyers, teachers and doctors are sitting in their garrets freezing and starving, you get revolution. Now, in their garrets, they have a laptop and broadband connection.*

The historian, of course, was Taine (see Chapter 3) and the comparison has been borne out during the events of 2012.

*12. The weakness of organized labour means there's a changed relationship between the radicalized middle class, the poor and the organized workforce. The world looks more like nineteenth-century Paris—heavy predominance of the 'progressive' intelligentsia, intermixing with the slum-dwellers at numerous social interfaces (cabarets in the nineteenth century, raves today); huge social fear of the excluded poor but also many rags-to-riches stories celebrated in the media (50 Cent, etc); meanwhile the solidaristic culture and respectability of organized labour is still there but, as in Egypt, they find themselves a 'stage army' to be marched on and off the scene of history.*

Since that was written, there have been massive strikes and demonstrations led by unions and workers' parties. The million-strong trade union demos in Portugal on 15 September 2012 were forceful enough to achieve, for the first time, the reversal of an EU-mandated austerity measure. In the USA a rolling strike by Walmart employees tipped the psychological balance between unions and employers there.

In Egypt, by late 2011, a strike wave had begun to force the renationalization of enterprises sold off under Mubarak to his regime cronies. In China, repeated walkouts at the iconic Foxconn plant in Zhengzhou, which makes the iPhone, are just the most high-profile of the strikes that have continued in the PRC during the economic recovery.

Yet nowhere has organized labour broken out of the patterns imposed on it under neoliberalism.

Unlimited strike action remains rare; sustained workplace occupations—as at the takeover of the general hospital in Kilkis, Greece, in the spring of 2012—have remained isolated and often defeated. The narrative of working-class resistance to austerity is strong in southern Europe. But the narrative of a working-class alternative to capitalism, namely socialism or communism, is extremely weak.

Consequently Europe and the USA are in a period of stasis, in view of the loss of momentum by the horizontalist occupation movements and their collision with the brick wall of official politics, police repression and far-right violence. We must also acknowledge the slow-motion radicalization of organized workers; their consciousness of their own weakness, and their preparedness to subordinate direct action to lobbying the Democrats in Congress or socialists in various European parliaments.

In Egypt, the workers' movement has grown faster. Early in 2012 the number of struggles—as counted by the Egyptian Centre for Economic and Social Rights—hovered around 250 disputes a month. The months of the presidential election witnessed a relative lull. But the first three months of Morsi's presidency saw around 1,600 strikes and occupations.

This movement is led partly by growing new unions, partly by local rank and file figures. However, it is disunited and not politicized. Apart from the demand for the minimum wage, there are no general demands that unite the movement. And although new unions are springing up, they still represent a small minority of workers and can easily become immersed in debilitating internal disputes.

At present, many of the local leaders of this new union movement are sceptical of politics and politicians, and keen to distance themselves from any kind of political taint.

In the original 'Twenty Reasons' I amplified a positive spin-off from this weakness of organized labour as follows:

*13. This leads to a loss of fear among the young radicals of any movement: they can pick and choose; there is no confrontation they can't retreat from. They can 'have a day off' from protesting, occupying: whereas with the old working-class-based movements, their place in the ranks of battle was determined, and they couldn't retreat once things started. You couldn't 'have a day off' from the miners' strike if you lived in a pit village.*

Since then, across the globe those tasked with policing the new protest movements have recognized this 'loss of fear' and, through trial and error, evolved an effective response: the aggressive and offensive use of non-lethal force.

The Occupy camp in Zuccotti Park was cleared with maximum

theatrical impact on 15 November: when I visited it a few weeks later, with my press pass on display, I was not even allowed to film inside the privately-owned concrete piazza. But the clearance of Zuccotti was only a foretaste of the way in which US police forces would deal with the now mobile and sporadic protests that followed.

On 18 November 2012, when around twenty students at UC Davis sat cross-legged and immobile to block a pathway, police drew batons and shotguns and then pepper-sprayed the entirely peaceful protesters. Video and still images of the protest, which went viral, show one officer forcing open the mouth of a protester and squirting pepper spray down their throat.[14] Geoffrey Wildanger, on the receiving end, wrote later:

> Pepper spray hurts a lot. Apparently it was military grade pepper spray, which causes a fatality in one out of every 600 uses. One young woman was hospitalized for chemical burns … one of us, sprayed in the mouth, vomited blood for 45 minutes … for two days my eyes burned when I took a shower.[15]

The demeanour of the police as they then break up a much larger crowd assembled to support the sit-down protest is clear: one missile, blow or act of aggression would have brought even greater force to bear. By now this was part of a global pattern of policing response to non-violent direct action that stood in marked contrast to the way such events had been handled while the economy was booming.

In Greece, police had already crossed a line in the summer of 2011, towards massive and indiscriminate use of tear gas and stun grenades against peaceful crowds. With the election of a New Democracy–led coalition, in June 2012, the stage was set for a radical erosion of democratic rights under the stewardship of the incoming Greek public order minister, Nikolaos Dendias.

Now began a crackdown on free speech. After the *Guardian* published the allegations that anti-fascists were tortured by pro–Golden Dawn police officers, Dendias threatened to sue the newspaper.

Magazine editor Kostas Vaxevanis was arrested (by more than fifty officers) after publishing the infamous 'Lagarde List' of Greeks with Swiss bank accounts. Vaxevanis was acquitted within days after an international outcry and a trial at which state prosecutors, having mobilized such heavy policing powers, offered no evidence. Meanwhile two TV journalists were pulled off air in mid-programme and suspended, when they began analysing Dendias's handling of the crises live on air.

Greece may be the laboratory experiment of curtailed democracy, but it shows what the effect of such repression can be on activists in the social movements and the journalists who cover them: it can force them into various states of retreat, fear and fatalism, and foster a semi-underground lifestyle.

However, the most important effect of the pepper spray, the arrests, the tear gas and rubber bullets has not been on the activists, but on the wider milieu of discontented young people. It has chased them out of the public arena and suffocated the expression of their anger. In this way it has—to use a famous internet meme as metaphor—put one giant Pop Tart of discontent into the microwave, and switched the dial to maximum.

That is where we are. And that is why the final story of the period that opened up with the Arab Spring cannot yet be told.

In February 2011 I wrote:

*14. In addition to a day off, you can 'mix and match': I have met people who do community organizing one day, and the next are on a flotilla to Gaza; then they pop up working for a think tank on sustainable energy, then they're writing a book about something completely different. I was astonished to find people I had interviewed inside the UCL occupation blogging from Tahrir Square this week.*

This is in part due to the ability of people to adopt multiple and parallel identities, but it is also the result of the following: it is easy to mix and match if you can upload and disseminate the basic knowledge needed to be an activist in different sectors. Because, as I pointed out:

*15. People just know more than they used to. Dictatorships rely not just on the suppression of news, but on the suppression of narratives and truth. More or less everything you need to know to make sense of the world is available as freely downloadable content on the internet—and it's not pre-digested for you by your teachers, parents, priests, imams. For example there are huge numbers of facts available to me now about the subjects I studied at university, that were not known when I was there in the 1980s. Then whole academic terms would be spent disputing basic facts, or trying to research them. Now that is still true, but the plane of reasoning can be more complex, because people have an instant reference source for the undisputed premises of arguments. It's as if physics has been replaced by quantum physics, but in every discipline.*

I expanded on this in Chapter 7 above. But it is worth considering here what the impact of this instant knowledge—and a wide repository of knowledge—has been on the protest movements themselves.

Castells has described the social movements of 2011–12 as highly 'self-reflexive'. That is, the activists are prepared to quickly analyse what's happened, gather evidence, change tactics, adapt slogans. By contrast the old left soldiered on with one fetishized tactic or slogan after another for years: Labour entryism, the rank and file movement, and so on.

So by late 2011 you have the beginnings of a re-evaluation of horizontalism. Activists became aware of the boredom engendered by the perpetual use of the 'human mic'. They began to understand the limitations of the communal kitchen in actually advancing the communal. They became weary of tent camps, which began to attract the dispossessed and deranged. Their 'tyranny of consensus' became, itself, a meme.

At the time of writing, in mid-November 2012, there is a clearly posed question: what next? But no answer. The rest of the conditions I outlined in February 2011 still prevail:

*16. There is no Cold War, and the War on Terror is not as effective as the Cold War was in solidifying elites against change. Egypt is proving to be a worked example of this: though it is highly likely things will spiral out of control, post Mubarak—as in all the colour revolutions— the dire warnings of the US right that this will lead to Islamism are a meme that has not taken off. In fact you could make an interesting study of how the meme starts, blossoms and fades away over the space of twelve days. To be clear: I am not saying they are wrong—only that the fear of an Islamist takeover in Egypt has not been strong enough to swing the US presidency or the media behind Mubarak.*

As it turned out, Islamists won the election in Egypt. They dominate the post-revolutionary government of Tunisia, are heavily represented inside the post-Gaddafi Libyan government, and increasingly prominent among the Free Syrian Army. Through it all, at not one moment did concern about Islamism force the USA to pull back from tacit support for liberation movements, or indeed to switch support back to the dictators on whom the world order had previously relied.

If you look at this conundrum through the eyes of the old foreign policy elite, it is puzzling: it seems as if the Clinton-led State Department opened up one client state after another to the possibility of an Islamist government—promoting alongside it the interests of a more Westernized, secular, liberal group which was never able to wield power, but accepting the Islamist outcome. The logic is that the State Department has fundamentally rethought its concept of soft power. It believes, after the Arab Spring, that there's a global marketplace in images and ideas and that its raison d'être is to influence that.

The next three 'reasons' are, I think, self-explanatory and stand the test of events.

*17. It is—with international pressure and some powerful NGOs—possible to bring down a repressive government without having to spend years in the jungle as a guerrilla, or years in the urban underground: instead the oppositional youth—both in the West in repressive regimes like Tunisia or Egypt, and above all in China—live in a virtual undergrowth online and through digital comms networks. The internet is not key here—more important are the things people exchange by text message, the music they swap with each other, etc.: the hidden meanings in graffiti, street art and so on which those in authority fail to spot.*

*18. People have a better understanding of power. The activists have read their Chomsky and their Hardt–Negri, but the ideas therein have become mimetic: young people believe the issues are no longer class and economics, but simply power: they are clever to the point of expertise in knowing how to mess up hierarchies and see the various 'revolutions' in their own lives as part of an 'exodus' from oppression, not—as previous generations did—as a 'diversion into the personal'. In 1972 Foucault could tell Gilles Deleuze: 'We had to wait until the nineteenth century before we began to understand the nature of exploitation, and to this day, we have yet to fully comprehend the nature of power.'[16]—that's probably changed.*

*19. As the algebraic sum of all these factors it feels like the protest 'meme' that is sweeping the world—if that premise is indeed true—is profoundly less radical on economics than the one that swept the world in the 1910s and 1920s; they don't seek a total overturn, they seek a moderation of excesses. However, on politics the common theme is the dissolution of centralized power and the demand for 'autonomy' and personal freedom, in addition to formal democracy and an end to corrupt, family-based power elites.*

With the experience of two more years of protest and instability, however, we have seen the emergence of what Castells calls 'alternative economic practice': informal lending between non-family members, sharing of tools, bartering of goods and services. Castells argues that it is out of such makeshift practices that a non-capitalist economics can emerge; at the very least, these tactics of necessity can be the ground on which the radicalized youth meet the dispossessed poor:

> Those who dared to live alternative ways of life ... built networks of solidarity, support and experimentation ... For many others who had accepted an existence sustained by the dream of consumption and the fear of departing from normality, when the crisis disrupted their lives a window of hope appeared through examples that offered glimpses of a different life. Not so much because of a sudden ideological conversion but as a result of the impossibility of living by the rules of the market.[17]

Certainly, during 2011–12, the impact of Occupy was to push the mainstream discourse to the left. In the UK you now have senior regulators openly discussing the write-off of the country's debt, and in the case of Andrew Haldane, head of financial stability at the Bank of England, admitting that Occupy had a point:

> Occupy has been successful in its efforts to popularize the problems of the global financial system for one very simple reason: they are right ... For the hard-headed facts suggest that, at the heart of the global financial crisis, were and are problems of deep and rising inequality.[18]

Haldane went on to argue that the regulatory reforms to banking begun in the UK would contribute to a more socially responsible and useful banking system, and appealed for the movement's support. He was not the only figure among the 1% to conceive of a radically redesigned— and essentially de-financialized—capitalism emerging from this crisis.

However, the weakness of Haldane's argument is obvious: all narratives of change are currently premised on the survival of globalization.

As I argue in Chapter 6 above, the survival of globalization is no longer a given. National routes out of the crisis are entirely possible, and are beginning to present themselves, despite the banishment of economic nationalism from official politics.

*20. Technology has—in many ways, from the contraceptive pill to the iPod, the blog and the CCTV camera—expanded the space and power of the individual.*

If you could only list one reason for what's happened in the past two years, it would be this: the networked individual colliding with the economic crisis. And yet it is the most contentious, being the hardest to quantify.

As I argue in Chapter 7, something fundamental has happened—a shift in human consciousness and behaviour as momentous as that triggered by the arrival of mass consumption and mass culture in the 1900s.

The sociological tradition tends to emphasize a continuous process of 'individuation'—from the lifestyle changes of the 1970s through the extreme consumerism of the pre-bust 2000s. By contrast I am drawn to Virginia Woolf's comment: 'On or about December 1910 human character changed.'[19] She was referring to a revolution in social life and art, which made the literary tools and conventions of the Edwardian era 'dead for us'. Cumulative micro-changes in technology and behaviour interacted with each other, then as now, to produce a tipping point.

Castells documents the tipping points more thoroughly in his 2012 book, *Networks of Outrage and Hope*.[20] For him, the model for real-world networked social movements was the Internet-based movement or community; this ethos then gets projected into space and time—the occupation, the demo, the meeting. The moment of physical projection itself is critical, because it is the point at which what he calls 'counter-power'—opposition to the status quo—moves from the realm of ideas to action:

> From the safety of cyberspace, people from all ages and conditions moved towards occupying urban space, on a blind date with each other and with the destiny they wanted to forge as they claimed their right to make history.[21]

Castells's analysis allows us to answer some of the difficult questions posed in this book. If he is right, the networked individual and her behaviour patterns are not just the product of youth, or generational change: there are numerous over-fifties who live the full, untrammelled life of the netizen. The change, Castells argues, is one-off and irreversible, like electrification, and it will condition all politics going forward.

On this basis he offers the following dire news to those—like Malcolm Gladwell during the Arab Spring, and more recently the British writer Mark Fisher—who want the movement to break with autonomy and horizontalism:

> Networked social movements, as all social movements in history, bear the mark of their society. They could not exist without the internet. But their significance is much deeper. They are suited for their role as agents of change in the network society, in sharp contrast with the obsolete political institutions inherited from a historically superseded social structure.[22]

If this is correct, we can expect horizontalism to survive its first winter of discontent, and to resist absorption into the trade unions or the liberal and social-democratic parties. But having exhausted tent camps and general assemblies with their dearth of demands—having begun the move into 'everyday life'—what happens next?

## *Where next?*

The movements that took to the streets in 2011–12 are at a turning point. They have created a strong counter-culture, which resonates among much wider masses of people than actually turn up to erect tents in squares, defend abortion clinics, attend picket lines.

Yet the revolution remains trapped at the phase of ideology, culture, political debate. The real changes in the world desired by those who protest are still only achievable by those with hierarchical power: be it Mohamed Morsi dictating peace terms to Israel over Gaza, President Obama shielding the women and minorities of the 'red' states of America from legal onslaught, Syriza's leader Alexis Tsipras, waiting nervously in the wings of Greek parliamentary politics.

It is no surprise to the social historian to find this extreme vigour of critical thought alongside seeping powerlessness. Marx himself identified the same problem with German radicalism in the early 1840s. Prevented from staging a revolution in politics, Germans had opted for a revolution of the mind: through the Romantic movement in music and poetry, student radicalism and left-wing philosophy: 'In politics, the Germans thought what other nations did. Germany was their theoretical conscience. The abstraction and presumption of its thought was always in step with the one-sidedness and lowliness of its reality.'[23] Marx and his contemporaries proposed that this could not long persist in a revolutionary period, and they were right: by the second month of the 1848 revolutions, Germany was at the centre of the action.

Today, however, the predominance of cultural over physical politics has survived twenty-four months of social upheaval, and the reason is clear. The radical youth do not disdain 'ordinary' or 'everyday' life, or the uneducated masses; nor do they fear to go up against batons and even bullets. What they disdain and fear are the politics of power. It is this logjam that will have to be broken for the social movements to go from being influencers to a decisive force. In the process, they will have to engage with the things they despise: compromise, parliamentary politics, the art of the possible, political Islam, organized labour. The question then will be, on whose terms and with what politics?

Here, there is a parallel with the 1930s that is worth exploring. The first four years of the crisis, from 1929 to 1933, were not a period of effective mass resistance. That happened later.

The first phase of the 1930s Depression was marked—in most places—by social disorientation, catastrophic policy choices, dysfunctional and autocratic governments and the rapid rise of the far right. Thinking on the left was dominated by the 'Third Period' line dictated by Moscow, which said that socialist parties were as bad as fascists and denied any possibility of reforming capitalism; this ensured, by the early 1930s, that most of the Communist Parties would become isolated sects that would have made today's Occupy protest look positively moderate.

It was Hitler's rise to power that focused minds, amid the fear that something similar could happen in France, Austria and Spain. At the same time, Roosevelt's New Deal signalled the possibility of a progressive liberal government after all, capitalism reformed—albeit at the price of a retreat to economic nationalism.

After a huge far-right demonstration in Paris in February 1934, in which sixteen demonstrators and counter-demonstrators were killed, the intellectual climate changed. The socialist and communist masses forced their parties to work together, despite cultural differences and physical antagonism. The Comintern rapidly switched to a strategy of alliances with 'liberal' mainstream parties—the so-called Popular Front. The unions went on the offensive, culminating in a workplace occupation movement that stretched from Poland, Spain and France to the USA in 1936–37.[24] Beyond the formalities, during this period, the masses took control of opposition politics: dictating new lines to their leaders; softening the rigid doctrines they were presented with.

Up to now, in today's crisis, protest has been driven by narratives of hope and outrage, not of fear. The horizontalists' self-isolation, indeed self-obsession, is not the result of a dictated party line, as in the 1930s, but of something equally strong in today's conditions: the inner zeit-geist. But as Castells points out, it is fear that, neurologically, impels us to take greater risks. As austerity pushes parts of Europe towards social meltdown, as fascism revives there and as democracy is eroded, maybe it is this that drives the workers' movement beyond the one-day strike and the social movements beyond the temporary occupation of space, as well as goading the existing parties beyond the comfort zone dictated by the global order.

It was the ninety-three-year-old French Resistance fighter Stéphane Hessel who gave the *indignado* movement its title, in the iconic October 2010 pamphlet '*Indignez-vous!*' Hessel identified the rise of Nazism, not the economic depression that produced Nazism, as the key radicalizing factor for his generation:

> I wish for you all, each of you, to have your own motive for indigna-tion. It is precious. When something outrages you, as I was outraged by Nazism, then people become militant, strong, and engaged. They join this current of history … and this current goes towards more justice, more freedom.

It took the rise of fascism to force humanity to fight for the progressive world it created after 1945. Flawed as it was, it is this world—of human rights, democracy and affluence in the West—that is now in jeopardy.

And though you can—as the anarchist slogan says—'live despite capitalism', you can't live 'despite' fascism, genocidal racism, extreme sexual counter-revolution and war. As the gears of mainstream politics and economic crisis clash and grind above their heads, I would expect this realization to be the guiding factor in where the mass movements turn next.

·

# Acknowledgements

When this crisis is over I will be able to publish a full list of the people who have helped me in the writing of this book. For now, as the situation darkens even in some democratic countries, I will just thank them anonymously as requested: the Greek and Spanish journalists who have gone massively more than the extra mile to help me get to where the action is; the numerous writers and artists around Occupy who welcomed me into their networks; numerous fellow MSM journalists who helped me out, including in Russia; two fixers in Cairo who were senior professionals displaced by the revolution, plus all the camera crews and producers I have worked with at these events. And of course my colleagues at the BBC who gave me the time and space to write this book. Andrew Kidd, my agent at Aitken Alexander, and successive Verso editors Tom Penn and Leo Hollis, together with Verso's redoubtable activist/publicist Sarah Shin can be named in person. Everybody on my Twitter and Tumblr feeds. And a big thanks to 500 or so activists and journalists who refrained from rioting at the launch party of the book, in London's Waterloo in January 2012, despite it being closed down by the authorities.

Paul Mason
November 2012

# Notes

## Introduction

1. *Occupy Everywhere: Reflections on Why It's Kicking Off Everywhere*, London 2012 (forthcoming).
2. Robert Cohen, *Freedom's Orator: Mario Savio and the Radical Legacy of the 1960s*, New York 2009, p. 100.

## Chapter 1

1. 'Meet Asmaa Mahfouz and the vlog that helped spark the revolution', youtube.com/watch?v=SgjIgMdsEuk (last accessed 18 October 2011).
2. Nadia Idle and Alex Nunns, *Tweets from Tahrir*, New York 2011.
3. 'Amazing courage of Egyptian Protesters! Must see!', youtube.com/watch?v=6VXP0FnTwZE&feature=related (last accessed 18 October 2011).
4. S. Radwan, 'Economic and social impact of the financial and economic Crisis on Egypt', International Labour Organization paper, April 2009.
5. Ibid.
6. Kara N. Tina, 'We're Not Leaving Until Mubarak Leaves', occupiedlondon.org/cairo/?p=300, 5 February 2011.
7. The Masry Shebin El-Kom workers would force the renationalization of their factory through legal action on 21 September 2011.

*Chapter 2*

1. 'The World in 2011', *Economist*, December 2010.
2. Stephen M. Walt, 'Why the Tunisian revolution won't spread', ForeignPolicy.com, 16 January 2011.
3. Reuters, 25 January 2011, 18:25 GMT.
4. Jonathan Lis, 'New IDF intelligence chief failed to predict Egypt uprising', *Haaretz*, 30 January 2011.
5. Edward Said, 'Islam through Western eyes', *Nation*, 26 April 1980.
6. Tarek Masoud, 'The road to (and from) Liberation Square', *Journal of Democracy*, vol. 22, no. 3, July 2011.
7. Fredric Jameson, 'Future City', *New Left Review* 21, May–June 2003.
8. Fredric Jameson, *The Cultural Turn: Selected Writings on the Postmodern, 1983–1998*, London 1998, p. 59.
9. N. Chomsky and E. Herman, 'Preface to the 2002 Edition', *Manufacturing Consent: The Political Economy of the Mass Media*, London 2002, p. xii.
10. Quoted in Mark Fisher, *Capitalist Realism: Is There No Alternative?*, Ropley 2009.
11. Fisher, *Capitalist Realism*, pp. 3–16.
12. Ron Suskind, 'Faith, certainty and the presidency of George W. Bush', *New York Times Magazine*, 17 October 2004.
13. Anthony Giddens, 'My chat with the colonel', *Guardian*, 9 March 2007.
14. Paul Mason, *Meltdown: The End of the Age of Greed*, London 2010, p. 233.
15. Quoted in Y. Kallianos, 'December as an event in Greek radical politics', in Antonis Vradis and Dimitris Dalakoglou, *Revolt and Crisis in Greece: Between a Present Yet to Pass and a Future Still to Come*, London 2011.
16. Alan Woods, 'The crisis of capitalism and the tasks of Marxists, Part III', 29 September 2009, ireland.marxist.com.
17. youtube.com/watch?v=gC2YCgDaL10&feature
18. 'Iran's Twitter Revolution', *Washington Times* editorial, 16 June 2009.
19. youtube.com/watch?v=xlu-qx8ohL8&feature
20. Krista Mahr, 'Neda Agha-Soltan', *Time*, 8 December 2009.
21. The poems and other rooftop videos were collected at mightierthan.com/2009/07/rooftop.
22. 'UCSC Occupation—Friday Night', indybay.org/newsitems/2009/09/25/18623281.php#18623394 (last accessed 18 October 2011).

23. Berkeley student statement, wewanteverything.wordpress.com, 18 November 2009.
24. 'Communiqué from an Absent Future', in Claire Solomon and Tania Palmieri (eds), *Springtime: The New Student Rebellions*, London 2011.

## Chapter 3

1. Woollard was sentenced to 32 months jail after giving himself up to the police.
2. Sophie Burge, 'I was held at a student protest for five hours', in Dan Hancox, *Fight Back!*, London 2010.
3. Jonathan Moses, 'Postmodernism in the streets', in Hancox, *Fight Back!*.
4. dan-hancox.blogspot.com
5. BBC Newsnight, 9 December 2010.
6. *The Nomadic Hive Manifesto*, criticallegalthinking.com, 9 December 2010.
7. Ibid.
8. Rory Rowan, 'Geographies of the Kettle: Containment, Spectacle & Counter-Strategy', criticallegalthinking.com.
9. 'The Rise of Street Extremism', Ideas Space, policyexchange.org.uk, 10 January 2011.

## Chapter 4

1. Keith Kahn-Harris, 'Naming the movement', openDemocracy.net, 22 June 2011.
2. Paulo dos Santos, 'On the Content of Banking in Contemporary Capitalism', Research on Money and Finance Discussion Paper No. 3, February 2009.
3. Richard Sennett, *The Culture of the New Capitalism*, New Haven 2006.
4. 'Live Reporting from Tahrir Sq, Egyptian Revolution', fifthinternational.org, 2 February 2011.
5. P. Altbach et al., 'Trends in Global Higher Education: Tracking an Academic Revolution', UNESCO.org, 2009.
6. Peter Beaumont, 'Mohamed Bouazizi: the dutiful son whose death changed Tunisia's fate', *Guardian*, 20 January 2011.

7. Ta Paidia Tis Galarias (TPTG), 'The rebellious passage of a proletarian minority through a brief period of time', in Vradis and Dalakoglou, *Revolt and Crisis in Greece*, p. 116.

8. Hippolyte Taine, *The French Revolution* (1896), vol. 2, trans. J. Durand, Indianapolis 2002, p. 419.

9. Robert Faris et al., 'Online Security in the Middle East and North Africa: A Survey of Perceptions, Knowledge, and Practice', cyber.law.harvard. edu, Harvard, August 2011.

10. Walter Powell, 'Neither Market nor Hierarchy: Network Forms of Organization', *Research on Organizational Behavior*, vol. 12, 1990, pp. 295–336.

11. an.kaist.ac.kr

12. Saeid Golkar, 'Liberation or Suppression Technologies? The Internet, the Green Movement and the Regime in Iran', *International Journal of Emerging Technologies and Society*, vol. 9, no. 1, 2011, pp. 50–70.

13. Ibid.

14. André Gorz, *Farewell to the Working Class*, London 1982, p. 64.

15. Sennett, *Culture of the New Capitalism*, p. 2.

16. Malcolm Gladwell, 'Small change: why the revolution will not be tweeted', *New Yorker*, 4 October 2010.

17. Ibid.

18. Sean Naylor, 'War games rigged?' *Army Times*, 16 August 2002.

19. Essam Fadl, 'Asharq al-Awsat talks to Egypt's April 6 Youth Movement founder', asharq-e.com/news, 10 February 2011.

20. libcom.org/library (undated). First transcribed in Donald Bouchard (ed.), *Language, Counter-Memory, Practice*, New York 1980.

*Chapter 5*

1. Ian Traynor, 'Greek debt crisis: eurozone ministers delay decision on €12bn lifeline', *Guardian*, 20 June 2011.

2. Takis Michas, 'Athens descends into anarchy', *Wall Street Journal*, 13 April 2011.

3. Alexander Trocchi, 'For the insurrection to succeed we must first destroy ourselves', quoted in Vradis and Dalakoglou, *Revolt and Crisis in Greece*, p. 303.

*Chapter 6*

1. Rupert Murdoch, 'Free markets and free minds: the security of opportunity', speech to the Centre of Policy Studies, 21 October 2010.
2. Martin Feldstein and Charles Horioka, 'Domestic Saving and International Capital Flows', *Economic Journal*, vol. 90, no. 358 (June 1980), pp. 314–29.
3. Andrew Haldane, 'The global imbalances in retrospect and prospect', Bank of England, speech, 3 November 2010.
4. Richard Freeman, 'The Great Doubling: Labor in the New Global Economy', Usery Lecture in Labor Policy, University of Atlanta, 8 April 2005.
5. Jared Bernstein et al., *The State of Working America*, Ithaca 2007.
6. *Global Wage Report*, December 2010, International Labour Organisation; Finfacts Ireland, 31 January 2008.
7. 'Real wages in Germany: numerous years of decline', DIW Weekly Report, 23 October 2009.
8. Gordon Brown, Mansion House speech, 20 June 2007.
9. K.-M. Yi, 'The Collapse of Global Trade: The Role of Vertical Specialisation', in Richard Baldwin and Simon Evenett (eds), *The Collapse of Global Trade, Murky Protectionism, and the Crisis: Recommendations for the G20*, London 2009; and Barry Eichengreen and Kevin O'Rourke, voxeu.org.
10. Costas Lapavitsas et al., 'Eurozone crisis: beggar thyself and thy neighbour', *Research on Money and Finance Report*, March 2010.
11. Ewald Engelen et al., 'After the Great Complacence', Oxford 2011, p. 209.
12. Andrew Haldane, speech, November 2010, op cit.
13. Child and Working Tax Credit Statistics, HMRC, hmrc.gov.uk/stats, April 2010.
14. BBC News, 'Labour attacks Nick Clegg over social mobility plan', 5 April 2011.
15. Stephanie Flanders, 'Have British jobs gone to British workers?', BBC website, 21 April 2010.
16. See Jared Bernstein and Christina Romer, 'The Job Impact of the American Recovery and Reinvestment Plan', Council of Economic Advisers, Washington 2009.

17. Andrey Korotayev and Julia Zinkina, 'Egyptian Revolution: A Demographic Structural Analysis', *Entelequia. Revista Interdisciplinar*, no. 13, spring 2011.
18. Economist.com, 3 February 2011; GlobalSecurity.org, 28 February 2011.
19. Andrew Lilico, 'How the Fed triggered the Arab Spring uprisings in two easy graphs', Telegraph.co.uk, 4 May 2011.
20. World Bank Food Price Watch, worldbank.org, April 2011.
21. Toby Nangle, 'The Sugar Rush and the Jasmine Wave', Barings Asset Management, 20 April 2011.
22. Jonathan Wheatley, 'Trade War Looming, Warns Brazil', *Financial Times*, 10 January 2011.
23. Ben Bernanke, *Essays on the Great Depression*, New York 2004.
24. Charles Kindleberger, *The World in Depression, 1929–1939*, Harmondsworth 1987, p. 9.

*Chapter 7*

1. J. M. Keynes, 'The Economic Consequences of the Peace', New York 1920.
2. Stefan Zweig, *The World of Yesterday*, London 2009, p. 219.
3. *Port Huron Statement of the Students for a Democratic Society*, June 1962.
4. Barry Wellman et al., 'The Social Affordances of the Internet for Networked Individualism', *Journal of Computer-Mediated Communication* 8, April 2003.
5. Manuel Castells, 'Communication, Power and Counter-power in the Network Society', *International Journal of Communication*, ijoc.org, 8 February 2007.
6. Edmund White, *Rimbaud: The Double Life of a Rebel*, New York 2008.
7. Zweig, *The World of Yesterday*, p. 20.
8. Robert Putnam, *Bowling Alone: The Collapse and Revival of American Community*, New York 2000.
9. See facebook.com.
10. blog.twitter.com/2011/03/numbers
11. 'Civil Movements: The impact of Facebook and Twitter', Arab Social Media Report, Dubai School of Government, vol. 1, no. 2, May 2011.

12. Sherry Turkle, *Life on the Screen: Identity in the Age of the Internet*, New York 1995, p. 14.

13. Margaret Wertheim, *The Pearly Gates of Cyberspace: A History of Space from Dante to the Internet*, London 1999, p. 249.

14. Castells, 'Communication, Power and Counter-power'.

15. Becky Hogge 'Barefoot into Cyberspace: Adventures in search of techno-Utopia', London 2011.

16. Karl Marx, *Selected Writings in Sociology and Social Philosophy*, T. B. Bottomore and Maximilian Rubel (eds), London 1963, p. 241.

17. This question has been explored by Nick Dyer-Witherford in a series of papers, the most recent of which is 'Twenty-First-Century Species-Being', presented at the Sixth Annual Marx and Philosophy Conference, 6 June 2009, Institute of Education, University of London.

18. Karl Marx, *Grundrisse*, Harmondsworth 1973, p. 704–11.

19. Paolo Virno, 'General Intellect', *Lessico Postfordista*, Milan 2001, trans. generation-online.org/p/fpvirno10.htm.

20. Franco Berardi and Geert Lovinck, 'A Call to the Army of Love and to the Army of Software', 13 October 2011, lists.thing.net/pipermail/idc/2011-October/004867.html.

21. Arif Jinha, 'Article 50 Million: An Estimate of the Number of Scholarly Articles in Existence', stratongina.net, 2009.

22. Bo-Christer Björk et al., 'Scientific Journal Publishing: Yearly Volume and Open Access Availability', *Information Research*, vol. 14, no.1 (2009), paper 391.

23. Robin Grant, 'The NOTW's social media downfall', wearesocial.net, 11 July 2011.

24. Amelia Arsenault and Manuel Castells, 'Switching Power: Rupert Murdoch and the Global Business of Media Politics: A Sociological Analysis', *International Sociology*, vol. 23, no. 4 (2008), p. 488.

25. Richard Dawkins, *The Selfish Gene*, Oxford 1989, p. 192.

26. Disgusting Solitary Gonad, untitled and undated text. See *Occupy Everywhere*.

## Chapter 8

1. All references from John Steinbeck, *The Grapes of Wrath*, Harmondsworth 2000.

2. Binyamin Appelbaum, 'From spending to cuts', *New York Times*, 1 August 2011.

## Chapter 9

1. Gustave Flaubert, *Sentimental Education*, trans. Robert Baldick, London 2004, p. 38.

2. Thibault, 'The Barricade in rue Saint-Maur-Popincourt after the attack by General Lamoricière's troops, Monday 26 June 1848', Musée d'Orsay, Paris.

3. Leo A. Loubere, 'The Emergence of the Extreme Left in Lower Languedoc, 1848–51: Social and Economic Factors in Politics', *American Historical Review*, vol. 73, no. 4 (April 1968), p. 1019–51.

4. Quoted in James Boyle, 'The Minimum Wage and Syndicalism: An Independent Survey', Cincinnati 1913.

5. Dimi Reider, 'J14 may challenge something even deeper than the occupation', 972mag.com, 7 August 2011.

6. Naftali Kaminski, 'How Israel's democracy might be revitalized from the Arab Spring', *Pittsburgh Post-Gazette*, 15 August 2011.

7. Philip Rucker, 'Former militiaman unapologetic for calls to vandalize offices over health care', *Washington Post*, 25 March 2010.

8. Glenn Beck, Fox News, 23 March 2010.

9. James McPherson, 'Antebellum Southern Exceptionalism: A New Look at an Old Question', *Civil War History* 29 (September 1983).

10. Erica Sagrans (ed.), *We Are Wisconsin*, Minneapolis 2011, p. 35.

11. Ben Brandzel, 'The unbreakable culture of the occupied Capitol', *Huffington Post*, 1 March 2011.

12. Ibid.

13. Glennbeck.com, 'Anarchists, socialists and communists party in Wisconsin', 21 February 2011, glennbeck.com/2011/02/21/anarchists-socialists-and-communists-party-in-wisconsin/.

14. All quotes from *The Coming Insurrection*, web version, tarnac9.wordpress.com.

15. Stephen King and Karen Ward, 'The New Economic Permafrost: How Ben Bernanke's Analysis of Japan Has Returned to Haunt the West', HSBC research paper, 23 August 2011.
16. Alexis de Tocqueville, *Souvenirs*, Paris 1893, pp. 15–18. Translated in Mike Rapport, *1848: Year of Revolution*, London 2008.

## Chapter 10

1. Ke Tang and Wei Xiong, 'Index Investment and the Financialization of Commodities', Princeton, September 2009.
2. UN-Habitat, *The Challenge of Slums: Global Report on Human Settlements*, 2003.
3. 'F A Hayek—Social Justice', youtube.com/watch?v=K1MC4ag9wOc (last accessed 20 October 2011).
4. George Orwell, *Looking Back on the Spanish War*, London 1943.

## Chapter 12

1. Quoted in A. J. Nicholls, *Weimar and the Rise of Hitler*, New York 2000, p. 160.
2. Ian Kershaw, *Hitler: Hubris, 1889–1936*, New York 2004, p. 322.
3. Laurie Penny and Molly Crabapple, *Discordia*, London 2012 (ebook).
4. Quoted in Foster Hirsch, *Kurt Weill On Stage*, New York 2002, p. 105.

## Chapter 13

1. 'Securing Stability and Growth', World Bank Report, June 2011, p. 5.
2. Gleb Bryanski, 'No Occupy Wall Street protests for Russia: Putin', Reuters, 17 October 2011.
3. S. Tipaldou and F. Serra i Massansalvador, 'Violent Protests in Undemocratic Settings: The Riot in Moscow's Manezh Square', ECPR Paper, cprnet.eu/conferences, August 2011.
4. premier.gov.ru.
5. youtube.com/watch?v=hLs8kv3u1hw&feature=youtu.be.
6. levada.ru/25-11-2011/vybory-v-gosdumu.
7. navalny-en.livejournal.com, 5 December 2011.

8. Tom Balmforth, 'Russian Health Inspector Warns Would-Be Protesters of Risk from Cold', Radio Free Europe/Radio Liberty, 2 February 2012.

9. 'Brève histoire de l'oligarchie en Russie', *Dissonance*, alexandrelatsa.ru, 17 November 2010.

10. Interview, *Philosophie*, 5 July 2012.

11. Daniel Tovrov, 'Manifesto of Free Russia: How to Rid the Country of Putinism', *International Business Times*, 12 June 2012.

12. blogs.waytorussia.net/herbariums/the-networks-and-russian-protest-movement.

13. Julia Ioffe, 'The End of Putin', *Foreign Policy*, 28 December 2011.

14. Sergey Chernov, 'Female Fury', *St. Petersburg Times*, 1 February 2012.

15. youtube.com/watch?v=ALS92big4TY.

## *Afterword*

1. Manuel Castells et al., *Aftermath: The Cultures of the Economic Crisis*, Oxford 2012, p. 211.

2. bbc.co.uk/blogs/newsnight/paulmason.

3. uwcforum.org/live/ (at 02.32.00).

4. Speech at 'The Egyptian Revolution: Results and Prospects', 12 July 2012, Marxism festival.

5. Laurie Penny, 'Notes from a Feminist Book Tour', *New Statesman*, 31 October 2012.

6. August Bebel, *Woman and Socialism*, translated by M. L. Stern, New York 1910.

7. Imposemagazine.com, 25 October 2011.

8. Thomas Frank, 'To the Precinct Station: How Theory Met Practice ... and Drove It Absolutely Crazy', *Baffler* 21, November 2012, thebaffler.com.

9. Manuel Castells, 'Where are the Indignados Going?', *Irish Left Review*, 27 January 2012.

10. Quoted in Robert Service, *Trotsky: A Biography*, p. 45.

11. Suby Raman, blog post, subyraman.com, 2 March 2012.

12. mideast.foreignpolicy.com, 24 February 2011.

13. K. Marx, 'The Eighteenth Brumaire of Louis Bonaparte' in *The Revolutions of 1848*, Harmondsworth 1973, p. 146.

14. newsfeed.time.com, 19 November 2011.
15. Geoffrey Wildanger, 'Occupy UC Davis', in Occupy #3, undated.
16. http://libcom.org/library/intellectuals-power-a-conversation-between-michel-foucault-and-gilles-deleuze.
17. Castells, *Aftermath*, p. 211.
18. Andrew Haldane, 'A Leaf Being Turned', Speech, Bank of England, 29 October 2012.
19. Virginia Woolf, 'Mr Bennett and Mrs Brown', London 1924.
20. Manuel Castells, *Networks of Outrage and Hope*, Cambridge 2012.
21. Castells, *Networks*, p. 2.
22. Ibid., p. 234.
23. K. Marx, 'A Contribution to the Critique of Hegel's Philosophy of Right' (1844) http://www.marxists.org/archive/marx/works/1843/critique-hpr/intro.htm.
24. See P. Mason, *Live Working or Die Fighting: How the Working Class Went Global*, London 2007.

# Index